The Responsive Workplace

THE RESPONSIVE WORKPLACE
Employers and a Changing Labor Force

Sheila B. Kamerman and
Alfred J. Kahn

Columbia University Press
New York   1987

Library of Congress Cataloging-in-Publication Data

Kamerman, Sheila B.
  The responsive workplace.

  Includes index.
  1. Personnel management. 2. Employee fringe benefits.
I. Kahn, Alfred J., 1919-   . II. Title.
HF5549.K253   1987   658.3   87-6636
ISBN 0-231-06480-2

Columbia University Press
New York   Guildford, Surrey
Copyright©1987 Columbia University Press

Printed in the United States of America

Book design by Ken Venezio

Contents

List of Tables

Preface

The idea that employment policies, practices, and fringe benefits should be responsive to the personal and family needs of employees is a theme that was first discussed in the latter part of the 1970s. It was featured as a major recommendation at the 1980 White House Conference on Families. By the mid-1980s it had become part of the popular culture, urged by working parents, by the women's movement, by social and family policy advocates, and even by some corporate leaders. The message is that the society has changed, work has changed, families have changed, and the work force has changed; therefore, the *workplace* should change, too. Given all that has occurred elsewhere in the society, people have asked, why hasn't the workplace changed? What can be done to make the workplace a better environment for today's workers without reducing the country's capacity to compete in the world economy?

There is no denying that the society has changed in the decades since World War II, especially since the beginning of the 1960s. In all the industrialized countries, there are smaller households, smaller families, fewer children in each family, higher rates of divorce and single parenthood, greater longevity, more women in the paid work force, a longer period of preadult education, and longer periods of postwork retirement. All these changes are both the consequences of changes occurring elsewhere in the society and the catalysts for other changes.

Often cited as the most dramatic social change, women are in the work force as never before. Labor force participation rates of women in the United States increased from 28 percent in 1940 to 38 percent in 1960, 41 percent in 1970, and 55 percent now. The most dramatic increase has been among married women with young children. More than half of all married women with children aged one and older are now in the labor force.

There is no denying that the nature of work has changed also. Since World War II, employment in the service sector has grown from 55 percent to more than 70 percent of total employment, while employment in the manufacturing sector has experienced a concomitant decline. With the growth in the service sector have come expanded job opportunities for women and an economy that is increasingly dependent on women in the work force. Women constituted 25 percent of the labor force in 1940, 32 percent in 1960, 37 percent in 1970, and 44 percent in 1986, an 80 percent increase over these years. It is almost inconceivable to think of a work force today without women.

The social role of government has expanded enormously throughout the industrialized world during these years, as every industrialized country has developed a package of social security and social protection programs, and as all people—not just the poor—have turned to government for a variety of protections and benefits. The social role of employers has expanded at the same time also. The costs of employee benefits in the United States increased by two thirds between 1960 and 1981, sometimes in response to government pressures, sometimes in response to government incentives, sometimes in response to collective bargaining, and sometimes voluntarily.

The Reagan Administration picked up the theme of employer responsiveness, too, in the context of its privatization initiative. The Administration had come to Washington carrying a general preference for less government, especially less in the way of governmental social programs. Where there were to be social services, they were better left to the voluntary and private sectors, and that included business.

What, in fact, has occurred or should be expected? What is desirable and possible? This book is a study of what is going on at the workplace and how the workplace has responded to social change. We have explored fringe benefits, services, and policies at the workplace, and we have assessed their adequacy in assisting mothers and fathers of young children to manage simultaneously the requirements of their work roles and their family lives. We have attempted to separate wish lists from reality, claims of impact from observed results. We have also looked at some critical benefits and services in detail in order to delineate what is useful and practical.

And we have asked about fairness and equity. Will a workplace-based pattern of provision meet everyone's needs? If not, what is possible? The reader will learn why we believe that a serious role for employers, which we endorse, is not an excuse for simultaneous governmental load shedding. Neither government nor the firm can escape from attention to family policy.

We are in the debt of the Foundation for Child Development, which saw the possible relationship between workplace family responsiveness and wholesome child development and therefore financed this research. Bert Brim and Jane Dustan raised stimulating questions and then let us work unhindered.

Sheila B. Kamerman worked on the book while in residence at the Center for Advanced Study in the Behavioral Sciences at Stanford, California, and expresses her appreciation to the Foundation's Fund for Research in Psychiatry for financial support during that year, and to the Center, for the very special, all-pervasive support it provided.

Six major companies gave access in return for confidentiality, and their staffs at all levels participated in interviews and general discussion. Two communities cooperated as we studied small employers. As indicated in chapter 1, many others agreed to interviews, while cooperative colleagues in many national organizations helped us monitor trends. Staff members at the U.S. Bureau of Labor Statistics were very helpful. We wish to thank, especially, Elizabeth Waldman and Howard Hayghe.

We wish particularly to acknowledge the contribution of Dr. Aileen Hart, who both completed one of the case studies and supervised one of the community studies. Frances Freedman took responsibility for the other community study and carried it out with high competence.

Karen Abbott and then Zandra Jones helped to complete the many versions of our reports and final manuscript. We appreciate their competence and good spirits. We remain responsible for the final results.

Sheila B. Kamerman and Alfred J. Kahn

The Responsive Workplace

1. Why Employers Should Care

Should employers be concerned with the personal and familial needs of their employees? If so, why and in what sense?

Experts in business administration and management concerned with productivity have recently discovered, or rediscovered, the importance of paying attention to employees. Human resource management has become more visible in the corporate structure and in business school curricula as people-oriented employment policies are increasingly touted.

Conservative politicians urge that employers participate in private sector initiatives to solve social problems, claiming that such efforts are far more effective and efficient than government programs. Social welfare professionals turn to business—to employers—to develop an alternative delivery system for social benefits and services or to provide financial support for existing services, when public services do not exist or when governmental funds are not forthcoming.

Industrial and labor relations experts talk of a changing labor force and the need for employers to develop new policies in response to the changing needs of their employees, if they wish to remain competitive in an increasingly world economy. And working mothers, working parents, and employees who are thinking about becoming parents look for signals that their employers will become more sensitive to their needs. They often face serious problems unless a measure of employer responsiveness helps them to manage both work and family life simultaneously.

Discussion abounds in the media and in professional journals about changes in the family, in the society, and at the workplace, and about the ways in which employers are beginning to take account of all this.[1] Much of what is written, however, is anecdotal, impressionistic, or limited to a small number of leading companies, and many of these leading companies are in the high-technology industry or in those parts of the country where high-tech companies dominate the corporate culture. Sometimes the reports are overstated or misinterpreted.

While some employers are being urged to do more, there are those who are convinced that the reverse is in fact occurring, or should be occurring. Thus, for example, some corporate executives are discussing cutting back on benefits now provided to employees in order to reduce labor costs and avoid further productivity losses. Small business owners are complaining that there is no way they can afford to provide many of the benefits employees of large firms take for granted and certainly not any of the new, special benefits now being discussed. Some executives are announcing that while business must assume a larger social role, this does not mean that business can substitute for government in carrying the primary responsibility for social welfare. Some go further and argue that business has no social responsibility role at all; they say that "the business of business is business," not social welfare. And many working parents say, "I hear all this talk about what employers are doing for their employees, but I sure don't see much going on where I work."

What is really happening at the workplace today? Why do many people in and out of business think that there should be and is a new, responsive posture? Are major changes occurring in employment policies and practices that make them more responsive to the personal and family lives of employees? What if anything is known about the consequences of such changes as are made? Is all of this a good idea? Should employers, in fact, have a role in meeting the personal and family needs of their employees? If so, what should it be?

This book is an effort to respond to such questions. In it we assess the different positions taken concerning the role employers should have and why. We examine what is in fact occurring or why some people think something is. We suggest what the consequences might be if current trends continue. Our review of the debate is based on what people have written and said. Our assessment of what exists is derived from many existing data sources, enriched by observations and several hundred interviews in both leading companies and less progressive ones, in small businesses and in large firms, and with human resource officers and labor union leaders throughout the country.

Between 75 and 100 interviews were completed in each of six large companies in different parts of the country and in different industries, selected to provide a range of insights on these issues. We included both national and multinational firms, those with large establishments and those with small establishments. Our interviewees were at all levels, from clerical and line workers to top executives. In each case these interviews are supplemented by observations, reports, studies, and documents provided by the company. In addition, we draw on data collected from extensive interviews in 15 other companies, studied earlier in 1980-81 as part of a survey of maternity and parenting policies in U.S. industry. All these interviews are supplemented further by interviews carried out with 200 small employers and some of their employees in two different communities, one located in the Northeast and the second in a Middle Atlantic state. We also interviewed presidents and senior officials in 10 unions and more than 25 human resource executives from major companies not included in our study. We explored the different perspectives of senior management, of middle management, and of nonmanagement personnel. Finally, we attended dozens of meetings where these and related subjects were discussed.

Our objective is to lay the groundwork for a more realistic assessment of what an appropriate role for employers might be. We begin with a discussion of the arguments for and against an expanded social role for employers. We proceed from an examination of this debate to an overview of what is happening in the labor force and in the society at large that suggests the emergence of new types of employee needs. In chapter 2, we look briefly at what is known about what employers have provided for their employees in the past—and why, followed by a more extensive discussion of what they are providing now. Where are there "gaps" in provision and for whom?

In chapter 3, we discuss major U.S. companies with good and relatively generous benefits, which nonetheless have missed the opportunity to be more responsive to employee needs. What these companies are doing wrong, and why this occurs, is the focus of this chapter. In chapter 4 we describe how a large employer can be responsive to the needs of a diverse labor force and how employment policy and practice innovations can be developed and implemented. In chapter 5 we turn to an examination of small employers. Here we present the first picture of what very small employers do for their employees. How does this compare with our national picture of what most employers provide? How do small employers assess their advantages and disadvantages as employers, and how do their employees view their situation? In chapter 6 we explore what large and medium-sized companies do in a work situation involving small establishments. In one sense these are large companies, yet the work environment is like that of a small employer; there are only relatively few employees in one location. What difference does this make?

In chapters 7 and 8 we turn to the issue of employers' responses to employees' new needs. Here, we examine certain selected new developments in more detail: child care services and counseling services, part-time and other alternative work schedules, vacations and personal and parental leaves, and flexible benefit plans. Are these truly responsive to family needs? Why are some firms providing these benefits? How extensive are they? Then, in chapter 9 we review what we have learned about the process by which decisions are and could be made concerning new policies. Who and what is shaping these new developments? We examine the different actors: management, unions, government, and consulting firms. Finally, in chapter 10 we present our overall assessment of what is happening now in the United States, what the issues are, and what options are open. We conclude with some recommendations for employees and employers concerned with responsiveness to employees, fairness, equity, as well as with productivity.

The Debate: Productivity, Privatization, and Social Change

Three developments are driving the current debate about what employers should be doing: a desire to raise productivity, an interest in reducing public social expenditures, and a concern about social and demographic changes occurring in the society.

Here we discuss these developments and identify the major issues. At the close of this chapter we pose the question of employer responsiveness in a form that we think realistic and in accord with the interests of employers, employees, and the larger society. The exploration of such responsiveness is reported in the remainder of the book.

Productivity Through People. There is general agreement today that the U.S. productivity growth rate has been declining since the mid-1960s and that several other countries are rapidly approaching, perhaps even overtaking, us. Productivity, as commonly defined, is the dollar value of output per employee per hour and is a function of labor, capital, and management—individually or in some combination.[2] Because of its significance for improving living standards and national and international competitiveness, productivity and the factors contributing to its declining growth rate have become an issue of major importance on the public agenda in the United States. While there is recognition that in some industries (such as steel) our problem is, at least in part, obsolescent equipment, many other factors are cited. Among these are the movement of workers from manufacturing to service industries; the changed composition of the labor force, in particular the increased numbers of women, youth, and minorities; the low levels of education and training for some groups in our labor force; the decline in capital investment in research and development (R&D); the increase in government regulation and taxation; and the rise in energy prices in the 1970s.[3]

Although there is consensus that the productivity rate has declined, there is no consensus on the extent of the decline, on which of the above-listed factors—or any number of others—bears primary responsibility for this development, and on whether the decline has the significance attributed to it. Nonetheless, there are some who are convinced that the key to economic improvement is concern with raising productivity and that the solution lies in management's ability to motivate workers to produce more. Indeed, this is a major theme in many recent books and articles.

In one of the most successful books of the early 1980s, excellent companies are characterized as those with the capacity to be continuously innovative, and innovation is defined as the continuing capacity to respond to changes in the environment.[4]. One essential attribute of excellent, innovative companies is identified as "productivity through people." Moreover, the authors say, "it is *attention to employees*, not work conditions per se, that has the dominant impact on productivity."[5] The authors stress that "excellent companies treat the rank and file as the root source of quality and productivity gain."[6] They acknowledge, however, that even if all employers agreed that "people are our most important asset," few really live this way.

Any number of other experts take a similar approach, stressing the importance of a changed attitude toward workers as being the key factor in raising productivity. For example, Rosabeth Kanter, a sociologist and well-known management consultant, argues that innovation is the touchstone of increased productivity, and the key to innovation is progressive human resource policies.[7] Her conclusion is that progressive human resource policies lead to such benefits as higher productivity, better quality, lower absenteeism, fewer grievances, improved morale, and positive image building and public relations in the media. Many experts reject the concept that it is technology that drives productivity, insisting instead on the need for a "redirection of attention to *human relations* in the corporate world" and a major change in management and the culture of the workplace.[8] Looking toward the experiences of several European countries, some urge participation in management as a way to ensure greater responsiveness to employees' needs and preferences.[9] Others believe that profit-sharing options and stock ownership plans are important incentives to create worker concern with company success.[10] And still others stress a wider range of employment policies and practices.[11]

Also calling upon managers to pay more attention to their workers, one labor management expert takes a somewhat different approach: O'Toole insists that at the core of declining productivity in the United States is "the failure of scholars, managers and union leaders to recognize that worker values are diverse and changing."[12] He argues that if the goal is to increase productivity, then management must learn how to become more responsive to the diverse and changing values of the work force. The real challenge for management in the 1980s is to redesign the philosophy and organization of work. He is convinced that only when managers are prepared to support a new culture at work, one based on the values of "diversity, choice, flexibility, mobility, participation, security, and rights tied to responsibilities," will workers be motivated to work harder and will innovation and productivity increase.[13]

Whether and which of the experts are right remains to be seen. We find no hard evidence in firm support of any of these theories regarding increased productivity. But clearly, there is agreement that something different is going on within the work force and something new is needed on the part of management. What implications are derived for the workplace merits exploration.

Privatization. On the one hand, industry is called upon to be more responsive to employee needs in order to increase productivity. On the other hand, it is urged to do more so as to enable government to do less.

President Reagan, early in his Administration, enunciated a policy of privatization as being a fundamental tenet for his Administration's social policy.[14] His objective was to reduce federal social expenditures (and public social expenditures generally) and to get the private sector to carry out many of the social welfare programs the society viewed as important. He established a Task Force on Private Sector Initiatives in 1981 with the goal of identifying successful model school, church, business, union, foundation, and civic programs that could help communities meet some needs that previously had been addressed by governmental programs. The Task Force presented its final report in December 1982.

The initiative elicited a variety of responses. On the level of philosophy and ideology, the President received considerable backing. But there were differences, and the action was less impressive than the endorsements. Some said that there is no way that business *could* become the mainstay of social welfare in the

United States. Others said that even if it could, it should not, and still others said whether or not it could or should, it was the only game in town.

One form that the privatization push took was the Administration's encouragement of employer provision of human services as a more efficient and effective alternative to government operations and as a possible substitute for some public programs. Thus, for example, the Administration urged employers to do more in the way of providing child care and counseling services, as well as a variety of other services many people have come to expect from government (see chapter 7). The White House Office of Private Sector Initiatives launched an employer-supported child care project in 1983, in collaboration with the Department of Health and Human Services (DHHS), Administration for Children, Youth and Families (ACYF). The first phase of this effort involved a series of forums held in five cities, with participation of chief executive officers of leading corporations; the objective was to explore the feasibility of introducing employer-supported child care. DHHS and ACYF also provided funding for studies of employer-supported child care and for a series of additional meetings. Many child care professionals participated—or tried to participate—in a variety of such endeavors organized under the auspices of local child advocacy organizations, as well as of local chambers of commerce. There was a second round of White House-initiated forums. In short, there was publicity, a sense of activity, encouragement to act. By 1985 the initiative was largely abandoned. There was no machinery for federal follow-through, and with a few exceptions, the brief, inspirational luncheons had modest payoff.

A second component of the new thrust urged increased corporate philanthropy as an alternative to public financing of social programs. Legislation permitting corporations to contribute up to 5 percent of taxable income to charity and exempting that amount from taxation has existed since 1935; yet corporate giving remained at about the 1 percent level throughout the intervening years. In a gesture of encouragement, 1981 tax legislation raised the maximum to 10 percent and President Reagan's Task Force urged corporations to double their average annual contribution to 2 percent. The American Association of Fund-Raising Counsel noted in 1984 that preliminary reports on corporate giving of $3.1 billion in 1983 represented about 1.5 percent of corporate income, down slightly from 1.7 percent in 1982, the highest rate of all time.[15] The Conference Board reported a surge in corporate giving for 1984, to $3.8 billion, representing an after-inflation increase of 11 percent. The corporation share of charitable giving had reached 5.4 percent, equal to that of private foundations but still considerably below individual giving. Health and human services contributions were a declining share in these totals, however, from 41 to 28 percent between 1974 and 1984, while civic and community activities received larger shares. The 1984 jump in all private giving was impressive, but the Urban Institute estimated that individuals, corporations, and foundations, combined, could offset only 25 percent of federal cuts.

A business spokesman said that corporate giving would have had to increase 1100 percent to make up for the 1982 cutbacks in social service funding. Instead, although there was an increase that year, it was 15 percent! His conclusion was that it was not only unrealistic to expect business to fill the gap, but also, he emphasized it would be a mistake, since the real business of business is business, not social welfare.[16] Some others were even more vehement in their rejection of a social role for business. One conservative spokesman said, to expect business to do more because government is doing less is to miss the point. The point is that the goal is to reduce formal provision generally and to turn more toward informal, volunteer, nonmonetized activities, self-help initiatives, and so forth. In an even stronger position, Milton Friedman has long stated that in fact corporations have a duty *not* to use shareholders' money for charitable purposes.[17]

Still a third development that occurred as part of the stress on privatization was the decision of some professionals, given the cutbacks in federal resources for social programs and the new ideology, to seek employer sponsorship and funding as an alternative to government. Some social welfare professionals urged employers to establish such services at the workplace as family, alcohol and drug, preretirement, and stress management counseling; child care services; legal aid; information and referral services; and so forth. Others suggested that even if employers did not provide such help directly, at least they should provide financial assistance to service providers or the employees who need help.

Making their case, such advocates insisted that if employers were to move in this direction, the company itself would benefit. They argued that supporting such programs constituted enlightened self-interest on the part of employers because they would lead to: "reduced worker turnover, reduced absenteeism, improved recruitment of needed employees, increased productivity and enhanced public relations and company image."[18] Apart from some reported employer and employee testimonials and a few small-scale accountings, at this writing no one has hard data to document such extravagant claims.[19] Of some interest, moreover, is the observation that the same list of positive impacts is produced every time someone wants to confirm the value of a particular workplace policy, whether it be flexitime, employee counseling services, child care services, or "progressive human resource" philosophies generally. The evidence is weak and the *relative* efficacy of these different strategies (which carry different costs and implications) is not even the subject of speculation.

Thus, the pressures for business to do more comes from an Administration in Washington that wants to spend—and do—less for social programs, from professionals who seek new sources of financial support for what they were doing earlier and want to continue doing, and from some in the society who see increased need for certain types of social programs. However, a survey of leading corporate executives found what many had assumed: little enthusiasm for or even interest in a social policy gap-filling role of business.[20] Employers understand there is a problem but are not sure what their role should be in the solution.

We would argue, as some corporate leaders have also, that regardless of any prior excesses or inefficiencies in governmental social programs, government still has a major role to play. Certainly employers do have an important contribution to make, but they cannot and should not be expected to be a substitute for government in the social arena. What the appropriate role for employers is and how it should relate to what government does, is what we explore in this book.

Social Change: A Changing Labor Force, A Changing Society, and Changing Values. The large-scale entry of women into the work force has had a dramatic impact on the workplace, the family, and the society. The changing roles of women at home and at work are affecting men and their roles and are changing the value system of the whole society. We are only just beginning to understand this and to recognize all the potential implications for the workplace (tables 1.1, 1.2).

Certainly, the most dramatic change in the work force has been its growing feminization. Women now constitute 44 percent of

Table 1.1. U.S. Labor Force, July 1986.   (in thousands)

Total population (1985)	238,000
Population over age 16, non-inst.	182,350
Resident armed forces	1,670
Civilian employees	109,880
Employed in agriculture	3,110
Public employees	16,720
Private sector, nonagriculture	83,530
Unemployed	8,190
Total employed	111,554
Total labor force	119,740

Source: Monthly Labor Review (September, 1986), 109(9).

Table 1.2. Percentages of All Men and Women Aged 16 and Over in the Labor Force, 1960-1985.

Years	Males	Females	Women as % of Labor Force
1960	83.3	37.7	32.3
1970	79.7	43.3	36.7
1975	77.9	46.3	39.0
1980	77.2	51.5	41.9
1985	76.7	54.5	43.7

Source: Bureau of Labor Statistics.

the labor force (and a projected 45 percent by the end of the decade).[21] Sixty percent of labor force growth in each of the two preceding decades is accounted for by women; and women are likely to constitute more than 70 percent of the increase in the size of the labor force in the 1980s. Some 70 percent of the labor force is now made up of persons who live in married-couple families. About 20 percent of the work force—women as well as men—have preschool-aged children.

More than half of all women, including 63 percent of women with children under age 18 and 54 percent of those with children under age 6, were in the labor force in 1986 (tables 1.3, 1.4, 1.5). For the first time in 1986, more than half the married mothers of children aged 1 and older were in the labor force, too; and most of these women worked full time. In contrast to earlier years, women are increasingly likely to remain at work regardless of pregnancy, maternity, and/or child care.

More than 70 percent of women in the work force are in their prime childbearing years (18–44) and 80 percent of these will

Table 1.3. Percentage of Mothers With Children Under Age 6, in the Labor Force in March, 1980, and March, 1985, by Marital Status

Marital Status of Mother	*Percentage in the Labor Force*	
	1980	*1985*
All mothers with children under age 6	47	54
Married mothers, husband present	45	53
Women heading families alone	55	59
All mothers with children under age 3	42	50
Married mothers, husband present	41	51
Women heading families alone	45	45

Source: Bureau of Labor Statistics.

Table 1.4. Labor Force Participation Rates of Wives, Husband Present, by Age of Youngest Child Under 6, March of Selected Years 1970-1985

Presence and Age of Child	Labor Force Participation Rate			
	1970	1975	1980	1985
Wives, total	40.8	44.5	50.2	54.3
No children under 18	42.2	44.0	46.0	48.2
With children under 18	39.8	44.9	54.3	61.0
With children under 6, total	30.3	36.8	45.3	53.7
With children under 3, total	25.8	32.6	41.5	50.7
3 to 5 years total	36.9	42.2	51.7	58.6
3 years	34.5	41.2	51.5	55.1
4 years	39.4	41.2	51.4	59.7
5 years	36.9	44.4	42.4	62.1
With children age 2 years	30.5	37.1	48.1	54.0
With children age 1 & under	24.0	30.8	39.0	49.4

Source: Adapted from Howard Hayghe, "Rise in Mothers' Labor Force Activity Includes Those with Infants," *Monthly Labor Review* (February, 1986), vol. 109, no. 2.

become pregnant at some point in their working lives. Those who become pregnant are now likely to work throughout their pregnancy, or at least until their ninth month, and they are likely to return to work soon after childbirth. Pregnancy and childbirth are now becoming workplace phenomena. Among those women who had a child in the year preceding a 1985 survey, 48.4 percent were in the labor force. Some of these women may have given birth only weeks before (table 1.6).[22] Half of all married mothers were at work within one year after childbirth in 1986. Labor force participation rates for mothers of children under one had an astonishing increase from 26 to 50 percent, between 1975 and 1986. Most women who were working at the time of childbirth were back at their jobs in less than six months after maternity and many returned much sooner.

All this makes for a very different work force, family life, and society.

The proportion of adult males in the work force is decreasing

Table 1.5. Number and Percentage of Children Under Age 6 by Type of Family and Labor Force Status of Mother, March, 1980, and March, 1986.

Labor Force Status of Mothers	1980		1986	
	Number*	Percentage	Number*	Percentage
Total children under 6 living with Mother	17,741	100	19,392	100
Mother in labor force	7,703	43	9,974	51
In married couple families	15,123	100	16,167	100
mother in labor force	6,385	42	8,241	51
In families maintained by women	2,620	100	3,226	100
mother in labor force	1,317	50	1,733	54
Total children under 3	8,979	100	9,528	100
Mother in labor force	3,597	40	4,680	49
In married couple families,	7,871	100	8,166	100
mother in labor force	3,597	40	4,028	50
In families maintained by women,	1,108	100	1,362	100
mother in labor force	472	43	652	48

Source: Bureau of Labor Statistics,
*Numbers in thousands.

as more are in school longer or retire earlier. There are fewer young people in the population generally. Thus the need for adult women in the labor force is likely to remain high and to continue growing. For those who think this situation will change, and women will once again leave the work force and return to the home, Janet Norwood, Commissioner of Labor Statistics, reminds us, "Women are in the labor force to stay; as we move forward into the 1990s, they will be a larger proportion of the work force than they were before."[23]

The baby boom population, a cohort that has left a significant mark on the society of each decade as it ages, is now in the 25 to 44 age group. These are the years in which marriage, childbearing, childrearing, child care—as well as job and career development—are dominant in individual and family lives.

Society is now being shaped by a different family life-style. Working families—two-earner married couples or sole-parent single-earner families, usually female-headed—are increasingly

Table 1.6. Women Who Had a Child in the Last Year and the Percentage Who Were in the Labor Force: 1976 and 1980 to 1985. (Number in thousands)

Age of Woman and Survey Year	Number of Women	Percent in Labor Force
18 to 44 years old:		
1985	3,497	48.4
1984	3,311	46.7
1983	3,625	43.1
1982	3,433	43.9
1981	3,381	41.7
1980	3,247	38.0
1976	2,797	30.9
18 to 29 years old:		
1985	2,512	47.9
1984	2,375	44.5
1983	2,682	42.4
1982	2,445	42.5
1981	2,499	40.2
1980	2,476	38.2
1976	2,220	31.8
30 to 44 years old:		
1985	984	49.6
1984	936	52.2
1983	942	45.1
1982	888	47.5
1981	881	46.2
1980	770	37.3
1976	577	27.6

Source: June Current Population Surveys of 1976, and 1980 to 1985.

the dominant family pattern in the United States as in the industrialized world generally. Families with two or more earners constituted more than half of all families in the United States in 1986 and 61 percent of all husband/wife families; in most of these families, both husbands and wives are working.

Some of these families are not only dual earner — two-paycheck — families but are also part of the much smaller group of dual-career families. For such couples, jobs — work — represent far more than a source of income. Investment in work — and the achievements and accomplishments related to work — are an important part of how they feel and how they think about themselves.

Finally, a growing proportion of families are single-parent families, and that group is likely to increase over the next decade. One quarter of all families with children were single-parent families in 1986, overwhelmingly headed by women. Half of all marriages now end in divorce; young women have about a 40 percent chance of becoming a single parent by the time their children grow up. Clearly, if young women want to assure themselves of economic security, work — full-time work and continued labor force attachment — is essential. Single parents will constitute a growing proportion of the work force, too.

Values and Choices. From now until the end of the century, the work force will look and behave very differently than in earlier years. Apart from the increased presence of women and mothers, it is a work force dominated heavily by the baby boom cohort and socialized with a very different set of values, albeit values now tempered by age and new economic realities. According to experts, among the values characterizing today's workers are an acceptance of changed gender roles and greater equality for women; an acceptance of diverse family structures; and a commitment to individualism, flexibility, and diversity.[24] Such values are supplemented now by a new and more realistic assessment of economic and political realities, a diminished respect for government and its ability to solve problems, and a concomitant increase in respect for technology and for business and the private sector.

O'Toole says that many experts make a major mistake by overgeneralizing about what people now want from and at work. He stresses, instead, the enormous diversity of the American work force today:

Indeed, by aggregating the countless studies of worker attitudes, values and satisfaction that were conducted in the 1970s, one arrives at a singularly significant conclusion: *Workers are not all alike; they have different needs, interests, and motivations. Moreover, these characteristics constantly change over the career of each worker, much as the modal work values of the society as a whole shift over time.*[25]

This generation of workers has very different values regarding authority and subordinate-superordinate relationships than recent cohorts, and they have very different expectations regarding male-female roles. Large numbers of women are now coming out of graduate programs in business and professional schools, constituting 40 percent or more of new hires in law, accounting, and some businesses, changing the look of professional and corporate organizations. Some young adults who delayed getting married until completing graduate and/or professional education are now facing the dilemma of deciding whose career takes precedence or how two careers can be managed simultaneously. Some married couples who deferred having children until well established in their careers face a "now or never" dilemma: to have children or not. Many of those who married and had children are now wildly juggling complicated daily routines, dependent on superb organizational abilities, boundless energy, and luck. Some couples who lived through the most recent recession learned to appreciate the safety net provided by having two earners in the labor force, as female unemployment rates remained lower than male, and as many blue-collar families experienced extensive unemployment. The consequences of all this for children, marriage, and work are not yet known.

What is known, however, is that employees are expressing a new view of the workplace and a new set of expectations. Thus, for example, participants at the 1980 White House Conference on Families, regardless of gender, employment status, or ideology, were in overwhelming agreement on issues related to the workplace. Their number one recommendation was that "Business, labor and government should encourage and implement employment opportunities and personnel policies that enable persons to hold jobs while maintaining a strong family life."[26] General Mills, in its American Family Report of findings from a representative national survey of family members, noted that family members do not single out one solution to the conflicting demands of work and family responsibilities, but "there is a desire for recognition of their needs and concerns by employers and understanding in working out approaches to meet them."[27]

This would seem to imply that any company that expects its workers to be efficient, motivated, and productive (or at least not disgruntled) must consider their needs and problems and find appropriate responses. What an appropriate response might be to this different and diverse labor force is a topic requiring exploration and testing.

Toward a New Perspective on Employers and Their Social Role

And so the arguments go: For productivity to increase—for American industry to remain competitive in a world market—management should start paying more attention to employees. To be responsive to employees means recognizing that today's labor force is not the same as yesterday's and that labor has a whole series of new and different needs and expectations. Those who prefer private sector activity to public, on ideological or other grounds, view employers as an important source of new private sector initiatives, and those who are concerned about the reductions in federal support for social programs view employers as a possible alternative source of support.

Some use the productivity argument as a rationale for employer activity; employees themselves think their employers should (or hope that they will) be more responsive because personally they are now facing new problems in their daily lives and wish to manage better. Other observers urge that notice of such needs be taken, not necessarily because it is proved that productivity will increase, but rather, because society has changed visibly and its component institutions must constantly adjust their fit if the whole is to function well. Adaptations are occurring elsewhere, even within families, they argue; therefore it is inevitable that the workplace will have to change, too.

Where, then, do these arguments leave us?

Management experts admit it is easier to *describe* excellent companies than *explain* how they got that way and how some stay that way. (Indeed, several of Peters and Waterman's excellent companies were not so excellent a few years later.) Inevitably, leadership emerges as an important component of corporate excellence, too.[28] Strong leaders do develop personnel strategies.

A survey of 850 working Americans found that one reason why Americans may not be working so hard is a "persistent confusion between job satisfaction and productivity, that may have led employers to offer workers the wrong incentives."[29] The point may be relevant; when asked about various features of their jobs, workers made clear distinctions between those features that made a job more agreeable and those they would work harder for. Although workers said that both aspects were essential components of good jobs, they clearly distinguished between the two. Of the eight features they listed highest as contributing to job improvement, four had to do with work motivation: good pay (chosen by 77 percent), recognition for good work (70 percent), the chance for advancement (65 percent), and pay tied to performance (61 percent). Two were linked to agreeability: good fringe benefits (68 percent) and job security (65 percent). Two were mixtures: interesting work (62 percent) and the chance to learn new things (61 percent). Other aspects of a job contributing to agreeability but not to work motivation included flexible working hours, a convenient location, congenial co-workers and supervisors, and freedom from stress.[30]

For those convinced of the importance of "attention to employees" whether as an important factor in improving productivity or for other management reasons, it is unclear whether the above-mentioned distinctions go beyond worker opinions and attitudes. If attention to worker needs affects productivity, what kind of "attention" is determining? There is no general agreement on what "progressive" human resource policies are or that they are the same for all types of employees, in companies of all sizes, in all industries, and at all times. The policy substance requires serious consideration. At the present level of discourse there in fact can be no rigorous test of impacts.

Obviously, this does not mean that the business world should stop and wait. As suggested, the idea of paying attention to employees would seem to make good sense even if there is no standardized definition of what this means and even if the results are not always visible, let alone measurable in productivity terms. We suggest only that there are other good reasons for such policy and that family responsiveness in the workplace is hardly a universal panacea for all problems of productivity and profitability. Nor are these, of course, the same thing, either. Moreover, we call attention to a hazard: those who oversell attentiveness to employees—who oversell fringe benefits, or scheduling flexibility, or employee-counseling services, or child care programs—as *the route to productivity* flirt with disaster if there is no visible and immediate payoff to the specific action taken or policy enacted. The business world is too complex for simplistic forecasts.

It may be shown ultimately that specific workplace responses pay off in the rigorous cost/benefit sense. One assumes intuitively that there should be a formula that ties benefits and provisions to satisfaction and to efficient and productive work. Life is, however, much more complex than this. In the interim, we hold that the workplace cannot, should not, indeed, *does not*, ignore current (and new) employee circumstances and needs in any case. The real issues are: *what, how much, at what pace*, and *with what rationales?*

What of the other arguments? Regardless of the current infatuation with public-private partnerships, employers are not going to become a substitute for government in the general social welfare arena, whether it is because they cannot realistically respond on so grand a scale or because they do not choose to do so philosophically. If business is to do very much more, it will be along one of three routes: through programs of corporate charitable giving, which are important but modest as compared with individual giving and government funding; through activities specifically important to the company in terms of image, local community relations, and so forth; and through action within its own firm and with its own employees, as discussed below. This is the central focus of our exploration—as it is the historical core of what business has always done.

Thus, we argue that to describe employers as a group as providing an alternative to the social safety net is unrealistic and misleading; there is no valid rationale or opportunity here for employers to do substantially more. This much said, it is important to remember how much employers already do in the way of delivering social welfare, indirectly, invisibly, or at least in ways that are not usually thought of as social welfare. We show in what follows (chapter 2) that employers are an important institution for the delivery of social benefits and services and are becoming still more important. While it certainly cannot take on the burden of a social safety net, the corporate welfare system already plays a far more significant role than most people realize.

One issue to be addressed is where this system and the statutory provision fit in relation to one another. In other words, how does the social policy of the firm relate to the social policy of the state? More specifically: How does or might management think about what it does for its employees and why? And how do employees view all this? More basically, perhaps, who pays for provision in this system and who benefits from it, and what does this imply? A second issue we address is whether employers should not be reassessing some of what they are now doing and providing. Eliminating or reducing nonwage labor costs in some areas, while expanding provision or establishing new policies in other areas, may lead to much more "responsive" employment policies and practices.

In short, we agree completely with those who say that changes in the labor force do require significant changes in labor/management relations and in employment policies and practices. Obviously, the labor force is changing, and just as obviously these changes are important. Unfortunately, too much of the discussion concerning the need for management to become more responsive to the needs of a changing work force is directed at the same message as that of the management experts: this is how productivity can be increased. We would reiterate: awareness of labor force changes and responsiveness and sensitivity to workers' needs and values are important components of good management per se, but they are not a productivity panacea or a magic lamp.

What is important to remember is that the major demographic change occurring is the decline in significance of the traditional family—the male breadwinner with an at-home wife. What has emerged as dominant is the working family, but this family may be a childless couple, a single parent, a couple with an aged parent, or a dual-earner couple with young children. And there are still single individuals in the labor force. Traditional families, while no longer dominant, remain an important component of the work force, too. In effect, what we are seeing is a trend toward a diversity of family types among employees and an emerging challenge for the workplace to consider the implications of such diversity for smooth daily and long-term operations.

The Centrality of Work and a Job in Daily Life. These labor force changes are related to still another development, one that has not received attention yet in this debate and one that we believe is of critical importance. We refer to the growing recognition of work as a central component in the lives of all adults, regardless of gender, and to the acknowledgment of a job and attendant benefits as a major source of personal satisfaction and social relationships, as well as income, and thus as critical to the total security of the individual and of families. Indeed, this development underscores the need to reassess the role of employers and employment in relation to the personal and familial needs of employees in a way that has not been done heretofore.

Some years ago, in an influential article published in 1964, Charles Reich, a Yale University law professor, wrote that for most people, work-related benefits such as pensions have become a principal form of wealth, while for those who are unable to work or to find work, government entitlements fulfill the same function.[31] Peter Drucker, the management expert, writing more than a decade later, concurred, identifying pensions as possibly the largest single asset of the middle-aged American, exceeding in value both the family home and the automobile.[32]

Reich's purpose in calling attention to the increasing importance of this "new property" as the basis for social status and economic security was to underscore the need for legal protections analogous to that provided for more traditional forms of wealth. Mary Ann Glendon, a legal scholar writing in 1981, documents the developments since then in law directed at assuring protections for these new forms of property, and she stresses their growing importance.[33] Since, as she points out, the most desirable forms of new property are contingent on labor force participation, it is inevitable that for most people, "plans and expectations for future security are centered about good jobs with good fringe benefits."[34] Indeed, even among the wealthy, new property (in the form of prestigious employment and special perks) has become more important and old property (in the form of land, bank accounts, etc.) less so. In addition, she says, new property in the form of government largesse supplants old property at all income levels as the platform on which an individual's security rests.

Most non-aged adults today, regardless of gender, are in the labor force. The most valuable asset for most employees is likely to be their job. Coupled with the benefits provided directly by employers (pensions, health insurance, paid vacation time) or by government as a concomitant of work (social security, disability insurance, unemployment insurance, medicare), employment, in particular a good job, has now become central to individual economic security, and, increasingly, more important than family and familial relationships in guaranteeing such security.[35] However, as we see in the next chapter, not all people have equal access to the preferred forms of new property (good jobs and good fringe benefits) that now are viewed as the most important sources of economic security in our society. Some have limited access to jobs, while others may have jobs but no—or inadequate—fringe benefits.

Those who worry about the loss of the work ethic in the United States should take heart. If anything, work is becoming more important to individuals as it assumes a central role in all aspects of daily life. Indeed, it is becoming so important that those who are excluded from this form of property will find themselves seriously disadvantaged. This gives rise to important questions: What can or should be done about those for whom access is limited?

Should work-related benefits continue to be a central part of the standard of living today? Should their roles increase? What alternatives exist or can be developed? These are among the issues that we address. Apart from anything else, the disparity in access raises fundamental questions of fairness, an issue on the public agenda.

A growing case is often made for the importance of solidarity in the society and of the need for industry, labor, and government to work together to bring the American economy to new heights of prosperity and competitiveness following recent downturns. Efforts at changing what has historically been an adversarial relationship between labor and management are growing, as can be seen from recent work reform developments.[36] All these reforms are focused on the workplace but in fact do not consider small firms, unorganized sites, or people with intermittent attachments. How should thinking about the social policy of the firm consider them, too? Or are such questions beyond solidarity?

Summary

The current concern with the role of the United States in a world economy, the current rethinking of the social role of modern government, and the major social changes occurring in the society, the work force, and the family are the catalysts in forcing a reexamination of the role of employers in relation to their employees. The growing recognition of work and the workplace as a central component of an individual's personal identity and economic security has highlighted the increased importance of work and work-related benefits and the problems attendant on limited or inequitable access to this new and important form of property. A growing concern with fairness requires an examination of what exists, for whom, and with what consequences. Ultimately, our goal here is to develop a fresh perspective on the social role of employers, one that will accrue to the benefit of management and labor, as well as to the society at large.

Clearly, the workplace must be reflective of changing societal norms of equity. It cannot ignore changing standards of living and patterns of consumption. It cannot ignore the role it plays in employees' personal and familial lives. Once adequate health services, pensions, vacation standards, availability of personal and emergency time, and flexibility in rules and regulations begin to prevail in the society at large, all workers expect a certain minimum, and, where possible, they select employers who provide more. A given employer who wants to be competitive does not dare do less, if only to stabilize his/her work force and to keep morale at a level that permits reasonable daily operations. Whether because management perceives this as essential to maintain competitiveness or because legislation or labor unions will impose requirements in the future, as they have in the past, we are certain that responses will continue. The job place will change with the society.

No U.S. employer today would expect to be able to recruit workers for a 60-hour, 6-day week, for example; what was once a standard is no longer. Almost 45 percent of the work force is female, and close to 70 percent of labor force growth over the next decade is likely to come from women entering the work force. No employer wants to be closed out of two thirds of his or her potential pool of workers. He must ask what kinds of benefits or policies will attract women who may also be mothers, men who may also be fathers, and employees who care about both jobs and families.

We suggest that standards for employment policies are changing now, just as the work force is changing. Many workplace changes are now being put in place, some by leading companies and others by smaller and far less visible employers, and still other changes have yet to emerge. Some of these may involve new roles and responsibilities for employers, and some may involve modifications in and reallocations of existing roles. We are convinced that payoffs can occur for those employers who want to be leaders.

We begin, here, with a look at the present corporate welfare system and how and why it evolved.

2. Employers' Responses to Their Employees

There is mixed or incomplete evidence in regard to whether employer responsiveness to the personal circumstances and needs of their employees pays off in productivity or in other ways with positive financial results for the company. There are certainly debates about whether the employer is obligated to be concerned about such matters. Nonetheless, it is clear that many employers do provide work-related benefits and services and that these are extraordinarily important to their employees.

Nor should this occasion any surprise. When men and women are in the labor force in advanced industrialized societies, they are also likely to be parents and parents of minor children for some of the time. Certain benefits, adjustments, and adaptations may be needed at the workplace and elsewhere in the society if parents are to fulfill home and work tasks adequately and rear their children well. If such responses are not forthcoming, adults may have difficulty in one, the other, or both domains; employers may experience problems at the workplace; and children may suffer, as may the society, ultimately.

In thinking about specific responses, how they are offered, and by whom, it is useful to recall that:

- At any given moment it is more likely than not that a given married employee has a spouse working outside the home.
- For the first time, there are more two-earner than one-earner families with children in the labor force.[1]
- The vast majority of single mothers rearing children under 18 is also in the labor force.

From the perspective of families as a group, work relatedness is an overwhelming fact of life. As seen from the workplace, however, they and their concerns are not necessarily dominant. Husbands and wives constitute 70 percent of the labor force, but parents of minor children constitute only 40 percent, and parents with very young children, under age 6, constitute less than 20 percent.

Of the 64 million males in the labor force in 1986, only 11 million (18 percent) had children under age 6. Only 8.5 million of 52 million women in the labor force that same year (16.5 percent) also had children under 6. These numbers obviously affect the strength of the constituency concerned with child care, availability of leave to take care of a sick child, and other benefits especially relevant to the parents of the young. On the other hand, 64 percent of the males are husbands, 55 percent of the females are wives, and 38 percent of the former and 40 percent of the latter have children under 18. Family concerns are hardly invisible.

The brief case summary that follows is interesting because it is unexceptional. We sometimes forget how firmly assumptions about benefits, work schedules, workplace cooperation, and family adaptations can be built into daily life.

This attractive, articulate young woman, born in Trinidad, is in her early 30s. She is a customer's representative taking orders for equipment. She has been in the company for 12 years, having worked her way up from clerk.

She is married, has children aged twelve, ten, and four, which means that all of the children were born during her association with the company.

She has worked throughout her married life, as has her husband. Her mother lived with them until the second of the children was old enough for kindergarten, so that made child care arrangements "very easy." Now her mother lives in Texas. The youngest child is in a day care center, which costs $45 a week. The hours are satisfactory and it is easy because it is only two blocks away from home. She can send the child with her ten year old who passes that way en route to school. The ten year old also is responsible for picking up the little one at 3:00. By 3:30 the twelve year old is at home; the husband gets home at 4:00 and the wife at 5:45. She talked about teaching the children to be responsible, and everything she described about the family routine suggests that they have achieved this very well.

The family has been healthy, but they do use the dental benefits and have been getting eyeglasses at discount through the union plan. She used the medical benefits for maternity, and "everything was paid." She particularly remembers the last birth, four years ago. She stayed home for six months and got the same job when she came back. If she stayed out more than six months, she could not be guaranteed the same job, but six months was enough. Six weeks were with full pay; the checks came on time.

Her husband, who is self-employed and has no health insurance of his own, used some of the medical benefits for a recent appendectomy.

If a child is ill, she will use an excused workday, of which she has five a year, one unpaid. They are asked to schedule these in advance, but if the supervisor cooperates, one can get it for real emergencies, and she has not had any problems. She has a very cooperative supervisor, and she thinks of herself as fortunate. Other women she knows have had problems in using their personal days.

Vacations depend on seniority. She has less flexibility here than her husband, but because of his flexibility they can coordinate times. They wait to see when she has to schedule her vacations and he then chooses his.

Summer is complicated. Two weeks of day camp, one week her husband takes charge, one or two weeks when she is responsible constitute a summertime child care "package." She and her husband, therefore, have only one week of vacation together.

She has not used the personal advice service at work but is aware of several people with financial problems who have received guidance there, as well as help with personal problems.

If a company offers an unusually supportive environment, in addition to benefits, that is helpful and appreciated.

Mrs. L. has worked for her company for 13 years, beginning as a senior secretary, and now is an executive secretary. She was born and grew up in California and initially came to this company at the suggestion of neighbors who told her about the job and about the firm. She said it was well known that this was an unusual employer even for secretaries. "You don't have to punch a time clock . . . it was really like a college campus . . ." She has two children, and when she first came to work for the company, her son was nine months old and her daughter three years old.

Earlier, she had worked as a secretary and then left her job two months before she gave birth to her first child. She then stopped working for about three and one half years.

She stressed how supportive the company, and her bosses in particular, have been. She said they really understood a mother's responsibilities. Sometimes she had to take days off in order to do something for the children and sometimes she would come to work very early in the morning and then go home at lunch in order to do certain personal or family-related tasks.

She commented that if a child is sick, there is no paid sick leave for a mother to take so that one uses either unpaid personal leave or vacation time. On the other hand, the advantage of flexitime for her was that she could work through lunch (although a half hour of it is mandatory) and can flex at either end. The problem is that though her own boss might permit her to take time off and say that she is sick if her child was ill, her peers notice and know about it and object.

With regard to current benefits, she selects the most comprehensive medical care program offered in the company plan. She said that her husband is in the Navy and she is entitled to use Champus, but she does not like it. Her son, who is now fourteen years old, is diabetic and needs good medical care.

She has also used her psychiatric coverage for her son, and treatment was partially paid for by the company plans.

She usually takes one vacation day at a time or long weekends. She commented, as did several others we interviewed in that firm, that the company's closing for Christmas week is a tremendous advantage for employees with children.

When asked what her "wish list" would be for the benefit/service area, she talked about the child care problems as being a particular concern even if she is past the "crisis" years. She thinks child care should be provided at the workplace because it is so hard to get decent care for children in the community. She said even if one has enough money, it still is a problem. She paid $75 a week even in the middle 1970s for the child care services she had, which included two meals a day for her children. At that time her salary was going largely for child care, and even then the quality and reliability were questionable. Later she paid for private school when her son was no longer eligible for the preferred public school and when he needed supplementary afternoon activities.

Our purpose in this chapter is to review what employers now do to ease the personal and family lives of employees and which employees benefit from such arrangements. The major spotlight is on nonstatutory employee benefits and services—what are often described as fringe benefits—as well as on policies having to do with the allocation of worktime. We include in our review those practices that have evolved over time from some implicit assumptions about employer/employee relationships and how compensation is to be allocated. Some policies and practices have emerged from specific and conscious concern for work redesign and the quality of work life. Others developed without any special theory, because they were introduced into collective bargaining. Thus, we include those policies that have been consciously adopted to respond to the personal and family needs of employees, as well as those that have such effect despite other purposes in their development, those policies and practices that employees have developed voluntarily as well as those negotiated as part of collective labor agreements.

Despite a focus on the employer, one cannot obtain adequate perspective without considering *statutory* benefits as well. Pension policy is intertwined with social security. Income replacement after childbirth can be covered by state Temporary Disability Insurance (TDI), by disability coverage under collective bargaining, or by an employer-initiated benefit system. Fringe benefit costs are factored into a total expenditure on labor that includes legally mandated benefits. As relevant, we shall, therefore, report coverage by the public system as the backdrop for employer provision. The large question about possible future relationships of these systems is deferred for the final chapter.

The Area of Concentration

Nonstatutory employee benefits and services, as well as policies having to do with the allocation of worktime, constitute a wide field. Yet we need to acknowledge at the start that a case could be made for even broader coverage.

Total compensation consists of wages/salaries plus fringe benefits, but we do not discuss the adequacy of compensation, the current level of the minimum wage, or the idea of a family wage, which has an interesting history, especially in the Netherlands.[2] We have explored elsewhere the potential role of family allowances in correcting for the lack of relationship of wage scales to family responsibilities.[3]

Indeed, one could argue as well that nothing is more important to families than the availability of work and job security.[4] That public policy issue, beyond the scope of most individual employers, is outside our present focus as well.

Still another important component of employer provision is related to the physical conditions of work. Issues of occupational health and safety are central components of company policy affecting employee well-being. These, too, are not covered in the present discussion.

Indeed, to focus adequately on our chosen topics, we also must forgo several developments that obviously interact quite directly with the areas to which we are giving attention: various efforts to restructure or redefine work, as well as work sharing (in the sense of spreading partial unemployment). We similarly put aside discussion of worker participation in management. Finally, we do not discuss such topics as corporate philanthropy and corporate investment policies, clearly relevant to country and community well-being and often not confined in their impact to company employees.

We have concentrated on family status and family responsibilities, yet family status is not the only relevant personal variable when one reviews workplace well-being. We do not here discuss affirmative action, equal opportunity, and other special measures that take into account sex and minority status in improving an individual's labor force status. A considerable body of law and an administrative/legal structure of enforcement have developed in this field and are widely discussed.

Again, our core concerns are the two aspects of what employers can and do provide their employees: (1) what we have described as the corporate social welfare system—the benefits or income supplements (cash and in-kind) and the direct or indirect services provided employees by their employers; and (2) policies related to the allocation of time: paid time off from work, unpaid but job-protected time off, and flexibility in the scheduling of work time (what is sometimes referred to as alternative work schedules or patterns). As will be seen, these alone are large and complex arenas. From the public or employer perspectives they are also expensive and potent policy domains.

The contemporary corporate social welfare system is the evolutionary product of earlier paternalistic practices. Despite the fact that employee benefits have been viewed primarily as providing protection for the individual worker, rather than as playing a significant role in meeting the family responsibilities of employees, in aggregate the diverse practices of this system do constitute specific and significant responses by some employers to the personal or family needs of large numbers of employees.

Looking Backward

Under the labels "welfare capitalism," "employee welfare," "industrial paternalism," and "industrial welfare," many have described the beneficence of employers in more or less positive terms. Regardless, it is clear that the concern of employers for their individual employees and their familial circumstances is as old as history.

Of more direct relevance, however, is the emergence of welfare capitalism in the United States in the late nineteenth century.[5] This welfare capitalism was the direct antecedent of the industrial social welfare developments of today. Concerned specifically with the amelioration of what employers viewed as their major problems—high employee turnover, an unsocialized foreign labor force, labor militancy, and the threat of government interference—some employers also espoused more lofty and altruistic individual and family-related goals. These initiatives paralleled the development of early welfare statism in Germany with the beginnings of social insurance. It was also the period of growth in the United States and elsewhere of a strong movement of voluntary social welfare agencies, such as the charity organization societies and the settlement houses.[6] These were in a sense three movements—statutory social welfare, voluntary social welfare, and industrial welfare—with common roots.

Several factors contributed to the spread of industrial welfarism as an institutional response to nineteenth-century industrialization. First there was the surge of immigration and the rapid expansion of a labor force that was viewed by some as intractable and even dangerous to the established order; there was desire to socialize these entering workers into very different life and work styles and thus to exercise social control through a variety of devices. Moreover, new factories, indeed new industries, were expanding in areas completely lacking a public infrastructure. The development could not proceed without some provision for housing and other public amenities.

In some areas the spreading social disorganization and worker discontent were attributed to the entry of women and children into the labor force. Some employers, in designing company welfare programs, were as much concerned with shoring up a weakening family structure, regarded as the source of many other problems, as with the amelioration of specific workplace problems. On the part of one group of employers as well, there was concern with adding a more benevolent and humanitarian component (and often a religiously generated ethic) into the harshness of the radically changing world of work and daily living.

In the United States, the major provision developed by employers included housing, medical care, schools, recreation services, community centers, religious facilities, advice and counseling services, food and clothing programs, pension plans, and even profit sharing.

Pullman, Illinois, is often thought of as the prototype of the nineteenth century company town.[7] Built in the 1880s, it was a showplace, widely heralded as an example of enlightened business policy. The total company investment in the town, which included a modern, ventilated factory, plus housing, an excellent school system, a library, parks, playgrounds, stores, a theater, a casino, and a church, was estimated at about $8 million, a large sum at the time. The standards of housing, lighting, and maintenance were considered to be far in advance of the day. Although Pullman's goal clearly was to attract skilled labor and to keep such workers beyond the reach of Chicago's trade unions and union organizers, many among the social reformers of the time were also convinced that he was sincerely interested in improving the living conditions of his employees.[8] Others who visited Pullman described a situation of fear and suspicion among the inhabitants, clearly a harbinger of future problems.[9] Company towns were often controlling in the extreme as they regulated norms and routines of daily life.

Corporate welfare grew most dramatically between 1910 and 1917, out of expressed concern for employees' well-being and its perceived link with efficiency and improved productivity. In language that sounds remarkably contemporary, some companies presented a rationale for why they decided to launch welfare and scientific management programs simultaneously. Others concentrated on one or the other but still viewed them as interrelated.[10]

Amoskeag Manufacturing Company, the large New Hampshire textile company, established its corporate welfare program in 1911.[11] According to Tamara Hareven, as with other companies, its objectives included curbing labor turnover, flagging troublemakers, preventing strikes, and encouraging company loyalty. Unlike some companies, however, in Amoskeag, efficiency and welfare programs coexisted as part of the same reform. Although the program is described as modest, it included housing, social and recreational activities, and health services, as well as the establishment of a centralized and increasingly professionalized personnel department.[12] Despite the fact that the company never introduced a profit sharing plan, and although its pension plan was only very limited, "Its image as a company that supported major welfare programs nevertheless survived in workers' memories because of the elaborately maintained housing activities sponsored by the corporation, and the overall grandeur and scale of the mill yard."[13]

Amoskeag's welfare programs left a far more positive impression among its employees than Pullman's and those of other companies primarily because they were not compulsory. Few constraints were placed on how and where workers lived and shopped. Of some interest, however, here as elsewhere, the welfare program does not seem to have curbed labor turnover, although it was viewed as increasing employees' identification with and loyalty to the company, as well as worker satisfaction. It probably served more as a recruitment device than as a strategy for assuring a stable work force.

The company welfare movement peaked during the 1920s, a decade of prosperity, leveling out during the latter half of the decade. Some ascribe the apparent slowdown in developments to growing individual employee resentment of employer paternalism or to union-organizer attacks upon it. Other factors may have included the growth in technology, lessening the importance of labor in many large industries; the expansion of voluntary agency and public community services, which reduced the need for company provision; and the growing availability of automobiles and public transportation, which expanded employee access to alternative services and reduced the need for company houses, stores, and towns.

Most important, the demise of business welfarism occurred because of the Depression. Employers could provide a variety of extras only when profits were high; the pressure to provide these benefits existed only when the labor market was tight and the competition for workers strenuous. Neither was the case in the 1930s. Furthermore, legislation and policies of the New Deal dealt a direct and final blow to such practices. The Wagner Act and other legislation made company unions illegal, while the Act, and the National Labor Relations Board created under it, encouraged the growth of trade or labor unions.[14] Thus, the one adversary that business had hoped to constrain through the development of company beneficence had won a significant victory. Once this struggle against the unions was lost, there was little reason for continuing welfare programs in the unionized, core sectors of the economy (and some company welfare programs could be declared illegal, as company unionism).

Finally, the economic and social havoc of the 1930s demonstrated the inability of private efforts, both profit (business) and nonprofit (voluntary social agencies), to meet the needs of a significant portion of the population faced with overwhelming financial and social problems. Only government, the federal government in particular, had the power, the wherewithal, the authority, and the mission to provide food, cash relief, or work relief on a large scale or to establish a social security system. In the United States the move toward government as the basic provider of a floor of essential benefits and services began with the New Deal. By the end of the Great Depression, primacy in this field of welfare benefits had moved from the private sector to the public sector. The growth in the role of government and in the nature, scope, range, and extent of its social provision, especially during the last 20 years, is an accepted, integral, and dramatic part of this picture that we must take account of in our discussion.

Nevertheless, despite the demise of company welfare in its paternalistic form and the concomitant trend toward government provision, the role of private industry was not to disappear in toto. It surfaced again in modified form after World War II and focused on a narrower range of provision than earlier. Before World War II, employee benefits plans were practically nonexistent, especially for production workers. The phenomenal upsurge in their growth soon after occurred largely as a result of four factors: (1) wage controls during World War II and in the immediate postwar period that permitted bargaining for benefits while denying wage increases; (2) the National Labor Relations Board's interpretation of the 1947 Labor Management Relations Act, permitting pensions to be included as a collective bargaining issue; (3) the 1949 report of the Steel Industry Fact Finding Board, which maintained that industry had both a social and an economic obligation to provide workers with social insurance and pensions; and (4) the wage freeze during the Korean War, continuing the earlier pattern set during World War II of permitting growth in benefit plans.

A second spur of company benefit growth occurred in the 1970s, paralleling the growth in statutory in-kind benefits. Favorable tax treatment of employers' retirement contributions dates from as far back as the 1920s, in fact, and the tax-free status of health insurance benefits was established in 1939. The 1970s and early 1980s saw a new move toward expanding the preferential tax treatment of employee benefits (stock ownership, legal assistance, van pools, educational assistance, dependent care,

cafeteria plans, and flexible spending accounts). As a severe inflation brought wage earners into high tax brackets, and Congress
enacted legislation providing new fringe benefit opportunities,
compensation in the form of tax-free benefits was clearly favored
by some employees as having greater value than higher wages. Industry increasingly understood the strategic role of benefits in
recruitment of categories of personnel for which there was competition, and unions routinely brought fringe benefits, as well as
wage demands, into bargaining sessions.

A Benefit Overview

An employee benefits plan is defined as:

Any type of plan sponsored or initiated unilaterally or jointly by employers or employees and providing benefits that stem from the employment relationship and are not underwritten or paid *directly* by government (Federal, State, Local).[15]

In general, such a plan provides (1) *income maintenance* (protection against loss of earnings) when regular earnings are cut off
because of death, accident, sickness, disability, retirement, or
unemployment; (2) *released time* with income continuance for
specified purposes such as vacations, holidays, and personal
needs; (3) *payment of medical expenses* associated with illness, in-
jury, and/or other types of health, medical, and dental care; and
(4) payment of expenses for certain *specified nonmedical services*,
such as legal services, education, and counseling. Some companies may also provide some services directly.

Richard Titmuss was among the first to note the significance of
such provisions. He described such benefits and services provided by employers to their employees as "occupational welfare," an
important contribution to the well-being of those fortunate
enough to be in the labor force.[16] He pointed out that these, as
well as benefits provided certain categories of taxpayers ("fiscal
welfare" in his terms), could be compared with the visible, more
traditional, and often more stigmatized form of "social welfare"
—the benefits and services provided directly by government,
often to those in particular need (table 2.1).

Timothy Smeeding proposes a useful definition of fringe

Table 2.1. Major Items on the Benefit Menu*†

	Nonstatutory Employee Benefits and Services	Related Statutory (Legally Required) Benefits (Non Means Tested)	Personal Benefits Supported by Tax Law (Incomplete)
Income maintenance	Insurance that provides income protection or replacement in instances of: • retirement	Social insurance federal and state	Supplementary retirement accounts IRAs Salary reduction plans Insurance benefits (sickness, accident, travel, disability)
	• death • long-term disability • sickness or short-term disability • accident, injury	Old Age Survivor Disability Insurance (OASDI) " Temporary Disability Insurance (5 states) Workers' Compensation (state)	
	• unemployment	Unemployment Insurance	
Released time	Vacations Guaranteed holidays Personal leaves	– Legal holidays[a]	–
Payment of medical expenses or medical services	Health and hospital coverage Major medical insurance Dental plans	Medicare[b] b –	All health and hospital insurance policies

Vision plans	—	
Health promotion programs	—	
Health services— employer or union operated	—	

Other Services		
Legal services	c	Dependent care assistance plans
Educational benefits	Public education [d] [e]	
Counseling and employee assistance programs		Child care tax credit (dependent care tax credit)
Child care information and referral or on-site child care services		

---

* For these purposes, federal, state, and local government employees may be thought of as having employee benefits provided by *their* employers, as well as benefits they share as citizens.

† Other public benefits include the Earned Income Tax Credit, tax deductions for mortgage interest and taxes paid on homes, etc. These are discussed as appropriate.

a However, the existence of a legal holiday does not ensure a paid day off.

b In addition, there is Medicaid, offering relatively comprehensive coverage to the poor on a means-tested basis, with eligibility ceilings varying by state.

c There are publicly funded and voluntary nonprofit legal services for the poor.

d There are also college-legal grants for the poor on a means-tested basis. Low-interest loans on a means-tested basis extend well into the middle class.

e Most publicly operated or publicly-financed counseling and community mental health programs concentrate on the poor or minorities or charge fees from those with health insurance coverage. However, all protective services (abuse and neglect), many services for the aged, and many information and referral services operate without regard to income.

benefits as "the amount of total employee hourly compensation not received as pay for time worked, but paid by employers to employees for time not worked, or paid by employers to intermediaries on behalf of employees."[17] There is no difference among economists in the view that total compensation is equal to wages/salary, plus pay for time not worked (vacations, personal days, and the like), plus supplements (including statutory social insurance contributions, private insurance and pensions, various other benefits.)

It is agreed among analysts that, depending upon the circumstances (strength of market, tightness of the labor market, political conditions), the nonwage labor costs may be shifted backward (reducing profits) or forward (increasing prices). From the employer's point of view they may decrease potential cash compensation or be irrelevant to cash compensation, depending on the potential for shifting. These considerations affect what a given company does at a given time, as does the tax status of the benefit.

We do not here report systematically on the more generous perquisites ("perks") of upper management, but these do not affect significantly the picture of coverage for the vast majority of the labor force. In recent years both pension and tax laws and regulations have increased the prohibitions on discrimination, so that similar categories of basic benefits have become available to most people in any given company, the unique upper-management perks aside.

Both private and statutory benefits in the United States are related to labor force status. The private fringe benefits are always related to such current status or — in the case of retirees, surviving spouses, and children or dependents of current employees — prior derived labor force status. The public social insurance benefits follow a similar pattern, but income-tested benefits like Medicaid or food stamps do not. Many other countries have more universal benefits independent of the work status than we do.

For most people, the labor force status connection of the benefit system poses no problem at all; for the minority of unemployed, underemployed, retired, or labor market-unrelated, the consequences can sometimes be disastrous. Women who have been lifelong homemakers are especially disadvantaged.

The work relatedness of health or child care benefits can have serious consequences. As we write, almost 120 million Americans are in the civilian plus military labor force, but of these, more than 8 million are unemployed. Moreover, these ratios understate the matter. The 1983 unemployment rate of 9.6 percent touched 26.5 million workers in the course of the year.[18] According to the University of Michigan's Panel Study on Income Dynamics, 40 percent of all prime-age men experienced a spell of unemployment over a ten-year period, even though most of the unemployment time was concentrated in a much smaller group.[19]

Data about benefit coverage tend to be incomplete. Many of the most generally cited sources report on the top 1,000 corporations, or companies with more than 500 or more than 250 employees. The business literature often defines a small business as one with fewer than 500 employees; yet half the private-sector work force is in companies with fewer than 250 employees and 40 percent in companies with fewer than 100.[20]

Nonetheless, the surveys tend to converge in the view that benefit availability and adequacy is affected not only by continuity of labor force attachment but also by:

- Employment by government, as contrasted with the private sector
- Employment in manufacturing and parts of the service sector, as contrasted with agriculture
- Employment in large and very large, not small, companies
- Employment in unionized, not unorganized, firms

Obviously the shifting economic status of a given branch of industry and the varying funding circumstances of nonprofit and religious agencies may also be significant.

There are, of course, refinements beyond our immediate scope. To illustrate: A study in the plastics industry reported that while "the overwhelming trend . . . is for fringe benefit levels to increase with increasing firm size," it is also of interest that "the largest firm size impact is on retirement pensions." Health benefits tend to be relatively uniform, with larger companies adding optical and dental benefits.[21]

Firm size, industry, and profitability must matter because benefit packages are not inexpensive. Chamber of Commerce data, as reanalyzed by Smeeding, add benefit costs to direct compensation to produce a total compensation figure. He finds the following distribution (1983):

- Cost of employer share of *mandated benefits* (social insurance, workmen's compensation, etc.)   7.2%
- *Discretionary fringe benefits* (medical, pensions, insurance, etc.)   12.4%
- Pay for *time not worked* (vacations, holidays, sick leave, lunch time, etc.)   9.8%
- Pay for *time worked*   70.6%

    Total Compensation   100.0%

A more traditional way to describe this is to note that mandatory and discretionary benefits, plus pay for time not worked, have been adding about 35 percent to a typical payroll in recent years. Large companies spend more, small companies less. The statutory component is the rock-bottom cost of doing business legally, no matter how small and shaky the enterprise.[22]

As we shall see in the chapters that follow, employer motivation, opportunity, and capacity in this field have enormous consequences for employees and their families.

Medical and Health Benefits[23]

In the United States the medical care benefit is plainly the most important benefit provided through the corporate social security system. This is the view of employees who are polled and of union leaders.[24] This was confirmed in our employee interviews, union contacts, and employer discussions.

If we list all the major components observed in the United States or elsewhere, full coverage of health and medical needs might consist of the following:

- Physician service — in and out of the hospital
- Hospital coverage — acute and long term

- Intermediate facility and nursing home coverage for short-and long-term care
- Catastrophic insurance to provide cost-free care or reimburse care costs for very expensive services, long term or short term
- Cash replacement of wages when one is unable to work because of illness, short-term disability, or childbirth
- Coverage for long-term disability
- Preventive care and health maintenance

These categories overlap somewhat. Benefits available may or may not cover dependents and may do so completely or partially. Some schemes emphasize cash replacement or fee payment. Others provide services. Few programs offer prevention except in the sense of coverage by a physician for a checkup or inoculations.

We begin with *physician, hospital,* and *related benefits,* deferring cash replacement during illness or short- and long-term disability to a separate section. The programs here described include catastrophic insurance, intermediate facilities, and nursing homes, if there is such coverage, but in all these latter categories far less is available than is offered with regard to hospital and in-hospital physician coverage.

The United States offers statutory hospital and physician coverage to the aged and permanently disabled through Medicare and to the very poor through Medicaid. For the most part, the vast middle in the United States have no legally required protection. What benefits, then, are associated with employment — the major alternative? The packaging is so complex and the categorization so involved that a listing will best serve as summary. Documentation is left to the notes.

- By the early 1980s, about three quarters of private-industry employees but four fifths of public workers (88 percent of state employees) had group health insurance. The coverage through group health plans reached about 57 percent of all persons.[25]

- In 1982, almost 60 percent of households had one or more covered members and two thirds of households with children had some coverage; there was moderate decline by 1984.

- Employment-related health plans involve family coverage (54 percent) more often than coverage for individuals alone (46 percent).

- With regard to the 57 percent of all persons who were covered by a private employer health plan in 1984, 5 percent of employees paid the full cost, 55 percent cost-shared, and 40 percent had coverage as an employer-paid benefit.[26]

- There are enormous differences in health benefit coverage by firm size, nature of the industry, and by whether there is a union contract, but a union's presence makes less difference in large firms.[27]

- Large firms are more likely to cover dependents than small firms are. Everywhere, dependent coverage is more likely than not to require an employee contribution or full payment. Large firms contribute or provide full coverage for dependents far more often than small firms do.

- The Urban Institute has reported that after a 15-year trend of health insurance coverage improvement, there was a decline from 1979 to 1982 and, again, from 1982 to 1984. By 1984, 35.1 million people (17.1 percent of the under 65s) were without coverage, compared with 28.7 million (14.6 percent of the under 65s) in 1980.[28] The decline could be continuing as we go to press.

All of this provision is for hospital care and for physician services for treatment of diagnosed illness and surgery. The other medical care categories have more limited attention. For example, in one year 73 percent of the population saw a physician on an ambulatory basis at least once and paid 57 percent of charges directly on an out-of-pocket basis; other public sources and private health insurance, most of it employment based, paid the remainder of these costs, almost coequally.[29]

Although counts vary from survey to survey and as unemployment rises and falls, there was expert convergence in 1983-85 on the following summation of health care coverage:

- 75 percent of the population is covered by employer plans, either cost-shared or fully employer-paid.

- 10 percent of the population is covered by Medicare, Medicaid, or both.
- 15 percent of the population has no coverage.

Who, then, are the more than 35 million Americans uncovered in this pattern? This percentage has grown by 20 percent in the 1980-84 period according to Urban Institute research. We summarize:

The largest group among those who have no health insurance coverage, more than half of those who are uncovered, according to 1982 and 1984 reports, are employed people and their non-working family members.[30] This includes between 6.6 and 8.5 million employees and their uninsured dependents (between 5.4 and 7 million). These people are found primarily working in agriculture, construction, retail trade, and personal services. Small employers are especially likely to provide no health insurance for their employees. In a 1981 survey of subscribers to *INC.*, a magazine aimed at small-business entrepreneurs, 21 percent of the respondents reported that their companies do not carry group health insurance.[31] During the economic difficulties of the early 1980s, a significant number of companies discontinued coverage or required new or increased cost sharing. In addition, more than half of all new jobs require a waiting period before health insurance benefits are received, and many of the 15 million part-time employees are excluded altogether.[32] Some low-paid workers reject health coverage in companies that expect them to share the costs because they do not feel able to do so. During economic difficulties in the mid-1980s, some workers ended coverage for family members because they could not afford to share costs. The lack of health insurance for this proportionately small but numerically significant group of the employed has greater ramifications than for any other group. In 1979, the uncovered employed had eight times as many dependents as the uncovered unemployed.

The second largest group among the uncovered are the unemployed. About one third of the unemployed (3 to 3.9 million out of a total of 11.5 million) were without health insurance coverage in 1983, approximately 7 million if their dependents are included.

This number is lower than some estimates because it reflects the health insurance coverage of other employed family members (more than one half of all husband-wife families have both spouses working), the extension of benefits by companies and unions (about 40 percent of workers have short-term layoff protection), and the availability of some government insurance programs (20 percent of the unemployed were covered by public insurance in 1982). Recent legislative efforts to help the unemployed have concentrated on requiring coverage for 18 months after job termination, but the former employee must pay the premium.[33]

The third largest group among the uninsured are those who are not in the labor force, largely low-income family members not seeking work and not qualifying for, or applying for, public assistance.

Young adults, aged 19-24, in or out of the labor force, are about twice as likely to be without health insurance as any other age group. Most are in families where the heads are covered, but even this leaves them with no or little protection.

Clearly, health insurance provided as an employee benefit in public or private employment is essential for individuals and families unless they are in poverty and thus eligible for Medicaid benefits or over 65 and covered by Medicare. The lack of coverage for employees who are parents, especially for young, unmarried women, can have severe and deleterious consequences for children. A major problem remains, therefore, for those employees and their families who do not receive such benefits through their jobs.

Employment status also affects the extent, the kind, and the adequacy of health care coverage. Even if *overall coverage rates* may be approximated, reliable data on the number of people with *adequate* coverage are unavailable. A 1984 study report from a 14,000-household sample tapped in 1977-78 found that while 80 percent of the civilian population did have private health insurance, their entitlements covered only one third of their total health care expenditures.[34] The percentage of unreimbursed expenditure has probably increased by the mid-1980s as companies add to the deductibles in health insurance (and government does in Medicare) in the belief that this discourages inappropriate use and helps contain costs. It is also estimated that about 15 percent or more of those with private health insurance, usually provided through their jobs, are not covered for major medical or catastrophic illness expenditures. This is the coverage that picks up when one has exhausted the hospital and surgical maximum of Blue Cross-Blue Shield and similar plans. After an annual deductible, it takes on the heavy burdens, which can multiply rapidly. For those not covered by major medical policies, given current physician fees, hospital rates, and health insurance limits, even a moderate spell of serious illness or an operation can be an economic catastrophe.

Finally, health coverage deals with acute and chronic illness, not, in most instances, with preventive medical care. Coverage for routine physician visits, pediatric care, prescriptions, and so forth is even more limited than the reports cited above suggest. Most people have no coverage for the routine check-up costs, the preventive services, or well-baby care. Recent switches to health insurance maintenance organizations, completely prepaid for prevention, acute care, and chronic care, are an improvement here but still cover only a minority of those with medical care coverage.

Although there are no reliable data for dental or eye care coverage, in the 1970s these were considered the new and popular benefits in companies viewed as having "Cadillac" employee benefits plans. In large firms, for example, dental insurance has become one of the most rapidly growing benefits. Nearly two thirds of the workers in the medium and large firms surveyed by the Bureau of Labor Statistics (BLS) had insurance for dental expenses in 1982, up from just under half in 1979.[35] Similarly, the Conference Board reported that "Dental insurance is so popular with both unions and employees that it has become widespread in a very short time." Its prevalence grew from about 8 percent of the sample surveyed in 1973, to 19 percent of a comparable 1975 sample, and to 41 percent in 1981.[36] The majority of the labor force lacks dental and optical protections.

Truly comprehensive health and medical care insurance is provided only to a small group of workers employed in a select group of industries and companies. As we move away from this elite core, health and medical coverage becomes less adequate both in range and extensiveness. A significant number of employees with family responsibilities still have no, or very limited, coverage for even the most basic services.

The Robert Wood Johnson Foundation has found that—including "free care" for the uncovered—almost 90 percent of Americans have a physician or *some* source of general medical care (but 24.5 million people were reported as not having care), that most Americans report satisfaction with their care experience, but that 23 percent of families with serious or chronic illness experience cite a "major financial problem" as a concomitant.

Clearly, there are differences in the exact counts, explained by method, target population, and calculations either of a one-time cross-section or a year-round rate. All agree, however, that unemployment, lack of labor force attachment, part-time work, employment in small companies, and ineligibility of the working-poor intact families for Medicaid explain the lack of coverage. To which we add that where family coverage depends on employee contributions, many low-income workers feel they cannot afford it.[37]

Inevitably, then, health coverage—its existence and its adequacy—is a major theme in the employee benefit system. The serious medical inflation of the 1980s has made employers very careful about expansion and has created interest in cutbacks, increased cost sharing, and cost control.

Pensions and Life Insurance

Pensions. When the Social Security Act was passed in 1935, one objective was to provide a minimum floor of income for the retired elderly. About 95 percent of the labor force today is covered by social security or a related public retirement program. However, the social security standard is still meant to provide only a floor of income. It has been assumed that for people to maintain their more comfortable prior living standards, social security income would have to be supplemented by other sources of retirement income, such as private pensions and personal savings. Dependence on social security alone, without coverage by an employer-provided pension, is increasingly likely to mean near-poverty or a very poor standard. Indeed, according to a report from the President's Commission on Pension Policy, "one of the results of the near universal coverage of social security and of the lack of coverage of employer pensions is the creation of a two-class retirement income system." Of those recently retiring, for example, about 53 percent of married men, 24 percent of married women, and 42 percent of unmarried persons were reported in 1984 by the Social Security Administration as having private pension supplementation. The significance of such supplementation varied enormously.

Employees themselves view entitlement to a pension as the second most important benefit they receive at work, after health and medical insurance; they also rank it second on their list of benefits they most desire to see improved.[38]

According to the 1985 BLS survey, 91 percent of the workers in the medium and large firms surveyed were covered by private retirement plans.[39] However, the most recent Census Bureau report, based on March 1985 data, estimates that 44 percent of all households and 58 percent of all households with a working member have some private employer or union-provided pension coverage at work.[40] Many American workers are not in the BLS "medium and large" firms. Many of the self-employed are in marginal enterprises — or try to save and invest but do not set up pension plans.

A distinction is drawn between employment in pension-connected jobs, expectation of a future pension, and the technical achievement of entitlement to future retirement benefits (vesting) by virtue of longevity. Federal law has required full vesting after 10 years, but reduction to 5 years was enacted in the 1986 tax reform. Analysis by the Employee Benefit Research Institute (EBRI) of a survey by the Bureau of the Census which it co-sponsored, disclosed that in 1983 pension coverage for all government-sector and private-sector workers was down to 52 percent, from 56 percent in 1979. Poor economic conditions, changes in American industry, and legislative changes may all have contributed to the decline. The system had developed over

50 years and was paying out at the rate of $91 billion in 1983, as compared with $149 billion in social security old age, retirement, and survivors' benefits.[41]

The overall coverage rate joins groups under differing circumstances, yet the percent who have actually achieved future benefit entitlement (a less precise number) is inevitably much lower. Thus the 1983 Census Bureau survey found that:[42]

• Of government employees, 83.0 percent were covered but only 47.7 percent had future benefit entitlement (by their reports).
• Of all civilian employees and self-employed, 52.1 percent were covered but only 24.4 percent reported future benefit entitlement.
• Of nonagricultural wage and salary workers, 56.2 percent were covered but only 25.2 percent reported future benefit entitlement.
• Of those in the work force core (aged 25-64, working 1,000 or more hours per year, and on the job at least one year), 70.0 percent were covered but only 36.8 percent reported future benefit entitlement.

The actual future pension situations of those with coverage and no vesting as yet will be determined by their employers' circumstances, their personal work histories, and impact of recent legislative changes in vesting rules.

As much may be said of male-female differences, as reported in the same EBRI overview. In 1983, 50 percent of employed men were covered by an employer-sponsored pension plan but only 27 percent reported entitlement to future benefits. Of employed women, 41 percent were included in a plan and 18 percent reported entitlement to future benefits. In the core 25-64 age group, 66 percent of women and 73 percent of men have pension coverage, while 41 percent of women and 51 percent of men are actually vested. The right to lump sum distributions (which may be quite limited) could be said to raise the vesting rate in the privileged work force sector to 62 percent for women and 70 percent for men. These data reflect recent progress for women.

There is considerable research documenting the importance of industry, firm size, and unionization in explaining variations. Available data disclose that, when surveyed in a comprehensive

1979 BLS survey, almost 80 percent of the noncovered workers were employed by companies in which pensions were not available to any employee and therefore are unlikely ever to have coverage on their current jobs unless their employers institute new plans. The others worked for companies providing pensions to some employees but not to the particular workers surveyed.

As might be expected, those workers who are well situated in the occupational-industrial structure are likely to have coverage. For example, more than 80 percent of union workers or of employees in companies with 500 or more employees have pension plans (but only a minority of the employed labor force are in this group). Coverage is highest in high-wage industries, such as communications and public utilities, and lowest in retail trade and service industries. Concomitantly, the unemployed and workers who are disproportionately concentrated in the peripheral sectors of the economy—young adults, racial minorities, part-time workers, and women, those with low incomes—generally lack coverage. Only 11.9 percent of workers under age 25 in the private labor force were covered in 1983. That percentage is substantially lower than the rate for those in the prime working years and working steadily (65 percent). Coverage for white workers is considerably better than for nonwhites.

Pension coverage is notably correlated with earnings, too: 32.3 percent of workers earning less than $10,000 a year were covered in 1983, while 67 percent of those earning between $10,000-25,000 per year were covered, as were 82.1 percent of those in the over $25,000 salary category.

In summary, about half the private labor force is currently covered by a private ERISA-regulated pension plan and fewer than half of this sector now have or believe they will have a vested pension. Experts projecting from trends prior to 1986 legislative changes foresee two thirds of current full-time nongovernmental workers retiring with a pension. The *National Journal* reports projections of a coverage rate of 77 percent in two years.[43] Yet more than half of the nonwhite members of the labor force and almost 60 percent of the women still do not have pension protection. Moreover, many who do have coverage, especially women, are likely to be entitled to low benefits. Workplace private benefits are important but, even with 1986 vesting reforms, hardly a substitute for statutory (social security) protection.

Life Insurance. For those who survive or those with longevity at the workplace, the pension provides "life insurance" for a spouse and sometimes for other dependents. The 1984 pension reforms added spouse protection in this regard. Otherwise, there are only survivor benefits under federal Social Security (OASI), which can be quite limited for the families of relatively young workers. Because of this, the group life insurance policy is another very popular benefit in private industry. The BLS 1985 survey reports that 96 percent of employers in large and medium firms have group life insurance; in fact, 86 percent of the workers in these firms are in plans completely paid by their employers. Some plans permit the individual to self-insure on the top of an employer-paid basic benefit. The Conference Board "large firm" survey (1981) is quite consistent with the BLS report. Some 98 percent of nonoffice workers and practically all office workers have life insurance coverage, and the "median" benefit is two times the annual salary. About one quarter of part-time workers do have coverage in these firms. There is a similar rate of coverage for dependents.

Employer coverage usually provides either survivor income plans or lump-sum payments. According to the Employee Benefit Research Institute, there were 635,000 master policy group contracts by 1983, providing $2.2 trillion of coverage.[44] We do not know, however, just how many employees have any coverage at all in smaller and poorer companies and what the level of coverage is among the self-employed.

Short-Term Disability and Sickness Benefits

Those who collect monthly or annual salaries, as contrasted with those paid on an hourly basis, can usually stay away from work for periods of brief illness or disability without any loss of income. For the hourly worker the time lost can involve major forfeit of earnings.

Many countries meet this problem by providing in their health insurance coverage for specified cash replacement of income for periods of illness or short-term disability. Plans vary in how soon after an absence they begin, how long they go on, and what portion of basic salary they cover. In the United States such protection may be provided by specified sick pay (benefits) plans or what are known as temporary disability insurance (TDI) plans. The latter, with six-month maxima, expire when employees become eligible for Federal Disability Insurance under Social Security and/or for benefits under company supplementary long-term disability insurance. Some companies' long-term plans come into effect after briefer periods, such as two months.

Unlike almost all the industrialized countries of the world, the United States does not protect against the risk of loss of income through illness and disability (the period before long-term Disability Insurance comes into effect) through a nationally mandated program. Five states (California, Hawaii, New Jersey, New York, and Rhode Island), as well as Puerto Rico and the railroad industry, have temporary disability insurance laws requiring employers to cover their workers under a plan that pays a benefit replacing part of the worker's wage, usually for a period not to exceed 26 weeks (39 in California). The 1985 benefit maxima in the five states ranged between $145 and $224 weekly, usually replacing about half the wage.

Most members of the labor force are dependent upon employer-supervisor benevolence or on sick pay-temporary disability fringe benefit insurance plans provided by the company (on its own initiative or through a collective bargaining agreement) if they are to be covered. Most large companies include both salaried and hourly workers in their plans.

National data on what employers provide or what employees receive are more limited concerning this benefit than for health insurance and pensions. There are some data for large and medium-sized firms, and there are estimates on employees' coverage. In 1983 almost 60 percent of all private wage and salary workers (45.2 million people) were estimated to have such insurance coverage.[45] This includes 27.8 million workers in voluntary sickness and disability plans in private industry in states that do not mandate temporary disability coverage, as well as 17.4 million more in states with mandatory TDI laws. In addition, 14 million government workers have coverage in the form of sick pay intended to cover income loss until long-term disability plans come into effect, and 7 million in private industry are covered only by sick pay plans. The private insurance plans offer partial wage replacement (1/2 to 2/3) after a 3 to 7 day wait, and usually lasting for 13 to 26 weeks. These are much like the TDI plans. For the 7 million private industry workers covered only by sick pay eligibility, the duration tends to range between 5 and 15 days. The replacement rate of 38 percent for income loss from short-term nonwork-related disability plans by private industry insurance or TDI has been stable for a decade. However, this figure includes public employees; for private employees the replacement rate is 29.2 percent in the states with temporary disability leave and 26 percent elsewhere.

These data tend to exaggerate the extent of protection against such risks because, as already noted, they include somewhat disparate types of provision. Coverage is limited in duration and in the rate of wage replacement, and many people are not covered. Typically, after five years of service an employee may be entitled to three weeks of sick leave in some firms but rarely any longer, even for very long-term workers. Some employers provide both sick leave and disability coverage, but others do not.[46]

Long-term disability benefits were started in large firms in the 1960s for managers, offering a supplement to, or a more generous plan than, social security. Plans began to be extended to clerical workers and blue-collar workers only in the 1970s. These benefits generally come into effect after six months of disability. The BLS survey found that only 48 percent of the firms in its survey provided this benefit—and often not to line personnel.

Maternity Disability and Parenting Benefits. Unlike almost all other advanced industrialized societies and many less developed countries, the United States has no nationwide statutory provision that guarantees a woman the right to a leave from employment for a specified period, protects her job while she is on leave, and provides a cash benefit equal to all or a significant portion of her wage while she is not working because of pregnancy and childbirth.[47] Although most countries provide these benefits through national health insurance, 16 countries have such benefits despite the absence of health insurance. Various policy instruments other than health insurance have been used to provide maternity benefits. These include unemployment insurance (Canada and Austria), a special maternity benefit (Israel), parent insurance (Sweden), employment benefit (Britain), and a benefit combining health insurance and mandated employer provision (Federal Republic of Germany). Among the continental European countries, three months' paid maternity leave is the minimum. The Federal Republic of Germany provides ten months of parental benefits, and Sweden, one year. The modal European pattern is increasingly moving toward six months.[48]

To the extent that maternity benefits—a cash benefit replacing all or a portion of earnings lost at the time of maternity—exist in the United States, they do so as a consequence of either state-mandated TDI, as discussed in the previous section, or the employment benefit system. The Pregnancy Disability Act of 1978 required that pregnant employees be treated the same as employees with any temporary disability. This is interpreted to mean that women employed in firms providing short-term sickness or disability insurance also have the right to paid maternity leaves. It does not mean, however, that all employers must provide disability insurance or even paid sick leaves; it means only that if they do, they cannot exclude pregnancy and maternity from coverage.

The 1978 Pregnancy Disability Act is mistakenly assumed by many in industry and in the society generally to have led to almost complete coverage of women employees, ensuring the replacement of at least some portion of their lost wages for some period of time around childbirth, usually up to eight weeks. Our own 1981 survey found, rather, that coverage was much less extensive than popularly believed. Including those states having TDI, about half the private-sector workers, at most, are covered by some form of disability or sickness benefits providing income replacement for about six to eight weeks at the time of a normal childbirth. (Doctors have found women medically "disabled" for about six to eight weeks after childbirth, longer only for

Caesarean births or where there are complications.) However, this survey, too, is somewhat biased toward medium and large firms. Since women are more apt to work for smaller firms, a more accurate coverage estimate would probably be that *fewer than 40 percent of working women have income protection at the time of maternity that will permit them a six-week leave without severe financial penalty.* By the standards of major industrial societies and in relation to a broader concept of what is needed, however, this is hardly an admirable picture. Even in the most generous situation, no firm and no state provides for paid maternity leave that lasts more than an absolute maximum of twelve weeks, and most provide far less or none at all. No country in Europe, even the least generous, provides less than twelve weeks, and most provide far more.

Furthermore, as with regard to health insurance and pensions, the issue of equity is ever present, too, perhaps even more so where maternity benefits are concerned. For most working women, whether or not they have any kind of job and income protection at the time of childbirth is a function of where they live, as well as where they work. Women who live in states with TDI have at least a minimum floor of protection. Women who do not, however, are totally dependent on what their employers provide, and most, as we have indicated, do not provide anything, or at best very little in the way of income protection at this time.

Where there is insurance coverage for medical and hospital care, childbirth is now uniformly included, and we have summarized coverage data in the previous section.

Nor do most women in the United States enjoy generous unpaid job-protected leaves following childbirth. Most working women have some leave, an improvement over the past, but it tends to be two or three months. Leading companies provide six months. (There are no precise national statistics.) Most European countries guarantee far longer unpaid leaves, some one or two years, but most working women in the United States could not afford to stay out much longer than they do for lack of more nearly adequate income replacement.

Currently there are also court challenges in regard to whether the right to a disability leave after childbirth also involves job protection.

In discussing maternity benefits we do not mean to slight the accommodation that might be made for fathers or the importance of such policies. We note, however, that despite attention to the subject in the media, the number of companies providing paternity benefits is very small; such leaves are rare even in the leading firms. In contrast, in Sweden, both parents are equally entitled to a parental paid leave after childbirth (deciding between themselves how it is to be shared), while in Norway and Finland, husbands may take a portion of their wife's maternity leave, and most European countries supplement their paid maternity leaves with extensive, job-protected, albeit unpaid, parental leaves.

Education

Although tuition assistance may not be as central to the employee standard of living or family life as the items thus far discussed, our interviews confirm that for some employees the aid is of major significance. For some it supports an important life transition; for others it opens opportunities to children that a parent's direct earnings cannot support.

In the mid-1980s a congressionally established study panel, the National Commission on Student Financial Assistance, estimated that 80 percent of companies with more than 500 employees offered some tuition assistance, usually in support of employee job-related training or to aid in payment for the education of their family members. Although about $7 billion in assistance is potentially available annually, only $400 million is actually used. The Commission commented that most workers did not know they were eligible for the benefit.[49] The 1986 tax legislation eliminates the favored tax position of these benefits beginning in 1987.

Time Off and Alternative Work Schedules

Released time, both paid and unpaid, is increasingly described as the "number one benefit of the future" for the full-time permanent work force. Included here are the various components of non-wage compensation (e.g., vacations and holidays; personal, parental, and child care leaves; sick leave), as well as alternative work schedules (part-time work; job sharing; flexitime). Few, if any, categories of benefits are as salient to the family life of employees. Here, too, data are limited on availability and coverage.

Paid Time Off. Vacations are of particular importance to employees with family responsibilities. Employees with children often find school vacations a particular problem as they struggle to cope with child care or supervision of children's activities. For working parents, even the ability to choose a vacation time that meets their needs is critical. In two-parent families, preferences may vary, some wanting to take vacations at the same time, to allow for joint activity, others preferring to take vacations sequentially, in order to extend child care coverage, and still others wanting some combination. No data exist concerning employees' rights to choose a convenient vacation time.

Although the 1970s saw a dramatic increase in the availability and length of paid vacations, the American tradition in the private sector, in contrast to European practice generally and public employment policy in the United States, is a short vacation. A Conference Board report states that "The liberalization of paid time-off practices is an uneven process, replete with variations by type of business, and with remnants of historic geographical differences."[50] Recent estimates indicate that the average American worker in private industry has two weeks of vacation plus some additional holidays. In large and medium-sized firms, a paid vacation is now standard practice for full-time workers, yet only workers with considerable service are eligible even for two weeks of vacation time (67 percent after one year and 94 percent after three). Almost three quarters of the workers with less than a year of service have a week or less of vacation time. Even after a year of service most production workers will have only a week of vacation, although most white-collar workers have two weeks. Only after 10 years of service does the three-week vacation become the rule for all classes of workers.[51] In contrast, the typical vacation in northern and western Europe is four to five weeks, for all employees, mandated by national legislation (and still longer for public employees). In large leading U.S. firms, the major difference in the vacation pattern is that employees in some industries, in some parts of the country, may quality for a three-week vacation in 5 or 7 years instead of 10.[52]

The average number of *paid holidays* reported by the BLS and Conference Board surveys is 10. The Conference Board reports, however, that almost 40 percent of its respondents provide 11 or more days.

Alternative Work Schedules. The predominant rhythm of contemporary American work life is provided by the 5-day, 40-hour work week, a pattern firmly institutionalized at least since the end of World War II. More than 80 percent of private wage and salary workers work full time (35 or more hours per week). Close to 80 percent of these work a 5-day week, and 64 percent, a 5-day, 40-hour week. Nineteen percent of private-sector employees work part time, slightly more than the percentage of part-time employees in the general labor force (about 17 percent). The major trend today is toward compression of weekly hours into fewer days, with the 5-day week overwhelmingly dominant, even for those working 41 to 48 hours per week.

The only other trend worth noting is the slight move toward a shorter week (4 to 4.5 days), especially for full-time employees working 35 to 39 hours per week.[53] This is, however, a rhythm plainly out of synchronization with the family lives of many workers, particularly at certain points in the life cycle. This pattern of work scheduling became the rule at a time when family responsibilities were generally divided along traditional lines—that is, the man served as breadwinner and the woman was expected to assume all family and home responsibilities, in particular, child care. Such scheduling obviously places enormous strains on the many contemporary families that differ from the traditional model, especially families with both parents or the only parent in the labor force. It gets a parent home too late for family or house-chore time.

Indeed, a third of all workers in the *1977 Quality of Employment Survey* reported a problem with inconvenient or excessive hours of work. They said that work schedules interfered with family life and that they had too little control over their hours of work. In a later 1980-1981 survey, 42 percent of respondents said part-time work (with full-time benefits) would help a great deal to reduce work/family tensions, and another 20 percent said it would help somewhat.[54] Coupled with the typical year-round com- mitment to work and brief vacations, the typical current work scheduling also constricts each individual employee's oppor- tunities to enjoy the personal satisfactions of a varied life.[55]

Among the changes that alternative work schedules permit in the standard schedule are: (1) changes in the length of work time, as in part-time work; (2) changes in allocation of work time, as in compressed work weeks; and (3) changes in the control of work time (from management to worker), as in flexitime.[56] We explore these options in greater detail in chapter 8.

There Are Data Gaps, Questions, and Issues

There is no comprehensive corporate social welfare system in the sense of a minimum of uniform private sector coverage for everybody in the labor force and including essential fringe benefits and services. Nor does anyone claim intent to create a system. As we have seen, although private pension plans repre- sent the most common way for workers to augment social securi- ty benefits, about half of the private labor force is not covered by them, and benefit levels vary enormously. Similarly, while the overwhelming majority of employed workers rely on their employers for medical care insurance (on a contributory or non- contributory basis), some have much more extensive coverage than others, and some have no coverage at all. For the most part, the well paid and the highly skilled are eligible for the most generous benefits, and levels of coverage vary significantly among sectors of the economy.

Particularly notable is the difference between the coverage ex- tended to those workers employed in the large corporate core sec- tor of the economy and those employed in small and very small businesses. Large firms have taken the lead in instituting virtual- ly all benefits, often in response to collective bargaining demands, and coverage remains far greater at such firms than at small firms. It must be remembered, however, that only 22 per- cent of the labor force work at firms with 500 or more employees, while, in contrast, about 27 percent are employed at firms with fewer than 20 employees. We are particularly lacking in any data on these small employers, what they provide, and what employees experience in working in such establishments.

Unionized establishments, especially in manufacturing and heavy industry, often set the lead in benefits and, generally, provide more coverage than the nonunionized, but union membership has declined from about a third to less than a fifth of the labor force in the past decade, with the decline of manufacturing employment and the increase of work in the less unionized service sector. Private-sector union membership was about 15 percent of the eligible in 1985.

The unskilled, racial minorities, and women—in general, the poorly paid—are concentrated in sectors of the economy that offer poor benefits. Thus, if employee benefits are counted as part of an employee's wage, income differentials between men and women, whites and blacks, the skilled and the unskilled, and the high-salaried and low-salaried workers are likely greater than commonly thought.

We have also noted that if benefits are connected to work and to workplace, millions of the unemployed lack coverage, as do those retired and disabled who left their place of employment without claims on significant fringe benefits or services. Nor do the many temporary and part-time employees enjoy significant benefit coverage, yet these are groups growing in size during the mid-1980s.

There exists, as well, a fundamental question about benefit design, the shaping of benefits, and the concentration of expenditures to yield maximum values for a very diverse labor force. As noted, most employee benefits do have family-related aspects and respond to some family needs. Dependents' coverage under health insurance, life insurance, and other survivor's benefits, pensions, and other types of retirement income protection all have obvious direct significance for the family members other than the company employee. Paid vacations and even paid sick leaves are benefits that accrue to family members, too, albeit indirectly either by protecting family income when a worker is ill or by assuring family time without financial penalty. However, these benefits as they have developed are largely set up and administered as though all workers lived in one type of family: a husband/wife family in which the husband is in the labor force and the wife is at home caring for several children. Over the past two decades, however, the family as an institution has undergone many changes. Now instead of one overwhelmingly dominant family type and a few scattered deviations, the traditional family has become a minority, and a diversity of family types characterizes the society and the families of employees.

Finally, we remind the reader: Much of what employers do in the benefits field is made possible by federal tax policy—by the deductibility or nontaxability of most fringes. It is simply not true, as the naive sometimes have believed, that what government does is paid out of payroll and other taxes, whereas what business offers is a private decision. The enormous fringe benefit development has been built on federal tax policy. (These items are known as tax expenditures). In a careful analysis of the federal budget for 1984-85-86, Stanford Ross has shown relevant tax expenditures, respectively, of $109.2, $112.7, and $128.6 billion. These are revenue loss estimates related to health, pension, insurance, education, and similar fringe benefits. This level of revenue forgone is one third of all tax expenditures for those years and also equal to about one third of public social insurance direct expenditures for the same years.[57]

In conclusion, the dominant family type today is the two-earner family in which both husband and wife are in the labor force. But this family type varies, too, by the presence or absence of children and the number and ages of these children. Another important family type is the single-parent family, usually a mother-only family, where the sole parent is employed. Of course, many families still follow the traditional model, but most of these, as well as most other types of families with children, are now likely to have only one or two children and rarely more. Some families are also caring for one or more frail elderly parents, living with them or nearby. The result of all this is that just as the families of employees are of diverse types, so are their needs, and, of course, so are their employers. If the corporate social welfare system is to use its investment well, it will need to shape benefits and services responsive to this diversity.

Is such shaping possible, practicable? Is it a task for employers, for government, for both? We need to examine some of the considerations affecting what large employers do or forgo and the forces behind the innovation and creativity that can be found in some companies. We also must better understand the smallest employers, the local shops and services, work locations for many women, and we need to know more about how employees view their benefits. The next several chapters, based on intensive case studies and two community studies, introduce these matters.

3. Opportunities Lost . . . and Found

This is a chapter about many companies, although we shall cite only a few. In an objective sense their benefits are generous and expensive. Some are viewed as outstanding companies and employers by the public and the media. Nonetheless, many of their employees see them as insensitive and unresponsive to their family situations, to their needs as individuals, or to the pressures in their daily lives.

High expenditure does not always mean optimum responsiveness and satisified employees. If it did, recent years would have seen fewer conferences, workshops, resolutions, explorations, and initiatives devoted to the "work and family" arena. Big and prosperous companies may miss opportunities to be fully responsive, and smaller and/or less affluent enterprises may not see a need or cannot afford to do so.

These case studies remind us that a company has many concerns other than creating a workplace for people. Moreover, organizational and leadership factors may overwhelm policy, even enlightened policy.

Good Benefits Are Not Enough: Atlantic Utility

We devote almost one third of the chapter to a major regional utility company (which we shall call "Atlantic Utility"), which employs tens of thousands of workers in many categories. In recent years the company's fringe benefit bill has varied between 47 and 50 percent of wage/salary totals, if one includes the cost of all time not worked, but not the heavy cafeteria subsidies at headquarters. And the wage/salary base is considered quite generous.

In survey after survey, somewhere between 70 and 86 percent of line workers and first, second, and third-level supervisors/managers in the company rate the benefit package as good or very good (but the available reports do not say how many selected each of these two favorable levels). A second-level manager told us, "Benefits are exceptional at Atlantic, and most people stay because of outstanding salaries and very high benefits." This is a commonly expressed opinion.

The Atlantic Utility Company intends to have a rich benefit package. The goal is a wage-benefit standard comparable to the top quarter of "Fortune 500" companies. For years the yardstick was calibrated by carrying out benefit trend surveys. Now they draw upon selected management consultant studies covering specific types of companies.

Since the nonmanagement employees are strongly unionized in a series of large unions with which the company has engaged in national bargaining, the benefit specifics and the investment among benefits are very much affected by union initiatives. Indeed, in informal prebargaining exchanges, each side learns what the other actually "needs" and what can be shaped and traded. Our study showed the company enters each bargaining cycle having decided what it can afford and will probably need to grant in the total wage-benefit package. It leaves the initiatives for specification to the unions. In general, management prefers benefits to wages, since the latter drive overtime costs; unions stress take-home pay but find that fringes are attractive and visible "goodies" to deliver to their members in each package. Both management and union are alert to the numbers and types of employees affected by each proposed benefit, but they refer to traditional categories: craft, seniority, exempt and nonexempt, outside and inside work, line workers and supervisors. Their data are not categorized by gender, and of course, not by family status and responsibility for young children.

We need not review here the benefit specifics except to note that they are comparatively generous and understood as such. The company has long had a reputation as an excellent employer. In recent years it has become a wage/salary leader, as well as a benefits leader. It is constantly flooded with job applicants and does not have to worry about recruitment. In is also generous in promotional opportunities and cooperative in facilitating lateral transfers for employees.

Understandably, many of our interviews reveal very content workers, proud of their company. Only Hi-tek, reported in the next chapter, is in fact more generous to employees in an objective dollar sense, but it needs to recruit and retain categories of personnel now scarce and in heavy demand. Located in a geographic area characterized by high unemployment, Atlantic Utility has confronted no personnel shortages for some years.

Yet our study also discloses that while personnel are held on the job by good weekly or monthly paychecks and benefits, there is a surprising amount of dissatisfaction with benefits and personnel policies in the company. And much of the dissatisfaction is precisely in areas relevant to the management of the intersection of work and personal/family life. We elaborate these dissatisifactions, not because they are the most important thing about Atlantic Utility, but because they are common, not rare, in American industry.

Employees Who Can't Access the Flexibility. We begin by citing some employees with complaints at Atlantic Utility:

Donald R. is a twice-married male with one eight-year-old son and one who is eight months old. He has 15 years of seniority with the company in a skilled job. He is sensitive to personnel policies and practices because he managed for several years as a single parent before remarrying. His present wife is at home. Active in the union and a shop steward, Donald reported that *personal days off* for emergencies and important business has long been a subject of tension in this company. Over ten years the benefit increased from one to two—and now to four—days that may be used for emergencies. "The trouble is that we still don't fully have it," he noted. "The contract provision says 'workload permitting'." An employee may draw upon four paid and one unpaid days as floating, contingency, or personal days, after a specified period of employment, according to the policy. But most supervisors interpret this to mean at their discretion *and* with adequate notice.

In a group interview in which Donald explained this history, John, a relatively new hire (with the company eighteen months) as a business office representative told of wanting to attend the funeral of an uncle to whom he was close. The request was refused, so he called in sick. The result was an administrative notation on his record, which could affect him on the promotional ladder. He was bitter.

During the same discussion, Helen Q., whose husband also works for the company in a technical job, reported a similar problem. A fourth participant, Yvette, said that she never stayed home with a sick child, because getting a personal day off at short notice was impossible, and her husband, who works for the state government, has no such problem at all. If she takes it off as a sick day, she is in danger of getting on the roster of people who use sick leave frequently and who are monitored closely and that affects promotion.

The rules are rigid. A mother with a problem at home with a child cannot get an emergency day off. But, another employee explains, if permitted to do so, she could actually work out arrangements in an hour or two and get to work at 10. The personal emergency system applies only to days, however, not to hours. If she arrives at 10 A.M. she must go home at the regular quitting time, even if willing to work late to make up the time, and the lateness shows as a blot on her record. This is a company with elaborate personnel records and rating systems. Such things affect one's future at the company.

Good Benefits but Administrative Rigidity. What on paper looks like a sound program of *sick leave and disability leave* is also spoiled for many employees by administrative rigidity and apparent suspicion. A large percentage in a sizable group of women whom we interviewed about postmaternity paid disability leaves told of being compelled to return after four weeks even though their doctors recommended that they remain at home longer. (The state policy expects six to eight weeks of "disability" after normal childbirth). They were called in to be examined by company doctors. Several told of "barely making it" because of their physical conditions, of coming in under protest, or of refusing to come and being penalized by not receiving cash benefits for more than the minimum of four weeks of postpartum disability following a normal delivery. Others took accumulated vacation time as the time of delivery approached only to find themselves on sick leave because of miscalculation—and the excessive number of sick days held against them, or so they thought. And without a formal disability leave, there was an interruption of their general benefit coverage.

Something like the following, from one of the women, was repeated by at least a dozen interviewees:

I did not come in for my company medical checkup after my delivery for seven weeks even though the company doctor's office called me. My own doctor said I was not ready to travel on a bus and that's the way I have to travel. When I did come in their doctor asked how I felt and I said "fine." I meant as fine as you can be seven weeks after a delivery. He didn't examine me. Not at all. He told me I was ready to come back to work. Oh, yes, he asked when I stopped bleeding and I said after four weeks. Then he said I would be paid for four weeks disability. That wasn't according to my own doctor's advice.

There were 64 cases in litigation at the time of our interviews because mothers and their doctors claimed longer disability than the number of weeks the company doctors felt they had a right to, given the physical conditions.

A male installation worker told of two incidents. Once, with his leg in a cast, he was made to come in to see the company physician. On another occasion he pulled a muscle in his back while working and went to the medical department. He was not examined. His interpretation was that medical staff was looking for cues that he really could work and that coming to be examined was a form of malingering.

The picture is more complicated than all of this, however. On paper, personal flexibility should be achievable and personal emergencies met through some combination of personal days, vacation time, sick leaves, and unpaid leave. The system often doesn't work, however, because vacation time and personal days are unavailable without advance scheduling, and low seniority blocks access to the time sought, or because the use of sick leave is often evaluated negatively.

Nor do the company's policies attend to all the major needs of parents with young children. Some experienced supervisors told us that six weeks' coverage, with income replacement after normal childbirth, is simply not enough. Low earners cannot afford to stay home thereafter for unpaid leave. The company's lack of attention to child care means that many employees face difficulty when they do return. And a vacation policy not ungenerous by American standards (three weeks of vacation after eight years of work) is still not enough to solve the problem of caring for a child out of school for twelve weeks, especially if one does not get the requested weeks.

Responsive Supervisors Can Make a Difference. However, almost each story of insensitivity and rigidity is matched by one of flexibility and responsiveness. The differentiating variable is often the next-level superior. But the determinant is not as simple as a superior's sympathy and understanding. Units also are different. In some, flexibility adds to attachment and morale. If problems are created, they are viewed as manageable. In other units, the supervisor or unit pays a price if there is a gap in staff coverage. Supervisors also are monitored for output!

A low-level supervisor in a personnel unit showed such flexibility. A secretary, mother of three young children, wife of a police officer, depended on her mother for child care. The mother had broken her arm and her husband could not cover; the mother's course of treatment would leave her unavailable for a month. The secretary asked for an unpaid leave. This would have negative consequences: loss of benefit coverage and administrative notation. The supervisor suggested immediate use of three weeks of vacation and then arranged a needed two-week supplementary unpaid emergency leave (and this is a company where vacation time is usually scheduled far in advance).

In several instances supervisors helped workers get time off to get a child to a doctor or to visit school and allowed make-up time, even though there is really no applicable policy.

Our exploration in various company units and with top management produced a mixed assessment. In large units, or if one had a cooperative supervisor, or if one had adequate seniority, it was possible to make optimum use of vacation time in relation to family plans: to coordinate with a spouse for a family trip, to take sequential vacations so that the children would have company, and so on. However, it simply did not work out well for some personnel at all. The policy is based on seniority, in the context of a unit's coverage needs. There is no family-support concept in vacation planning. For the latter, the informed note, American vacations generally would need to be longer.

Similarly, the need for constant coverage of the utility services and a management style that stresses schedules and control allow little by way of *flexible hours* (flexitime). Such a policy, as we have noted, can be helpful for employees who need to get their children off to school, deliver others to child care arrangements, shop for elderly parents, or do some family errands that cannot be managed evenings or weekends. Employees explain that there are exceptions at Atlantic, however, but these, too, are dependent on individual supervisors and supervisor empathy, cooperative co-workers, or informal trading between personnel. The type of work and kind of unit may be a constraint in some units but clearly need not be throughout the company.

Needed: Information That Works. One of the difficulties people face is the lack of adequate information resources in a large and diverse company with many work sites, written policies differentiated by job-levels and types, and yet adaptable and discretionary. Some interviewees told of supervisors of other local personnel who knew the system well and guided them through it. Others made poor choices because they believed obsolete policies to be still in effect or did not know of existence of provision. None of this was a problem arising from lack of written manuals, brochures, leaflets, and statements about benefits and policies. The company has information bulletins, newspapers, personnel who are responsible for supplying forms and brochures, and central office experts in specific policies and benefits. Nonetheless, there remains serious evidence of employees without information. Illustrations arise with reference to maternity leave, personal emergencies, early retirement, and transfers. In a few instances, employees spoke with resentment about what they assumed to be "all deliberate delay" in relaying information to their particular advantages. While intent was hardly shown, the results were certainly frustrating.

For example, a competent, articulate, middle-level supervisor in a customer-service operation spoke sympathetically about the company out of long years of experience. She was especially grateful for the generous medical coverage, since her husband had been ill for a long time, and she was the primary family income source. Later, as a widow, she managed time off for urgent child-related needs. She knew that in other jobs in the company she would have been fired, and she depended on the support of her district manager, who understood the problems and needs of single parents. Nonetheless, she was critical about the inadequate information flow to employees. For example, the maximum for dental plan coverage was $500. Subsequently it was raised to $1,000, but people under current treatment whose bills had gone beyond the old maximum were not told that they were now eligible for supplementary coverage. She had therefore circulated her own memo about this in her office, but told us that "management should have done this."

The Dilemmas. What are the problems in translating a reasonable, even generous, benefit from paper to reality? Why are some benefits truly responsive only when interpreted sympathetically? Why are other possibilities not pursued? A top personnel officer explained that the Atlantic Utility Company is responsible to the public for 24-hour coverage and must be sure to have skilled personnel present in sufficient numbers at all times. The personal days policy is best handled through advance scheduling and on a seniority basis. The policies make it difficult for people to get true emergency time "because it is easy for people to invent emergencies, and sometimes they simply can't be spared on days that they prefer because we need to be sure of coverage." The intent is to respond to real emergencies, but clearly many employees with such emergencies feel mistreated.

Similarly, the intent of the disability plan is to have a good benefit but to avoid abuse by having the company doctor monitor it. In the hands of some particular doctors, maternity and other disability leaves are always suspect and, from employee perspectives, often unnecessarily curtailed or not fully reimbursed.

As much is said for the very adequate personal sick leave: a good benefit on paper but not fully available because administrative controls to prevent abuse create an atmosphere of excessive suspicion and control. Elsewhere one's sick leave is properly used, by policy, to stay home on a sick-child emergency; here excessive but legitimate use even for one's own verifiable illness is a negative mark against advancement.

Individual supervisors can overcome all of this. Some may, in fact, be the most authentic implementors of company policy intent; but others are clearly viewed as rigid and restrictive. Despite good explicit policies, this company with good wages and an excellent benefit package has many disgruntled employees. Among those with the most difficulty are parents and family members attempting in some way to integrate work and family routines in a satisfying fashion.

Other Companies: Negotiated Benefits Without Responsiveness

Atlantic Utility has problems and limitations but has moved further toward meeting personal and family needs of employees than has "Midwest Oil," a large chemical and oil company with 25,000 employees. Because of the complex pattern of unionization and the several different types of operation and of technical specialization, Midwest Oil must carry from 60 to 70 different benefit plans.

Even though Midwest Oil, like much of the petroleum industry, shares a standard plan, there are just enough differences to make this a quite onerous task. The fertilizer, coal, and plastics companies are different enough for the plans to reflect this. Exempt and nonexempt employees have practically the same package, but it is not exactly the same. As much may be said of unionized and nonunionized locations or categories of employees.

The attempt to impose some control on all of this has yielded a terribly elaborate and bureaucratized system. This is exemplified by the enormous looseleaf binder consulted by the manager of Benefit Plan Development with whom we met. The Employee Relations Manual deals with policies in relation to all the benefits, and it must be looked at frequently in an extended discussion. Many contract issues arise as plans are implemented, and many compliance questions relating to federal law and directives also arise. When law is clarified, policies settled, agreements reached, manual language is perfected. An entire unit in the Benefit Plan Development office keeps the manual up to date. It is this authoritative source that is consulted in preparation of manuals, brochures, leaflets, and benefit statements.

So complex is the operation that there are separate organizational units for Benefit Plan Development and for Benefit Plan Implementation (administration). The responsible vice president has 140 people working under him, occupying an entire section in a midtown office building.

Although a management committee of inside directors reviews and approves benefit changes, the Benefit Development manager comments that for the most part it is a minor item for the directors. They will, however, carefully attend to occasional major changes or to what might be deemed "executive windfalls" not equitable from the perspectives of the rest of the staff.

The lack of major board attention, most of the time, may be connected in some part to the fact that in this industry the magnitude of capital investment per worker is far more significant than wages and benefits.

One might not know what to conclude after all this with regard to the benefit specifics: health insurance, pensions, short- and long-term disability, sick leave, vacations, holidays, life insurance, education, recreation, and cafeterias (all except mandated state and federal benefits). Comparisons within the headquarters city and nationally show that the "package" is generous and attractive, equal in cost at the time of our visit to 39 percent of payroll.

Yet the high expenditure level and richness of benefits, looked at item by item, do not result in a reputation for responsiveness, considerateness, or sensitivity. This is not a company considered to care about employees' personal and family needs. The benefits are taken for granted as an industry standard, and employees feel that they have little support if they are caring for frail elderly parents, handicapped relatives, or children; attempting to go to school while working; or coping with other work-family life tensions from time to time.

Women, for the most part, are in the clerical/secretarial

categories and constitute a small part of the primary production work force. The most discussed benefit issues relate to the discretionary personal leaves after postchildbirth disability, how these workers will be replaced, whether they will return, whether they are abusing personal leaves. The concern increases as some women reach levels of technical and management responsibility and are not readily replaceable by "temps," as clerks might be.

One notes, in the midst of this not overly supportive environment, two interesting, perhaps suggestive, developments:

First, at some of the smaller production locations, where women are not secretaries and clerks and do carry responsibility for primary production tasks, there are reports of greater flexibility, adaptation, and considerateness around pregnancy and child care issues. (Men are not mentioned in these regards.) As seen elsewhere, street-level administration finds that it functions best if it attends to employee morale. Here it is said, for example, that the refineries are "nice little homogeneous groups in which the personnel manager knows every single employee personally and takes a personal interest in everyone's individual entitlements." If team performance requires high morale, it seems responsiveness appears.

Second, the company has a contract for an anonymous, competent, Employee Assistance Referral telephone service, based on an annual per capita fee. The service is wide ranging, confidential, and accessible and apparently receives a positive response. It is a professional service delivered off site, covering a broad spectrum of employees' personal and family problems, and considered a helpful personal resource for all employees.

Decentralization as an Obstacle

Another brief illustration of missed opportunity comes from a multinational accounting firm. This is a company with 8,000 to 10,000 employees, of whom 7,000 are professionals; the firm has 160 different offices.

In the past, benefits were never an important issue. New hires out of college or graduate school come for training and hope of advancement. Few questions are asked about benefits. It has traditionally been considered unseemly to bother too much about rewards and protections in one's internship phase. Salaries in any case were and are the main thing. As one rises in the system one bargains. Partners in effect pay for their own fringes. There are generous educational benefits, the most important benefit here, because all the young professionals want to keep learning; this is a real recruitment plus.

If Midwest Oil and perhaps Atlantic Utility Company are tightly administered around benefits and feel the need to be in order to cope, this partnership seems the reverse. Even basic benefits have not been standardized, though by objective measures they tend to be quite good. Nonetheless, the benefits issue was not considered important in the past and has had little attention. Most important, the plans were not consistent across different locations and sites. For an organization of sophisticated professionals who know tax law and accounting, there is a surprising lack of information about laws, rulings, and practice in the benefits and personnel fields at fairly high levels in the company, and there have been no comprehensive cost calculations.

In the past, almost everything in this field has been somewhat decentralized to the operating locations, and these offices have been led by partners with different philosophies and degrees of interest. A few years ago, cost considerations led to the first coordinated attention to health and hospital plans, and that pushed the company to settle on a more nearly uniform approach, near the more generous end of their current variable practice. But new questions also have been suggested as needing attention. More women have been entering the company, and they now constitute 20 percent of employed professionals and a large percentage of the potential pool. In fact 50 percent of recent applicants have been female. Companies of this kind in a growing industry have a 20 percent professional and a 50 percent administrative turnover annually. Retention of promising new talent is a consideration.

Yet, some of the new employees have noted, concerns of women employees and of young families generally have not been specifically addressed. Even as medical and hospitalization benefits were standardized, the nature of the organization, of the partnership system, and the power left in the operating offices to the managing partner resulted in enormous, continuing informality in relation to sick leave and personal leaves. These are the policy arenas that most affect what happens at the time of childbirth and immediately thereafter and the ways in which the workplace does or does not offer supports when people are rearing young children. In some offices, the informality had good results; in others, people could not count on what they needed. It was discovered, when the exploration began, that even though it was illegal, one senior partner in one office did not permit the medical plan to cover maternity; this did not change until he retired. Another plan paid only $100 of the first $1,000 in hospital/medical costs for childbirth in an otherwise generous benefit package.

These anomalies have been corrected as new and younger partners press for change, more women professionals are hired, and the company explores how to create the national, guaranteed benefit and personnel policy base upon which local diversity and variability might build. The problem here is the obverse of that at Midwest Oil.

Paternalism May Need Updating

Without continued monitoring, even the most paternalistic employers can lose touch with their employees' needs and attitudes. "Fantasy" is the name we use to describe the entertainment company that has long been one of the first to come to mind when companies known for paternalistic, successful personnel policies are discussed. A new look suggests that even the most benign paternalism may need updating in some ways to ensure current responsiveness.

This national entertainment enterprise employs about 40,000 people permanently and more than 5,000 others seasonally at several locations. Many of its full-time workers, some in quite specialized crafts, and others in more usual occupations (electricians, carpenters, drivers, secretaries) are represented by more than 40 unions in different locations. Currently union contracts set the standards for nonunion benefits, and there are similar plans for exempt and nonexempt workers. (There is also important industry-wide bargaining.) Until a few years ago, the company successfully kept the basic health and welfare coverage better for the nonunion people than for union members, but this has changed. A close examination shows some advantages for each, but only at the margins. The basic benefits tend to converge.

Each employee at Fantasy receives an annual benefit statement. Like similar computer-generated statements in other large companies (Hi-tek, FoodStores, for example), the personalized statement very helpfully describes each employee's coverage in each field and summarizes his or her contributions and those made by the company. Here, the range of benefits and the levels of each, as well as the scope of coverage carried completely by the company, are all impressive. Fantasy is a benefits leader, as it is in the compensation field generally.

Apart from medical coverage, pensions, life insurance, long-term disability, dental insurance, and deferred compensation, the package also includes:

• Paid Holidays
• Social Security
• Worker's Compensation
• Unemployment Insurance
• Credit Union
• Scholarship Program
• Educational Reimbursement
• Group Auto & Home Owners Insurance
• Stock Purchase Plan
• Jury Duty Leave
• Employee Discounts
• Bereavement Leave
• Christmas Party
• Tickets to Company Recreational Activities
• Film Festivals
• Recreation Clubs
• Blood Bank
• Cafeteria
• Travel Accident Insurance (Company Business)

All of this successfully helps solve recruitment and retention problems. It provides a context in which Fantasy has no trouble each summer hiring the needed thousands of college students as temporary workers. Many like what they see and want to stay; they thus constitute an excellent recruitment pool. Indeed, the company finds it necessary to offer job counseling and placement services to ensure that permanents in public-contact jobs move on in sufficient numbers each year so as to sustain the desired youthful image. At the recreational sites, employees are highly visible and must look good, to establish the desired milieu.

The headquarters setting constitutes a comfortable campus environment. The individual recreation enterprises are also unusual and pleasant settings for visiting. The company's long tradition has been to cultivate a family-like environment in which everyone, from the president down, is on a first-name basis. It has been considered good for the company's image to cultivate the notion that the traditional paternalism associated with Fantasy for many decades still continues, despite enormous growth, geographic dispersion, unionization, and some labor conflict.

Much supports the theme of "we are a family." There is considerable family, even multigenerational, continuity in the labor force. Many couples work here, too, though there are no precise numbers. Weekend and seasonal family parties create close employee community ties generally. Heavily subsidized and attractive cafeterias encourage eating with one's colleagues. At least two of the recent expansions involved provision of company housing, amenities, and facilities and the establishment of nearby or on-site child care centers operated by a national proprietary chain, offering services at a modest discount to employees. Yet none of these arrangements are used to control daily living.

A secretary says: "Fantasy is a great place to work. It's not high-pressured and everybody is very laid back."

Why do we describe the picture one obtains as mixed?

A top manager comments: "The paternalism and the first names are for the public image. It's not for back-office restrooms and all the less visible stuff that makes people comfortable."

What is the real picture? The traditional benefits are good to excellent, but there have been no important new developments, and none seem likely, according to senior management.

Given the company's traditions and public posture, it is hardly to be characterized as completely unresponsive. For example, the company successfully helps employees maximize their cash benefit entitlements at the time of childbirth by helping them with a package that includes the state's temporary disability benefit and a paid sick leave benefit. The company's long-term disability plan, which replaces 60 percent of full wages and is not taxable, goes into effect after four weeks, so new mothers are then encouraged to shift from the state plan. What all this amounts to is that a woman who has been at the company for a year will receive full salary for about six weeks of postchildbirth leave and can supplement this with accumulated vacation time.

Jobs are protected, as is income, for the six to eight week post-childbirth period and longer if there are complications. There are also personnel policies involving job protection (the same or a comparable job) after an allowable medical leave for one year (when doctors affirm the need) and a personal leave for up to 30 days. This 30-day personal leave is fairly standard and is available throughout the firm for any reasonable purpose. It is, however, considerably less generous than what has become common in leading companies. On a discretionary and individualized basis longer leaves may be granted, as much as three months, but that is very infrequent. Instances were cited of someone with seniority permitted to plan a special two-month vacation, of use by someone who had to go elsewhere to settle an estate after a family death. On the other hand, it was agreed that the common desire to have extended leave after childbirth is not covered by the benefit. Sometimes flexibility around sick leave and vacation leave can be coupled with some medical or personal leave to serve such purpose.

Some employees find the available discretion working in their favor, the company's traditions supporting the creative packaging of entitlements on their behalf. Others find no policies that will meet their needs and supervisors who express understanding but stress the need to get the job done.

Clearly, there are significant numbers of enthusiastic employees and disappointed ones, as well. The manager quoted above for her cynical remark about public-image paternalism was praised by her own secretary for permitting an individualized arrangement involving her working three days a week for the first three months after childbirth. (The secretary did not know that the manager had described the arrangement to us as a burden to be reassessed in a few weeks.) At a desk in the same room, another secretary commented that if there is a home emergency, she can call in, arrive late, and stay after hours to make up the time, and there is no problem. However, it is not acceptable to stay out for a day because her child is ill.

Clearly, here as at the Atlantic Utility, the degree of responsiveness depends on the extent of discretion available to and exercised by supervisors and managers—something about which there are different perceptions. It is a large enough company for there to be contradictory facts.

A claims examiner in her late 30s is entitled to two weeks of sick leave each year, and when her baby is sick she can call in and say so, using her own sick leave time to cover the loss of pay. Similarly, when she needs to take one of the children to the doctor, she can use her own sick leave. She commented:

At [Fantasy] no lying is needed. You can be honest about a kid's illness. That's part of what makes this a wonderful place to work for...Maybe it's the supervisor more than the company policy but at least you can do it. At my previous job you had to lie.

Words such as these were employed by a travel coordinator, a bookkeeper, and several others, while in an adjacent building a receptionist said that when she stayed out on two occasions because her young son was ill, a notation was placed in her evaluation: "sick too often." She did not choose to lie! Her wish list had two priority items: The company should either provide on-site child care services for headquarters personnel (they do at entertainment sites) or support such services in nearby communities, even if employees are charged full operating costs; there should be some kind of back-up or crisis child care service at the workplace for emergencies, especially to care for a mildly ill child.

To this a career-counseling manager would add some kind of employee assistance counseling program. He meets personnel with problems on all levels; they avoid the drug and alcoholism treatment program because of the stigma. Marital problems, parent-child problems, or personal psychological difficulties interfere with work, career advancement, and happiness. "Management must stop pretending that personal problems don't exist at [Fantasy]," he summed up. (We were to hear some months later that a new program is being explored by management.)

Fantasy has good salaries, a strong basic benefits structure, a history of concern about employees, and much good will. In recent years, however, it has moved into a reactive posture, initiating benefits only when under union pressure for covered employees, later making them more generally available.

The company has not enacted a "cafeteria" or flexible benefits plan. (Several managers and administrators told us that they employ many immature workers who would lack a basis for wise choices.) Nor does the company have a flexitime policy. There are no formal provisions for getting time or using one's sick benefits to care for a sick child. Employees describe personal leaves after childbirth as too discretionary to meet everyone's needs reliably. After some talk a few years ago, the child care issue was dropped. Now there is some consideration of a child care needs survey. In others words, the company has not formally addressed the issues that make a difference for two-earner couples with children, working single mothers, and older working couples with elderly parents as they try to manage work and family life simultaneously.

Management has not taken on the task of achieving a new level of family or employee support through new initiatives. Some employees express the wish for something more. A divisional marketing manager, young, but with the company for 13 years, told us:

The people in top management use bad judgment in their benefit policy by not ever taking the initiative. Instead of deciding to be leaders and to pioneer, they are reactive. Not proactive. Many of the employees see that the ball is in the hands of the union and this diminishes the company's image.

The gap between the rhetoric and public relations image of Fantasy, on the one hand, and some of the operating realities, on the other, is considerable. Management seems to recognize that more attention to the personal needs of employees would make

an enormous difference for some workers. Even though there is
interest in annual turnover of the summer workers and turnover
generally in the public-serving entertainment cadres, there is
need for stability, loyalty, and enthusiasm for the ongoing core
force of creative workers, managers, administrators, and line
personnel. The company has already traveled so far that modest
increments would produce a considerable gain.

The Importance of Implementation

A multinational diversified manufacturing firm with about 50
U.S. units employing 20,000 workers in several parts of the country has capitalized on the favorable publicity surrounding its
policy announcements concerning family responsiveness. There
is no question about the sincerity of the intent, but the practical
steps taken thus far are few. Some new things have been done,
but they are modest by any standard. The obstacles cited are
hardly unique.

Corporate executives, political leaders, advocates, and experts
in the field often list the company as a work and family leader.
Many would be surprised at the reality. The speeches, brochures,
and workshop sponsorship, directed mostly at the importance of
the subject and at options for action, seem to divert most outsiders from observing the limited progress thus far made by the
company. The needs of working families are described as bottom
line issues, as productivity issues, and also as matters of value
and culture in the best sense. The company is proud of its leadership a decade ago in creating a division to focus on corporate and
community responsibility. Later, the charge was broadened; the
firm was committed to "social responsibility" and "social policy."
Initially, the department would place emphasis on educating
senior management about these matters rather than devoting
itself to public education or advocacy. More and more stress was
placed on changing company culture and focusing on social
policies calling for community improvement in areas where the
company is located. This would be good for employee morale (and
productivity?) and also for the company's public image, it was
claimed.

A new chief executive officer put his influence behind this departure in company culture, and staff in the responsible department were looking ahead to future public affairs initiatives on the federal and state level and to international activity as well.

On a macro level this is of interest and of potential effect. There has been valuable support for some governmental provision. Companies that are taxpayers can lobby with effect. However, relatively little has as yet occurred in the responsiveness of benefits or policies, certainly little to measure up to the level of talk. Again basic benefits here are strong and appropriate, but the add ons discussed as related to the meeting points of work with family life have not yet been initiated. The major exception is a corporation-wide flexitime policy. In one large city there has been cooperation with other firms in creating a local child care information and referral service and distributing useful information brochures. There have also been several noontime seminar series on aspects of family life and childrearing. A dependent care assistance plan as part of a flexible benefits package is being explored.

Why the slow pace, the modest initiatives, the gap between announced policy and accomplishments? Central-office second-level officers cite:

- The fear of interfering in employees' privacy
- An overwhelming orientation to bottom line and productivity issues
- Great difficulty in making individual managers sensitive to these issues, whatever the social policy of the firm in its head office
- The problems of implementing policy in a highly decentralized company in which the decentralization has an important purpose

One high-level executive told of how few in top management had as yet fully absorbed the facts about the changed labor force and the real significance of the policy area. The commitment may be formal, he said, but not deep:

It's not the rules we lay down; it's the signals we give employees that really make a difference. This is especially important for family issues in the corporate context....Whether or not middle and lower level managers are carrying out such policies [showing more responsibility toward the problems and needs of employees] should be part of the criteria by which they are evaluated.

The formal policy and the desire to be associated with it in the public mind signals an important first shift in corporate culture. Practical steps must now be selected and a complex implementation process planned. This is not yet a missed opportunity, nor should it be publicized as one already seized.

Seizing the Opportunity: Paternalism Takes the Next Step

We conclude this chapter with a description of one company that seized the opportunity. Paternalistic in the best sense of the term, this company has been among the leaders in recognizing the new needs emerging among its work force. Now under serious economic pressures, one wonders whether it can continue in its leadership position, at the forefront of the responsive firms, or whether economic constraints will change the picture.

"Sportswear" is a large manufacturing company with factories in 140 different places employing 44,000 people in several divisions. Most of its workers are semiskilled, but there are some skilled factory employees. There are also small creative and professional staffs, and the usual cadres in management, legal, bookkeeping, housekeeping, personnel, advertising, sales, finance, and public relations, which are essential to any large company.

Like Fantasy, Sportswear is a company with strong tradition and a dominant ideology. It is much older than Fantasy. It has long had a national reputation as a leading people-oriented company, concerned for employees and the many communities in which they live. The company has a corporate philanthropy program that concentrates on the small communities in which it does most of its manufacturing. Line employees and managers are encouraged and supported in volunteer activities for local health, recreation, and social service agencies.

Historically, the company's social responsibility philosophy has expressed itself in the provision of good working environments more than in competitive wage rates, in the opening of facilities in black communities and the creation of jobs there before the civil rights movement, and in constant attempts to create a people-oriented corporate culture. The founding family in this business and their heirs were responsible for this philosophy. They have managed to perpetuate it through personal influence and strong management traditions, even though the company went public more than a decade ago.

As we observed Sportswear's current responsiveness and contrasted it with some other corporate environments, the key differential seemed to be successful interpretation of the new times. If a tradition of sincere paternalism is not to deteriorate into public relations or fall behind what union initiatives or recruitment bargaining can achieve, it must work at the task of responsiveness. Sportswear seems to do that. It studies trends, and its work force keeps up with new policies and developments; it participates in numerous national and local forums, committees, and workshops; and it supports demonstration projects and related research.

By company policy, salaries are to be a bit more than competitive, and the traditional benefits (medical, life insurance, disability, pensions, etc.) are to be state of the art. With that as a starting point, the company tries to build greater sensitivity to changing needs as they emerge and are understood.

Thus, when federal policy, as expressed by the rulings and directives of the Equal Opportunities Commission, called for affirmative action, the task of recruitment and development of women and minority employees became a continuing major objective of the company, assigned to specific people and departments. When national discussions in the late 1970s specified possible approaches to the greater harmonization of work and family life as essential to implementation of opportunity for women and protection of children, the leads were taken seriously. As much has been accomplished by demonstration and research grants in this field as by policy innovation within the company. Program and policy ideas are often pilot tested at headquarters and then disseminated.

Currently, the company's standard benefits are priced at 35 percent of its wage and salary payroll, the highest in its industry.

There is no cafeteria plan, formulated as such, but there are several options within each major benefit plan, so a de facto modified flexible benefits system is emerging. They want to await federal tax policy clarification before moving further. Company personnel policies include flexitime (throughout almost all departments), job sharing (see below), part-time jobs with full or prorated fringe benefits, a five-month unpaid but job-protected child care leave available to fathers and mothers after the maternity disability leave, and the right of employees to use their own sick leave to care for an ill child or an elderly or handicapped dependent.

The company failed with an on-site child care program in the early 1970s when few employees made use of it. It has now reopened the issue and is considering child care support through other means. In the meantime, in recent years, it has supported community information and referral services, standard-setting, training, and efforts to improve the supply of services. Its responsible personnel have kept themselves informed about national developments. They recently surveyed their personnel in several locations around the country to determine what arrangements are currently used and what is wanted.

Job sharing has been a minor development in U.S. workplace flexibility thus far. Almost every development is unique, but it seems to take hold best for technical and professional work like teaching, drafting, and counseling, where people can do independent, delineated tasks sequentially to fill a shift. Sportswear had 9 or 10 job-sharing teams at headquarters when we were there and seemed poised for a major breakthrough: the first assembly line experiment. The plant manager believed that he had worked out the problem of line balance. A shift team learns mutual pacing, which balances the productivity of different people; a midday change for work sharing could throw off the balance if not planned carefully.

The pattern in job sharing appears to be a transitional one. Women (they are the ones involved thus far) who have worked full time want to cut back on their hours after childbirth and when the children are very young. After varied intervals, most want to resume full-time work.

We do not know whether, in fact, Sportswear will prove to have solved the line balance problem in assembly line job sharing. It is characteristic of the company, however, that modest head-quarters success with other types of jobs led to an exploration of adaptations in the factories. It is also characteristic that they will simultaneously explore the possibility that they may also have here a partial solution to the desire of some older assembly line workers to phase down after age 50 as they tire more quickly and find some decline in manual dexterity.

To round out the picture, mention should also be made of the large number of free, after-work and noontime courses and seminars ranging in subject matter from parenting and child care to retirement, health and diet, friendship, family trends, and hobbies. At the same hours, using excellent facilities, there are fitness courses and workouts. Participation is very high.

Cafeterias at headquarters provide wholesome, subsidized meals in congenial surroundings for personnel at all levels. An extensive, on-site employee-counseling program is broadly conceived for use by family members as well.

None of this occasions any regrets in the field, at headquarters, or at stockholders meetings. The forward-looking and responsive employment policies have been very good for recruitment and retention. The company has an excellent public image. Morale is good and has remained so even where fluctuations in the economy and in the export market have created some temporary declines in profits. In short, the updated paternalism has become employee responsiveness.

Thus we note that good pension, health, and related benefits do not always produce fully satisfied employees. Benefits must be understood and accessible, particularly those involving personal time and flexibility. They must be accessed through sympathetic supervisors, lest administrative rigidity appear to close off access. And benefits require constant updating as experience is gained about what is needed and how the workplace may accommodate.

4. Big Companies Can Be Flexible

Contrary to the picture of several companies in the previous chapter, large companies can recognize the value of individualization and flexibility. It is possible to offer good pay and good benefits and, in addition, to be responsive to the diversity of employees' needs and wants.

An example of a large company that has managed to integrate responsiveness to employees in the context of a formal, bureaucratic structure is "Hi-tek," a leading, mature, high-technology company, located on the West Coast, in an area replete with high-tech, aerospace, and defense companies. It is a large company with about 40,000 employees and more than $2 billion in annual net income, constituting close to half the business of the leading diversified conglomerate that is the parent company. This high-tech organization is relatively autonomous and includes within it several smaller subsidiaries in the electronics field. These subsidiaries are also relatively autonomous, in particular with regard to employment policies and practices. There is some tension between the high-tech and non-high-tech parts of the company because the former is in a growth industry and the latter in traditional heavy industry, which has been experiencing economic problems in an increasingly competitive world economy. There is also some tension resulting from the desire on the part of management at corporate headquarters to centralize human resource policies more, in order to contain costs, and the conviction of management in the high-tech organization that decentralized authority is critical if the company is to be able to compete for the skilled and professional labor force it needs.

The company has certain characteristics that clearly have played a role in the development of its special corporate culture. As a high-tech firm, it is in an expanding industry. As a research-oriented, professional technology company, it needs and has a highly skilled labor force. It is located in a part of the country where there are several other similar firms, drawing on the same labor pool. Thus, it is in an industry and in an area where both recruitment and retention of labor are problems. It is not union-ized and the possibility of unionization does not constitute a serious factor in its human resource planning. To attract the labor force it needs, however, it must be competitive with other companies in the industry and in the area.

Its work force is divided equally between men and women, but in contrast to other industries, about 60 percent of its employees are professionals. Typically, for a company in this industry, about 85 percent of its management and professional staff are male while 90 percent of its administrative support staff are female. The proportion of women professionals and managers is increasing, however, and senior management is convinced that this trend must be encouraged.

The company has a history of progressivism and innovation in its human resource policies. It is viewed by management, employees, and informed outsiders as a very people-oriented company with a corporate culture in which great stress is placed on creativity, individualism, and responsiveness to employees. Despite this, responsiveness to the *family* needs of employees has not been an explicit factor in the development of company policies. Responsiveness to employees generally—and to the per-sonal needs of a diverse labor force—has, however, played a role. As a result, family responsiveness has been an unexpected byproduct of company policies, as has been the even more impor-tant discovery that responsiveness, including responsiveness to the personal and/or familial needs and wants of employees, does not have to be a zero sum game. In other words, it is possible to do more for employees without necessarily spending more—an astonishing discovery! Creativity and innovation can pay in the human resource area, too. Policies can be so designed and implemented that employees are convinced that their employer is doing especially well for them, yet it does not have to be costly. Once again, flexibility is the key.

The Benefit/Service Package

In assessing its benefit package and planning for future developments, the Hi-tek management is caught between two conflicting pressures: corporate headquarters' concern with labor costs and its desire to contain, if not curtail, costs by taking advantage of labor's willingness to accept give backs, on the one hand, and Hi-tek's own need to remain competitive within the industry, on the other. (At the time of our field study, the general economic recovery and new problems for some branches of the industries in which Hi-tek competes had not yet changed any of this.) In maintaining a delicate balance between the two, management's approach to benefit planning is that the package as a whole must be competitive within the industry but not necessarily with regard to each and every individual benefit. To achieve this goal, however, each benefit must be reviewed annually, so that at the very least the most critical ones are competitive.

Planning begins with an assumption that the total compensation package must be within the top quartile of the industry. At a minimum, salaries have to be in that range, as does the overall benefit package. In assessing the competitiveness of the package, related benefits are clustered and analyzed in chunks. Paid time off (vacations, holidays, sick leave) represents one benefit cluster, health insurance (medical, dental, vision) another, retirement benefits another, and so forth. Once the whole package has been reviewed and a decision made with regard to the overall competitiveness or ranking of the package, attention is paid to the laggard areas.

Competitiveness is assessed through reports of what comparable companies are providing, based on surveys carried out by benefit consultants, and/or informal discussions with human resource personnel in other companies. In recent years, one major problem has been fixed maxima in health insurance coverage and in psychiatric coverage, during a period of rapidly escalating costs in the health care field generally. Since health insurance costs are a major problem in benefit costs everywhere, one problem has been to satisfy employee's needs for a more generous benefit at the same time as the corporate policies of cost containment are kept in mind.

The company provides what are usually described as excellent *standard* benefits. Only its special, flexible benefit program, Flexiplan, is unusual (see below). Several types of retirement benefits, including deferred income and savings plans, are provided outside of the Flexiplan benefits. The company is among the very few that provide an indexed pension. Vision care benefits are also provided, as is short- and long-term disability insurance. The former is mandated by the state, while the latter is voluntary and contributory.

Vacations are fairly standard for a large company in this community. Employees are entitled to two weeks until they have worked for the firm for 10 years, when they become entitled to a three-week vacation. Vacation time is accrued incrementally and can be accumulated over time; any time over one week may be cashed out. Employees get 14 holidays a year, including two personal days and the week between Christmas and New Year's, when the company closes completely. Sick leave is handled in an unusual fashion, through a pool. Employees earn a certain amount of credit over time and can draw from the pool as needed. The use of sick leave is highly visible and closely monitored. The system is probably a deterrent to possible abuse; at the same time, it is viewed as very fair by most employees.

A wide range of educational programs is covered under the company's tuition reimbursement plan, and many courses are given directly on the company's own campus-like premises. A variety of services is provided for employees, too, including a credit union, a counseling service, a service for purchasing theater and concert tickets, a travel agency, a shop, and even a service that takes care of paying employees' traffic tickets!

The cost of the total benefit package is equal to about 37 percent of the total costs of salaries and wages. This cost needs to be seen, also, in relation to a very high wage base. Personnel costs are high at the company and the *average wage* was about $32,000 per year in 1983. Ultimately, as one employee said, "The package represents what management says the company can afford, what competitors do, and what the company needs to do in order to obtain and hold on to the labor force it wants."

Family Responsiveness: Conscious Ploy or Serendipitous Consequence?

The company's expressed concern has been with responding to the needs of a diverse work force. A growing proportion of this work force consists of two-earner couples and dual-career and single-parent families. Obviously, one question is: To what extent have company policies, deliberately or by happenstance, responded to the special needs of these working families?

Flexiplan. During the 1980s, in the news media, in popular magazines, and in various conferences involving industry representatives, as well as representatives from benefit consulting firms, cafeteria-style or flexible benefits were touted as being designed for the new labor force, and as being particularly responsive to the needs and preferences of two-earner families. Hi-tek was among the first companies to establish such a benefit plan, and it has been in effect there for more than 10 years. A significant number of other companies have followed. Is this a prototypical family responsiveness measure? Did management see it this way? Do employees? Has it had positive effects on employees' family lives? Has it had any particular significance for working families? We begin by taking a more systematic look at the company's Flexiplan benefit program.

Background and Development. Discussion of the concept of a cafeteria-style benefit plan can be found in the literature as early as the early 1960s, but only two companies initiated a serious, systematic research effort to develop a plan. Hi-tek began a research and development project at the end of 1969 to explore the feasibility of the approach. At the time the company employed about 15,000 employees, most at one West Coast location.

Several problems were identified initially as needing attention: the design of the program, administration, satisfying tax and other federal and state regulations, communicating with employees to assure their understanding and acceptance of the plan, and costs. The *design* of the benefit package required the selection of benefits to be included, a decision about the number and nature of options within each benefit, and the development of a method by which employees could generate credits and make trade-offs between benefits.

The *feasibility* study included, in addition to the development of the plan, a careful employee survey designed to assess employees' reactions and responses to the possible development. Almost five years after the feasibility plan was initiated, the company's Flexiplan program was implemented. During the explorations, the company experienced a major recession, went through a period of significant layoffs, and reduced its work force by almost 50 percent. Yet despite this, the study of how such a plan could be designed and implemented continued, without being viewed as a threat by its work force.

The Plan. The company's flexible or cafeteria-style benefit plan is described as a program designed so that the employee has a major hand in the selection of benefits that will best fit the individual situation. It recognizes that not everyone's needs are the same, and that those needs may change over a period of time. The program places the employee in a decision-making role. It is up to the employee to decide which of the various plans he or she prefers.

The Flexiplan part of the total benefit package is limited to four major categories of benefits: health and medical care, dental care, life insurance, and accidental death. The overall benefit package includes, of course, far more benefits outside of the Flexiplan group, but the flexible components are expected to increase over time. (Many companies that instituted cafeteria plans later went further.) Management anticipates that shortly it will be able to include the stock saving plan in the package; vacation time had been expected to be included and still is expected to be, eventually, but is not yet.

The health and medical care component involves nine plans in total, including four insurance (indemnity) plans and five HMOs, as mentioned above. In each case, there is a core plan, which is the basic plan the company provides. Every employee is ensured this minimum amount of protection but can elect certain upward or downward modifications. The basic plan is fully paid by the company. On the other hand, one plan involves more nearly comprehensive coverage, including a very small deductible, longer hospital stay coverage, and a higher maximum major medical benefit; for this plan, the employee would have to pay additionally. It might, however, be very attractive to an individual who is the sole earner in a family, responsible for several dependents. Moreover, the additional costs to the employee would be in pretax dollars, and therefore, for a high wage earner—and there are many such at this company—much of the cost might be borne by the government through the tax system. Three other health insurance plans involve higher deductibles under major medical (ranging, for example, from a $150 per year family deductible to $2,000 per year) and more limited maximum coverage. The plans with the highest deductibles are likely to be attractive to two-earner couples with redundant coverage, when both employees work for companies providing very good benefits. Opting for one of these plans would give the employee a dollar credit to be applied against another benefit, or it can be taken out in cash. The difference in costs between the most nearly and least nearly comprehensive plans might be the difference betweeen an additional payment of $9.00 per week to a credit of $18.00 a week, but the extra cost would be in pretax dollars and, therefore, much cheaper in net cost to the employee. In addition to these four insurance plans, five HMOs are available to employees living in certain geographic locations.

Two options are available in dental care. One is a dental insurance plan while the other is a dental network, similar to an HMO.

Life insurance, a third component of Flexiplan, also has multiple plans, with several different options. Nine plans are available, with a range of coverage, including dependent life insurance. Individual employees may increase their life insurance coverage up to five times their salary, for example, and may pay for this additionally or by using credit from a cheaper medical plan, and vice versa. The accidental death plan also provides multiple options.

By and large, employees have tended to select the most comprehensive medical plan, regardless of need. And although cashing out is an available option when reduced benefits are chosen, few employees do so. Generally, employees in this highly paid labor force have tended to supplement the core plan in all areas, viewing the use of pretax dollars as an inexpensive way for them to improve their benefit package. Personnel department staff try to advise employees in dual-career families that it makes no sense for both to take high medical coverage. Yet some continue to select such plans, nevertheless. They stress that when a couple both work for the company, the spouse with the higher salary should take the more expensive plan, since the pretax dollars that go to pay for the benefits cost the higher wage earner less than the lower. One reason that some employees continue to carry higher insurance than seems necessary may be a combination of concern regarding the stability of marriage coupled with anxiety regarding whether more coverage could be obtained—and what the costs might be—if they do not take it now. The company is planning to cover cohabitating, as well as married couples—and their dependents—following a pattern already established by several other companies in the area.

Once a year, employees are given the opportunity to change their benefit choices. As one personnel counselor said, this is especially important because people's personal situations can change dramatically in the course of a year. An employee may marry or get divorced. An employee who gets married may marry someone who has children and needs benefit coverage. Divorce may leave a working mother with responsibility for covering minor children or may leave a man without responsibility for any dependents. About 80 percent of the employees take advantage of the opportunity for choice with Flexiplan. In a typical year, 6,000 changes may be made in a group of 18,000 employees. Personnel staff help employees by providing information and clarifying options. They do not, however, recommend options except by pointing out the consequences of alternative choices. The general impression is that although employees feel overwhelmed initially, both professionals and nonprofessionals rapidly become accustomed to making informed choices.

A Serendipitous Consequence. Family responsiveness neither was nor is a conscious factor in the company's employment policies and practices or in its benefit developments, many executives told us, including several who were involved in the initial development of the Flexiplan program. It was not a factor in the creation of Flexiplan nor part of the motivation leading to its development. However, Flexiplan has had a variety of positive consequences, one of which has been to prove especially attractive to two-earner and single-parent families. Two illustrations underscore the dramatic differences in how employees use the plan to satisfy their particular needs.

A female manager, unmarried, who has worked for the company for more than 20 years, takes the minimum life insurance plan because she has no dependents. Similarly, she takes the cheapest health insurance plan, with the largest deductible, because she thinks of herself as healthy and the maximum deductible poses no financial problem for her in the event of a medical emergency. She gets back about $25 a week by opting for these minimum plans.

A male engineer is married, has worked for the company for 25 years, and has two grown children, both of whom work for the company. He first chose an HMO plan, one that is less expensive than several other options, when his children were still at home and when he wanted to be sure that the whole family was fully covered, not just covered for medical emergencies. Pleased with the HMO, he continued it even after his children were no longer included in the plan. He receives a credit for its lower cost. He uses this credit to purchase more extensive (and more expensive) life insurance. One daughter and son-in-law, both of whom work for the company, have no children. They have opted for the minimum plans in each benefit category and have chosen cash for the money saved. Since they have just bought a house, this approach fits well with their needs. His second daughter, who also works for the company, is married to a lawyer who is practicing independently and therefore has no benefit coverage of his own.

They have two children. In contrast to her sister, and in contrast also to her father, she has chosen the most comprehensive health and dental insurance policies and the maximum amount of life insurance coverage both for herself and for her husband.

According to one executive,

People are different from one another and employers should be responsive to these differences ... Benefits costs are calculated on the basis of composite rates for families, rather than individuals, it is true; and there is some assumption of a family unit focus. So one could argue that there is some internal redistribution favoring families rather than single people. And large families get the largest amount of redistribution. But we have very few employees with large families, so that's not a real issue. On the other hand, about half our labor force is single, and we do get complaints from them that they are subsidizing other workers' children.

An executive involved in the early developments noted that

When we first explored the development of cafeteria-style benefits, the labor force changes that now seem so dramatic were nowhere near as visible. The concern then was to respond to the needs and wants of a diverse and individualistic labor force. As it happened, what was done was also very helpful to the one third of our employees today who are in dual-earner families. Employees with working spouses are among the most enthusiastic supporters of Flexiplan. But we certainly did not plan it this way.

Another executive spoke in a similar vein.

Becoming more responsive to the special needs of dual-career families and working mothers was just an incidental point, almost a peripheral issue, when the plan first went into effect, almost a decade ago. Now, however, when management talks about Flexiplan, it is one of the chief points made ... The point is made that this is important for all employees, not just for professionals, and that employees can make rational choices if they are given enough information. Employers need not and should not take the kind of paternalistic stance that is inherent in most benefit plans, where it is the employer (or the union) that is deciding what is good for the employee. Second, is that the labor force is changing and that Flexiplan is an ideal programmatic response to the growth in the numbers of dual-career families. A third point is that the labor force is increasingly diverse, including single workers, married or cohabitating but childless couples, single-mother families, married couples with children, and so forth. And Flexiplan permits all of these employees to make the choices that seem most appropriate to their needs and even to change the choice as their needs change.

Even though flexible benefits are now viewed as being especially responsive to the needs of two-earner and dual-career families, it is not working families with children who are the real beneficiaries. Just as this company's work force is disproportionately single, even among the half who are married and the one third who are dual-earner families, by far most are childless or have older children. There are some multigenerational families in which one parent (and sometimes two) and/or one or two children—and sometimes their spouses—work for the company. There are many divorced employees and remarried employees. And there are a significant group of single mothers. But only a very small proportion of the company's workforce has young children, and a still smaller group among them are working mothers with small children. It is these employees who feel the most intense work and family pressures, and it is their needs that have received little attention anywhere thus far.

A woman, who is among the few female department managers, characterized the situation at Hi-tek this way:

Having to care for children is what creates problems for some working women, but it is not a really visible problem. The only women at the company who have children, in particular young children, are nonprofessionals and low-wage earners. The professional women at the company and the few women in management are mostly single. Or if they are married, they are childless. Their perspectives are very different from the nonmanagement women, as are their needs.

"Child care is not a problem for professional women in this firm," she said, "because either they have no children, or very occasionally, if they do have any, the children are older. Less than a handful of these women have young children, and they are usually the superachievers, often managing with great difficulty and usually keeping it under wraps." Child care, in reality, is a problem for nonmanagement women. For such women, when they have young children, the problems are reliability and accessibility. Affordability is an issue for some, but it's much less important. Management views absence for children's illnesses as absenteeism, and this counts against the employee. Given the company's policy regarding sickness benefits and leaves, the reliability of a child care arrangement becomes critical. "If secretaries could take time off when a child is ill and not have it counted against their own sick time and against them personally, it would alleviate a lot of problems." In her estimation, this could be accomplished by increasing the secretarial pool and by allocating a separate sickness benefit for dependent care. As she acknowledged, however, it would also add to the firm's labor costs.

She stressed that benefits are not viewed as a woman's issue and that there are no apparent gender differences in the attitudes toward flexible benefits. "Child care is a woman's issue," she said,

but that's not likely to be included in our benefit package. Management might pay some attention to the issue if it was a problem for women managers or professionals, but it isn't. Management is not going to get concerned because secretaries have problems. *Maybe*, if some competing companies begin to pay attention to issues like child care, and sick leaves to care for sick children, and maternity or parent leaves, then *maybe*, we would get some action here.

Similarly, she commented,

It's not marriage that makes the difference in one's perspectives on things like benefits — it's children. When employees have children, that's when they begin to reassess a lot of employment policies. Benefits really only matter then.

Paid Time Off. Like Flexiplan, several other company benefits are now similarly identified as responsive to the needs of working families, though developed initially with other reasons in mind. Thus, for example, the fact that the company closes completely during Christmas week is viewed as enormously helpful by all employees — both the single workers who use this time for personal recreation and employees with school-aged and preschool-aged children, who would otherwise have to make some kind of special arrangements for their children at home for the week. And having the company closed for the week eliminates the problem of high absenteeism that occurred regularly before this became company policy.

A similarly appreciated benefit — and an appreciated policy of implementation — has to do with paid personal days and the right to use them when family emergencies arise.

Although sick leave policy is viewed as very fair, it does represent a potential problem for those with child illness emergencies.

Yet some employees have found the policy helpful even in this situation because of the discretion supervisors have concerning the policy. For example, one single mother described how well the policy had worked for her several years earlier. She had been working for the company for about two years, in a secretarial position, when her five-year-old son was in a serious automobile accident. Her supervisor telephoned her at home the day after the accident occurred to ask how her child was and to tell her that he had placed her on sick leave so that she could be with her son while he was in the hospital, during the immediate critical time and during his subsequent convalescence, yet not lose pay at that time. "It made all the difference in the world to me," she said.

I couldn't begin to figure out how I'd manage to be with Tommy at the hospital and yet not lose my job. Without my job we would have no income, yet I knew I had to be with my boy. I was still distraught even when they told me that he would recover, until that call came.

Maternity. Maternity policies at Hi-tek are similar to those in most progressive, very large companies. The policy involves both a paid disability leave and an unpaid personal leave. The standard period of maternity disability is six to eight weeks after childbirth, a standard now accepted in most places where there is disability insurance. If desired, and if their physician thinks it necessary, women can also take one or two weeks before they are due to give birth as part of their disability leave.

Because the company is located in California, its women employees benefit from state legislation that requires all employers in the private sector to participate in the state Temporary Disability Insurance (TDI) program (which since passage of federal legislation in 1978 must cover pregnancy and maternity), or, if they prefer, to have their own private insurance plan, which must provide the equivalent of the state plan, plus some additional protection.[1] The California TDI program is the most generous state short-term disability insurance program in the country, replacing a portion of salary from a minimum of $50 up to a maximum of $224 weekly in 1985 and lasting for up to 39 weeks. Almost all private employees are covered under this legislation.[2]

The company's short-term disability (STD) plan covers the first week of disability (normally not covered under the state TDI) under its sick leave plan, at full pay, and then the disability insurance plan goes into effect. The advantage provided by the California location is dramatic when one compares the STD benefit for Hi-tek employees working at non-California locations and discovers the benefit is only about 60 percent of that provided by the combination of the company plan and the state plan. Of course, all non-work-related disabilities are covered by these disability plans, not just maternity. STD is discussed here as a family-related benefit, because it is through this benefit that family income is protected at the time of pregnancy and maternity, an increasing occurrence as more and more women continue to work at that time.

Pregnant women are under no obligation to report their pregnancy. They may announce it as early or as late as they wish but need to present a physician's certificate when requesting disability leave. Most women work until the very last minute and return to work after six weeks. If a female employee claims to be disabled much beyond that time following a normal childbirth, staff in the personnel office may ask to speak to her physician. There is no expectation of a woman's returning before the six-week period is up, and there is some leeway depending on the nature of the childbirth. More time is allowed following a Caesarean, or for a difficult delivery, and so forth. But six weeks is the usual leave, and there is no indication of any abuse or of any particular problem. Both management and nonmanagement employees seem satisfied with existing policies. The contrast with Atlantic Utility (chapter 3) is dramatic.

A personal, unpaid leave of up to three months may also be taken for maternity purposes, with full job protection. Because the company has its own pool of temporary clerical and secretarial personnel in addition to the permanent part-time staff, women in such jobs can elect to come back on a part-time basis if they prefer, and many do so, at least for a while. Professional women can sometimes work out special arrangements to phase in their return, but most, by far, are back at work full time within two months of the time they give birth.

Mary Ann, a married budget analyst with two children, worked at the company during both her pregnancies and described the experience. An intense and articulate 29-year-old, she gave us a picture of what the experience was like both before and after passage of the federal legislation. Her older daughter was born just before passage of the Pregnancy Disability Amendment (1978); the younger one was just five months old at the time we talked to her. When pregnant with her first child, she worked until the beginning of her ninth month and returned to work when the baby was three months old. Thus, she was out of work for a little more than four months overall. She received full disability benefits for the whole period because the baby was born by a Caesarean section. If not for that, she would have received no cash benefits and been limited to having an unpaid but job-protected leave. Paid disability leaves were not available for normal pregnancies and childbirth in most California, and other, companies until after passage of the federal legislation.

During her second pregnancy she also left work at the beginning of her ninth month, again at her physician's suggestion. In retrospect, she said she regretted doing so because she felt well and would have preferred to have more flexibility regarding her return date after childbirth. As it happened, it would not have mattered, because the particular situation required that she return to work when her baby was two months old, even though it was sooner than she had hoped to and sooner than she had wanted to. She was offered a promotion, and the job could not be held open for her any longer. However, given her willingness to return before she had to, technically, her superior has been very flexible in permitting her to manage her particular child care needs. She is nursing this baby, just as she nursed her first child, and has organized her infant care arrangements so that the baby is cared for near where she works. She can take time off to go there and nurse the baby during her lunch hour and at other times, if it becomes necessary.

The company's response to maternity leaves often depends on who the employee is and what her job is. If it is a secretary, coping with her absence is easy, as is being flexible concerning her particular needs. Nor is it expensive. It just means having a temporary replacement for her. So if her boss is supportive and if she can manage with less income—a big if for many—she can adjust her schedule accordingly. On the other hand, if it is someone who is a professional or a skilled employee, she may be difficult to replace temporarily. Instead, her work may be covered by her co-workers. Generally, the job is carried for six weeks. Some of the work gets done and the rest is carried over awaiting the employee's return. If it is really urgent that the work be completed sooner, she may be replaced and then, on her return, given a similar job.

Assuring a professional a comparable job is not a problem for the company. As one manager who had been out on maternity leave said,

If you are sufficiently skilled you are too attractive to lose. For someone in that position, even taking a leave that is longer than company policy can be worked out, as could a phased-in return. I know, because I took off three months and then wanted to work part time for another six months. I worked it out with my superior. The reality is even if I had wanted to take off that extra six months, I could have because he knew that even if it meant quitting I'd have no trouble getting another job whenever I wanted to return, here or someplace else. But I didn't want to leave and I didn't want to stay home completely; I just wanted a little more time with my baby. She's likely to be the only one I ever have.

Child Care. Child care is described by both management and non-management as one of the two benefits that are central to the family responsiveness issue. The other is paid time off.

The company has no child care benefit at this time. There has been some discussion concerning inclusion of child care as a flexible benefit, but most people, both management and nonmanagement, seem to think it will be several years before any such development occurs. Most senior management are opposed to operating an on-site child care service because of costs, potential liability, and the negative experiences of the few large companies they know about that have gone that route. One human resource (HR) officer who agreed that management was not very supportive of doing anything concerning child care argued that the company's employees came from many different places and over great distances. It is difficult, if not impossible, to develop one uniform program for such a diverse group. What might be considered instead, in time, he suggested, would be some kind of child care subsidy, possibly inclusion of child care in the Flexi-plan package, as an optional benefit. A second possibility, sug-gested as something that might be done in the short run, would be to develop a child care information and referral service in con-junction with several state agencies.

One reason that child care is not viewed as likely to be included in the Flexiplan soon is the cost factor. An HR executive explain-ed that preliminary explorations indicated child care would be a very expensive benefit. "For example," he said,

if we were to give all employees $5.00 per week in a flexible benefit to use as a child care subsidy or for something else instead—clearly, the smallest amount that would constitute a subsidy—it would amount to close to $200,000 a week. It would also constitute a big hunk out of the total amount available for new benefit items for the coming year. Fur-thermore, child care is a problem that affects only a very small group within our work force. Some of us believe that one way to respond to this need, among some employees, would be to provide child care as an option in Flexiplan that employees could choose instead of something else, or that they could purchase. But that has not been the company policy where new benefits are concerned. Instead of trying them out within Flexiplan, the approach is to 'pioneer' first outside the plan. Then, if de-mand is high enough and we can assess who uses it and get a fix on it, we may include it in the plan.

A personnel counselor was convinced that child care is an enor-mous problem for women employees with preschool-aged chil-dren, especially single mothers and single fathers who have custody of their children. "Many parents strap themselves in order to pay for good nursery schools for their preschooler," she said, "and infant care is almost impossible to find or, if available, to afford." On the other hand, a woman in middle management in-sisted that in her experience

the child care problem is one of accessibility and reliability, not afford-ability. You think you have a good arrangement and then your child care woman gets sick or her child gets sick, and suddenly you are stuck—sometimes just as you are getting ready to leave the house. That's when the child care crisis occurs.

Several women employees, both management and nonmanage-ment, were convinced that one major reason management has not made further strides in developing a child care benefit is that child care is more of an issue for nonmanagement women than for managers.

"It is a class issue," said one articulate and insightful woman manager.

Until there are a significant number of women professionals and managers who have young children and who find child care a major problem, management will not identify child care as an important issue needing management attention and support. And until women feel secure as they move up the management ladder and do not feel that exposing their personal and family problems will make them vulnerable (as they now feel, often quite correctly), they will define their child care problems as personal, they will suffer in silence, and the women down the ladder for whom it is an overwhelming problem will be unlikely to get any help. In this company it will take time and something new happening before management provides a child care benefit.

Few of the male executives we spoke with had any sense of the personal child care problems and experiences of their secretaries, and none were aware of the child care details for any of their professional female staff. For most, this was another world, and not one that was expected to be brought to work. Some, but not all, women in management were more sensitive to the problems, but usually only those who had had personal experiences themselves.

Among the management people most likely to be informed of new benefit developments, none thought that child care was likely to receive attention in the near future, though all thought it would eventually. "The company has not been proactive on the child care issue thus far and is not likely to be soon," said one human resource executive.

First, it is expensive. Second, it does not have a "champion" within management. No one high up is pushing for it. Third, it doesn't have a big constituency in the company. We have a lot of single workers, or married but childless couples; we don't have a lot of employees who have young children. Fourth, those who have a problem are not influential in the company. It is not a problem of management personnel or of professionals. Finally, among senior management there is an ideological principle involved. There is some feeling that it is paternalistic to pay attention to personal and familial problems like child care. On the other hand, some others think a child care benefit would be a discriminatory benefit.

Regardless, even if some interest in child care builds up, it would only be either an information and referral program—which is inexpensive—or a modest voucher type of benefit, maybe included in the Flexiplan package. But it will take either a powerful groundswell or a powerful champion to get it moving soon.

Flexitime. The last new benefit innovation in the company was the establishment of flexitime as company policy in 1980. Here, the company did not play a leadership role at all, but instead, "hopped on the flexitime bandwagon, after several companies in the area had moved in this direction." Although it was not a major initiative, was not costly, and was already supported by more than half a dozen other companies in the industry, it still took one and one half years to institute it as company policy. Moreover, even though the impetus for flexitime came from top management, it took time to implement. A pilot project was carried out in one department. Six months later, the results were assessed. Subsequently, the policy was put into effect for the whole company. It is generally viewed as a very successful policy, liked by most employees and by most in management.

The standard work week at the company is 40 hours, excluding lunch breaks; the standard day is 8:00 A.M. to 5:00 P.M. with one hour for lunch. All employees must be at work between 10:00 A.M. and 3:00 P.M. and must take at least one half hour for lunch. Otherwise their schedules are adjustable, as long as they amount to 40 hours per week and meet with the supervisor's approval.

A middle-level manager, a single mother, discussed the importance of flexitime for managing her work and family schedule, saying,

Flexitime, for me, was a Godsend! I could take my children to nursery school before coming to work and get here at 9:00 A.M. instead of 8:00. It took all the morning pressure off once I could arrange that. Before, it meant depending on someone else and being late whenever there was a problem. I leave at 6:00 in the evening, but I have a friend who gets home earlier and he picks up the children and takes care of them while beginning dinner.

The flexitime policy varies across groups and departments. In most cases it is up to the specific supervisor to approve. Depending on the particular job, employees can change their schedules almost daily, but most, of course, do not. Most still work the standard 8:00 A.M.—5:00 P.M. day. If they flex, they tend to select a particular variation and keep to that schedule until something happens, such as a child changing school, or a new child care arrangement, or a spouse changing jobs, or a divorce. Some women work 7:00 A.M.—3:30 P.M., with a half hour for lunch, and some work 9:00 A.M.—6:00 P.M.

A man talked about how he and his wife managed to cope with their family and work responsibilities. Enthusiastically describing their use of flexitime, he explained how he takes the children to school and then goes to work. His wife begins work at 7:00 A.M. but leaves in time to pick up the children when school is over. They use individual vacation days to stay home on school vacations, alternating between them in taking days off so that one parent is always home when the children are. Similarly, they stagger part of their vacations to cover the part of the summer when the children are not in day camp. It leaves them with very little personal flexibility, but they view this as a temporary problem, with this the best solution given their options.

Flexitime can be used to respond to nonfamily needs too. For example, if a staff member has a class, a course that is being taken off site at a local university in either the morning or the afternoon, schedules can be adapted accordingly.

There are still no time clocks at the company, and the flexitime policy as it has been enunciated and carried out underscores the stated corporate culture with its emphasis on individual autonomy and choice, a response to diversity, and an assumption that individual employees are mature and responsible in how they handle autonomy. Thus, one result of the company's flexitime policy is that very different types of employees can benefit from the policy. To illustrate: One mature man with responsibility for elderly parents adjusts his schedule so that he can shop for his parents and stop by to prepare an early dinner for them three days a week; a couple with young children use flexitime so that one leaves later and brings the children to school while the other goes to work early but gets home in time to pick up the children when school ends; a young women working part time for an MBA takes courses early in the morning two days a week and late afternoon another two days. All three very different employees benefit from and are enthusiastic about flexitime.

Assessing Effects and Effectiveness

Employees' Views. Employees, uniformly, view the company's benefits as excellent. Except for child care—and that is mentioned only by a small number who have young children and are experiencing personal problems and some others who are aware and sensitive to their needs—most workers are remarkably satisfied with company policies.

Employees who come to the company from smaller firms are very conscious of a dramatic contrast. They are much better off, and they know it. "Smaller companies do not have comparable benefits," we were told again and again.

Low-wage women employees, whose spouses are self-employed or working for small companies, are especially aware of the value of the benefits the company provides. It is their benefits, provided through their jobs, that assure health and medical care, a decent retirement income, and so forth, for their families. For many, these benefits are an important part of what attracted them to the company. Yet regardless of the value and importance of the benefits, clearly no one comes to the company *because* of the benefits, although some, when leaving, acknowledge regretfully what they will be missing, unless they are going to another high-tech company.

Those employees who do come from another high-tech company are least cognizant of the benefits or of any other employment-related policy. "High tech, aerospace and defense companies all have excellent benefits," said one man who had worked for Hi-tek for ten years, left for a better job at one of the competing companies, and now, three years later, was returning here in response to the offer of still another promotion.

We aero braceros take top benefits for granted. Anything else is unheard of. In the benefit area, the most important thing is that here we have some choice in how we spend benefit dollars. What is really special here, however, is that for a big company, management is remarkably unauthoritarian and humanistic—people-oriented—in its policies. It is this corporate culture that makes the company such an attractive place to work at more than anything else.

Flexiplan Evaluation. A formal evaluation of Flexiplan was carried out in 1981 by a team of researchers from both inside and outside the company. One objective was to assess the extent to which the original goals that guided the plan's development had or had not been achieved.

The major reasons for launching Flexiplan were the following:

1. It would have a positive impact on employee relations.
2. It would eliminate the follow-the-leader approach concerning benefits that is so prevalent in most industries, but especially in this one.
3. It would improve employee motivation and raise productivity.

Both the first and the second goals were achieved. There is no evidence one way or another about the third goal.

Initially, management decided to begin the plan with only three benefits: health insurance, life insurance, and coverage for accidental death. Dental benefits were added only in the 1980s. Vacation time was considered but then deferred for subsequent attention. It was also decided that to avoid generating anxiety, suspicion, or hostility among employees, despite the problems in the company at that time, there would be no reduction in the core benefit package. Thus, the benefits then in place became the standard benefits in the Flexiplan package.

Flexiplan was designed to represent an opportunity for variations, based on individual needs, wants, and preferences. Options covering more or less than the standard package, and costing more or less, would be made available to employees. The initial plan was designed and implemented by an organization employing 11,000 people. When it was evaluated seven years later, 17,000 employees were potentially involved.

At the time that Flexiplan was put into effect, the total value of employer-paid benefits was not significantly different in value from those offered by a multiindustry group of companies. The total value of the plan, however, including the insurance options for which employees could pay additionally, did make the package worth more than what other comparable companies were offering, and of course, more than the company standard. By the early 1980s, when the plan was evaluated, however, the total of the employer-paid benefits was significantly less than those offered by the multiindustry standard, and the total value of the package, even including the options available, was no longer significantly better than that of other, comparable companies. Thus, whereas the total package was comparable to a multiindustry standard in 1974, it was not in 1981, although it was still comparable to its competitors within the industry.

Administration costs have remained modest throughout the period, and there has been no increase in the numbers of personnel required to administer the program or to counsel employees. The difference in staffing requirements between the regular benefit plan and Flexiplan is one full-time, nonexempt employee.

About 1,200 new, current, and former employees were surveyed regarding their attitudes toward the company's benefit package. The results revealed the following: Almost all current employees report that they are moderately or very satisfied with their benefits. Most feel that they understand the choices available to them and are not confused by the process. About 80 percent of both former and new employees think that the company's benefits are *better* than those offered by other companies, despite the reality that they are not and may even be a little worse. About the same percentage of current employees say that Flexiplan makes them feel more positive about the company. About 25 percent of new employees say that Flexiplan had a moderate or strong effect — but not a determining effect — on their decision to come to Hi-tek rather than accept a competitor's offer. Especially dramatic, 30 percent of the employees surveyed wrote in — in the absence of such a category — that the single most important benefit the company provided was the opportunity to choose!

Flexitime Assessed. Flexitime was implemented throughout the company in the beginning of 1980. To determine both management's and employees' perceptions of the impact of the policy, a study was carried out 2½ years later. The focus of the study was on perceptions only; no outcome measures were assessed. About 1,200 new and current employees, as well as supervisors, were surveyed by questionnaires, and 62 percent responded: 74 percent of new hires, 61 percent of current employees, and 55 percent of the supervisors.

The results indicate that there is a wide time band when people start and stop working, but 80 percent are at work by 8:30 A.M. and 60 percent leave by 5:30 P.M. How employees go about setting their schedules is unclear: 63 percent of supervisors say employees must obtain their approval before setting a work schedule, but only 30 percent of employees say this is the case. Half the employees say they set their schedules themselves.

The specified goals were achieved only in part. Most employees and supervisors said they liked the policy and believed it contributed to a more positive feeling about the company. Most supervisors, as well as new hires, believed it facilitated recruitment. Half the employees said it would lead them to remain at the company if offered a position elsewhere. About half believed that flexitime decreased their commuting time. About 40 percent of both employees and supervisors thought it improved productivity. On the other hand, most employees and supervisors did not think that it had any positive impact on absenteeism, tardiness, or turnover, and fewer than one third saw it as having any positive impact on any of the secondary outcome measures listed as unanticipated benefits.

It is noteworthy that nowhere among the primary or secondary objectives did this management-initiated evaluation of the impact of flexitime raise any questions about personal or family life vis à vis work, except marginally in relation to commuting time. Nonetheless, in the list of employees' responses, "decreased conflict between employees' job and personal life" is listed. Almost 40 percent of employees specified that they experienced less conflict between their job and their personal life after flexitime was implemented.

On the other hand, most supervisors found it more difficult to contact people and to schedule meetings, and almost half thought it was now more difficult to manage a project. Nevertheless, when they were asked whether flexitime should continue, 97 percent of the current employees, 99 percent of the new employees, and 99 percent of the supervisors said, "yes."

Management's Views. "Benefits have to reflect 'where labor comes from'—the geographic location of the company—as well as 'which labor you need'—the type of industry the company is in and the kind of work force it needs," according to the vice president for human resources.

Forty thousand people don't need the same benefits, and therefore the goal of benefit development should be to discover how to offer the greatest opportunity for diversity and individualization. This can be a problem in a company like Hi-tek because the absence of unions means that no one individual and no one organization represents all employees. There is no structure for dealing with multiple preferences and achieving consensus.

There are multiple constituencies in the company—even among groups where you would think there would be some unanimity. For example, there's not just one woman's constituency within the company but rather several different women's constituencies. And they rarely agree.

According to this vice president, these women's constituencies are:

• Exempt and nonexempt women
• Married and single women
• Mothers and childless women
• Old and young women
• Women in dual-career families and women in traditional single-earner families—some of whom may be working but really would like to be home
• Professional and nonprofessional women
• High-paid and low-paid women

In his view:

This complexity within each larger constituency is especially important in the benefits area. To respond to such diversity, what is needed is an enabling device that will permit access to certain benefits and services in an individualized way, and this is what the Flexiplan program permits.

Another human resource executive described Flexiplan as an ideal new social invention in the benefits field, because it is responsive to employee preferences and choice at the same time as it does not appear to increase costs to the company.

Flexiplan is an excellent cost management tool for a company that is committed to being a leader in the compensation field (pay and benefits) yet wants to do this as efficiently as possible. Flexible benefits permit managing the benefit program in such a way that it maximizes benefits for employees without costs being driven by the marketplace. It is nowhere near as expensive to administer as many think, since the basic costs involve merely preparing information material for employees and training personnel staff to be able to communicate clearly and properly. The real cost of the plan is when changes are made in the benefit options offered. When a major change is made, it can involve a cost of about $100,000 for reprogramming. However, a company must have a good computerized employee database to carry out a flexible benefit plan. With such a database, administrative costs are no more than they are for any other system, but most companies still do not have such a database.

"On the other hand," he continued,

flexible benefit growth has been negligible recently, and one issue is when and how it can break out of its concentration on insurance benefits and move into some new areas. Services such as child care, and paid time off, need to be addressed as important issues for the company's future labor force. Pensions are less important to include in Flexiplan because the company has already established a deferred compensation and salary reduction plan.

Management's ranking of benefits in the order of the value placed on them by employees places Flexiplan at the top. "The most important benefit is the opportunity to choose, to customize, to individualize one's benefits," according to a significant number of employees in the recently completed evaluation of the program. Indeed, employees list this ahead of any other single benefit. The second most important benefit is health insurance. Although the company is not at the forefront here, through Flexiplan a wide range of options is available. Third in their listing of important benefits is the category of time off—vacation, personal days, holidays, sick leave. Most people expected the time-off benefit to increase in the 1980s, but thus far it has not. Concern with productivity is pushing the other way, because paid time off is a very expensive benefit. Not only is pay involved, but nothing is produced during that time, so that it is almost a double cost to the employer. Fourth is the area of savings and retirement income—stock purchase, salary reduction, deferred income, pension plans, etc. (One reason this benefit cluster is so low down in rank may be because Hi-tek's work force is relatively young; regardless, this is a lower ranking for retirement-related benefits than would be found among most employees.)

At the service end, preretirement counseling and investment counseling are beginning to get some attention.

The Factors That Shape Benefits and Policies at Hi-tek

Concern with productivity is an important part of what is generating the current change at the workplace. Certainly it was an element in the development of Flexiplan, and it continues to be an element in any discussion of new benefit developments. But there is no real evidence that specific benefit policies affect productivity in specific ways.

On the other hand, there is evidence that labor costs are a barrier to raising productivity. If the parent company is to compete in a world economy, management is going to monitor labor costs—and therefore benefits costs—very closely. Part of what makes Flexiplan so attractive is that employees like it, they think they are getting *more* as a result, and yet it actually costs less! In effect, even if the amount of dollars spent does not increase, the available dollars are used for what employees want most.

Some benefits and policies are industry driven. "To get and keep our kind of labor force we must maintain competitiveness with other companies in our industry," is a constant refrain. The company assesses what is going on in the industry through national and industry-wide surveys. There is a good deal of informal networking among human resource staffs in different companies, also.

Some benefits develop as a consequence of legislation. "Our maternity policies were clearly shaped by federal and state legislation. And IRS rules and regulations have had a major impact on Flexiplan, and now on our salary reduction plan," said an executive.

"Labor force trends and the demography of the workplace also influence the development of new benefits," another said:

There are changes in the composition of the work force and there are changes in attitudes and values as today's new workers reflect the values of the 1960s and 1970s. These changes have to make a difference long term, but we are only just beginning to see the impact, and some in management would like to deny it is happening. At a recent meeting of senior management, there were 2,000 white males present—and no one else. Clearly, this cannot go on, and top management knows this.

Occasionally, top management takes a really creative leadership role, as happened with flexible benefits, or initiates an exploration of a new policy, as with flexitime. But this does not happen very often. Top management is usually responsive, not proactive, in this area.

Finally, some new developments occur by accident: a union contract is up and the union is bargaining in a particular company. Someone hears about a new development: "The union negotiators decide to throw that one on the table, and it sticks!" Once it exists in one company, the competition begins to know about it. If it seems worthwhile, management in other companies decide they have to adopt it, too. "In effect, there is a snowball effect; and that's probably a far more important factor in benefit policy developments than most people realize."

New developments can be initiated in Hi-tek at any one of four levels:

1. Top management (the CEO and the Board)
2. Top human resource management
3. Middle HR management
4. A "bottom up" approach (the least likely, yet much time and effort goes into encouraging employee self-expression)

The HR staff, who take primary responsibility for initiating new benefit developments, spend time monitoring or charting the industry generally. They also stay abreast of new developments by participating in professional organizations and reading professional journals. Informal contacts with their peers are an important source of new ideas and new trends. Inevitably, they listen to employees' comments, too—both their complaints and their preferences. Ultimately, they are responsible for agreeing among themselves, across the company's divisions, on what they think should be projected, in the context of how much money can be spent. Top HR staff then make an annual presentation to senior management describing where the company is vis-à-vis its benefits and where other companies in the industry are. They make suggestions concerning new initiatives for the next year, as well as for the next several years.

Among the likely future developments are the following: an increasing disappearance of any distinction between exempt and nonexempt employees in the benefits area; a greater stress on improving employee communication; exploration of several new benefits, perhaps as part of Flexiplan, including child care, subsidized transportation, subsidized housing (e.g., low-interest loans), and improved work environment.

On Balance

We began this chapter by suggesting that large companies could institute policies that were more individualized and personalized in responding to the diversity of needs in a large labor force. Small employers, we shall see, do this on an individual, discretionary basis. But Hi-tek, a large company, has accomplished some of this by becoming one of the first major companies to pioneer with a new social invention (which is by now a widespread development), a plan permitting employees to choose the benefits they want from a menu offered by the company and from a given price list. Clearly from all that was told us about the history of the plan and its implementation, and from all the reports and studies we reviewed, Flexiplan was not launched to respond to employees' changed family needs, but the program has been successful in responding to the diversity of employee needs. New types of employees, those who are carrying child and family responsibilities simultaneously with job responsibilities, are among the most positive beneficiaries.

Although management stresses the importance of these benefits for working families, there have been other benefits to management that management has been less comfortable in publicizing. At the same time that employees have enjoyed the opportunity to choose, Flexiplan also saved the company money. During the ten-year period that Flexiplan has been operating, the company kept its standard benefits while other companies improved theirs. Indeed, instead of increasing its standard benefits, the company, in effect, introduced cost sharing. For improved benefits, employee cost sharing is quite significant. In fact, this was a major serendipitous benefit of Flexiplan—the ability to expand cost sharing at a time when it was not being introduced any place else in the industry. It may be seen more widely as a wise policy in the 1980s as U.S. industry fights for its market niches and is necessarily concerned with health cost inflation as well.

Other aspects of Hi-tek company policy support the concept of flexibility in response to a diverse labor force, with similar results. Flexitime has a developmental history and impact evaluation that in broad terms is closely related to the Flexiplan experience, albeit with less significant results. Several factors led to its development; however, in contrast to Flexiplan, where the company was a leader, here it was a follower. Regardless, the policy is in place, and management and employees are pleased with it. It has had a positive effect on employees' attitudes toward the company but, like Flexiplan, no measurable impact on productivity, or on labor force recruitment or retention.

The company's general ambiance is clearly important to employees and can also be characterized as flexible. The culture is open and relatively nonhierarchical. There are almost no differences between management and nonmanagement employees' benefits. There are limited trappings of status. Employees use first names with their supervisors. Individual company policies are often modified on a discretionary basis as managers and supervisors respond to the needs and problems of individual employees.

Most in management acknowledge that the labor force—and the society generally—has changed and that these changes require different policies. Flexiplan and flexitime are valuable serendipitous responses, even though the company has not on a policy level explicitly decided to adapt policies generally to the changing demography of the labor force. Top management suggests that over time Flexiplan's reach will become broader; more clearly family-oriented benefits and services such as child care and paid time off will then be included.

Perhaps so. Maybe even probably so—in time. But for now we note that little in the way of explicit and direct attention to the new kinds of family/work issues has yet emerged. And here we got some important new insights. These issues do not characterize the needs of all working women, but rather of working mothers, especially those with young children—and working fathers, too, when they are sole parents or when they have working wives. It is a problem that is highly gender related but not exclusively so. More important, it is highly related to the presence of young children. Not only does just a relatively small proportion of Hi-tek's labor force have children, but more important, the women who do are not in the part of the labor force that Hi-tek is currently concerned with recruiting or retaining. Before management pays more serious attention to these child/family/work issues, there will need to be a change in the character of its professional/management female labor force. Perhaps when enough of these highly skilled young women begin having children, the pressure on this company—or on others in the industry—will lead to some new family-responsive initiatives at the workplace. Another factor influencing the company in this direction may be the growing needs of adults with older parents. It is possible that over time some pressure will come from employees with such needs, too. Regardless, until one or the other, or both, occur, little new is likely to happen. In the meanwhile, we should take appreciative note of the benefits to be derived from company policies that take flexibility as their guiding principle and lay the groundwork for a more individualized and personal response to employees, while still assuring them the foundation of social provision that good basic benefits make possible.

5. Trading on Tradeoffs: The Small Employer

The sportswear shop is owned by a woman who has another, larger shop elsewhere. Previously, she managed that shop, and her late husband managed this one. Now she manages both but has given the day-to-day responsibility for running the store to two young women, friends, who had worked for the owner for many years. They are employed "half on the books and half off," but they say they have no social security coverage and little in the way of other benefits. "We've been trying to get her [the employer] to get health insurance for us, but she says it's too expensive. Maybe someday she'll do it. We'd like at least hospitalization, and we have even said we would settle for her forming a group plan without contributing anything to it; we would pay for the whole thing. But she says that there aren't enough of us."

The two women can each take two weeks off in paid vacation time and can choose the times they want as long as they do not take off at the same time, and they avoid the peak seasonal times. They can take off "some holidays" and get paid, as long as it's not "too many." They have no specified number of days they can take off if ill, but they can cover for one another and get paid, as long as they do not "abuse" the privilege.

The issue of a maternity leave has not arisen for these women; but in a subsequent interview with the owner, she said that she would save the position if one of the "girls" got married and became pregnant—if "the girl" were out only "a couple of months" and "if she were serious about coming back." If an employee had a problem with a sick child at home, "of course she could take a day or two off," or if she had to visit a child's school, she would not lose any pay. Where flexible hours are concerned, an employee could come in an hour or so later—and keep the shop open later—but the owner could not keep someone who wanted to work only half time.

Clearly, this is a work environment that attracts some people and not others. It suggests a complex picture, with advantages and disadvantages, tradeoffs. In short, this is what work is like in very small enterprises.

Context

About 40 percent of American workers are employed in firms with fewer than 100 employees and an estimated 27 percent in firms with fewer than 25. What do they experience by way of fringe benefits, personal services, and policies regarding work time?

As we noted in chapter 2, the Small Business Administration defines a company with fewer than 500 employees as small, but that doesn't help us very much since a very high proportion of all businesses are in that category. Data about small company benefits and practices, when available, are usually limited to those with 250-500 workers, leaving out a large part of the labor force. And women, in particular, work even more often than men for very small businesses.

Yet our discussion clearly requires some attention to companies not included in Chamber of Commerce or Conference Board findings and often left out of Department of Labor surveys as well. Establishments with fewer than 25 employees are not even required to report to the Department of Labor on benefit provisions unless they are part of multiestablishment plans!

The research literature has extensive coverage on the differential rewards associated with the primary employment sector and the disadvantaged "dual labor market" of marginal jobs, most of them in relatively small or very small establishments and dominated by women and minority group members. Whatever the precision of the "dual labor market" concept, there is also strong research evidence of very significant wage differentials between large and small employers, as well as the serious problems of low wage workers in many jobs that do not provide the benefits taken for granted by the employees of large corporations. There is little detail about and little understanding of the thinking of employers and employees in quite small enterprises and of the dynamics of choices and coping.

To achieve some insight into what benefits are offered and what work policies and practices are like for those who work in very small firms, we therefore carried out interviews in more than 200 small establishments in two communities in the Northeast, one in New England ("Milltown") and one in New York ("Waterside").[1] Obviously, this process could not provide a picture that would be valid for the nation as a whole. Nonetheless, it could and did offer useful insight in a domain that is largely unknown and invisible. Some day a major governmental agency or large national research enterprise will find it rewarding to undertake the exhaustive and expensive research needed to provide fully representative, reliable, and valid statistics.

Our interviews with these small employers were carried out on a "door to door" basis, in two geographically circumscribed communities of shopkeepers, restaurants, banks, professional offices, and light industry. We, or those working with us, interviewed owners, managers, employers, and, of course, employees. The results, we think, are interesting, provocative, and often poignant. The contrast between the picture for one group of employees provided in what follows and that provided for other employees in the reports of the U.S. Chamber of Commerce, Bureau of National Affairs, or the Conference Board is dramatic.

These interviews took place in coffee shops, bakeries, photo shops, and all the other small businesses to be found in a neighborhood. The exact locale and the degree of privacy varied with the setting—the gas station, doctor's office, or large market. We talked to owners and to employees. We inquired about statutory benefits, other fringe benefits, vacation time, holidays, personal days, and work schedules. In owner-only shops with no employees, we asked about the proprietor's benefit coverage. We asked as well some hypothetical questions: Could an employee have personal time off to care for a sick child or to go to school so as to see his or her child perform in a school play? Could the employee's schedule be adjusted to take a child to school or pick up a child? Would part-time work be permitted? Why did employers think people worked in the neighborhood shops and businesses? What do the employees say about this?

Clearly work in the small enterprise or small establishment reflects among other things, tradeoffs made by both employers and employees. While a bit oversimplified, the generalization could be: trading some money and benefits for flexibility and individualization, and sometimes, for geographic proximity. The situation and the dynamics are worth understanding since they are relevant to the broader issues being explored.

Small Businesses: Owners, Employers, Employees

Who are the small employers in these two communities?

About half are retail establishments (clothing, food, small electronics), and another 30 percent are personal services (dry cleaners, barbers, hairdressers, photography studios, health clubs), professional services (physician, dentist, optometrist, attorney, accountant), or other types of services (auto repair, framing, upholstering). A few combine both (TV sales and repair; washing machine sales and repair). About 15 percent are restaurants, which range from franchise operations of national chains, branches of national chains, local coffee shops and pizza parlors, taverns and bars to family-type and a variety of ethnic restaurants. There are also several banks, a few insurance offices, a printing plant, and a medical laboratory. There are no significant differences in all this between the two communities, although Milltown has a few more restaurants than Waterside; and Waterside has a few more banks than Milltown.

About half the establishments are single, independent enterprises. About 40 percent are one of several establishments owned by one or two persons and either managed directly by the owner(s) or managed indirectly, with someone else responsible for the day-to-day operations. Less than 10 percent are part of a national or regional chain, or subsidiaries of a larger organization, with no direct involvement in management by the owner. The only difference between the communities is that Waterside has more single units and Milltown more multiple units.

Small Entrepreneurs, No Employees. About one fourth of the single-unit establishments (29) are managed and operated by their owners, with no paid employees. A substantial group of these small businesses, about 40 percent, operate without even basic statutory benefits (for example, no social security). Almost two thirds have no health insurance for themselves, including one third of the Milltown units and all of those in Waterside. More than half either take no vacations or remain open on most legal holidays, or both. More than 60 percent have no life insurance. For many in marginal local business operations, the dream of "being your own boss" contrasts with a reality of a tough seven-day-a-week, risk-ridden life-style. Many family pleasures in fact are sacrificed. There is inadequate time for children and for family and personal relationships. Government is considered by many to be unsupportive.

The experience is best perceived through some specifics:

A Korean family operates a greengrocers, open 7 days a week, 12 hours a day. The produce is fresh and beautiful and the owner and his wife are proud when told how beautiful the vegetables are. In limited English he tries to explain how they work and how the children help, too. His two adolescent sons help after school and on weekends, as does a brother-in-law who helps out after he finishes his job elsewhere. When we asked the owner how he manages when he or his wife is sick—can he or she take time off—he says, "We never sick—cannot be." In the 18 months since he bought the store from the previous owner, the store has never been closed except late at night.

"I've had this store for almost 25 years now. My wife's a teacher, that's why she's not here. But she has good benefits, and that's how I have health insurance. It's too expensive if I have to buy it for myself," says the owner of a small shoe store. "And she has a good pension, too. Her salary is low, but we depend on this business for our income and on her job for benefits," he said with some humor.

This children's clothing store just opened 6 months ago. The woman whose store it is has lived in the community for almost 15 years. Most of that time she worked at the nearby hospital, in a low-paid job, but one that carried with it all the standard benefits: health insurance, retirement benefits, life insurance. For almost all of those years she was a single mother, rearing her three daughters alone, and worrying what would happen to them if something happened to her. "The benefits," as she put it, "were very important; they more than made up for the low salary," since she didn't have the education or skills to get a better paying job. Last year she remarried, and her husband's job now provides the basic benefit coverage for herself and her children that she views as so important. She felt that she could launch this new venture, which she hopes will pay off, but which she knows is risky. She feels that she can afford to do this now whereas she could not when she had only herself to rely on.

Fewer Than Five Employees. We do know that the size of the enterprise is significant for benefit and personnel policy variations, but this exploration does not yield a definitive picture. Is the cutoff point 10, 50, 100, or what? Are there several? For present purposes, we differentiate the establishments with fewer than 25 employees and those with more, because of the ERISA rule. Among the small places, the categories "under 5," "5–9," and "10–24" appear useful. To remind ourselves of the sample limitations, we have rounded all numbers in table 5.1. They should be read only as suggestive.

About half of the small businesses (86) that have paid employees have fewer than five; often this means just one or two full-time workers. *This is the largest single type of employer in both communities.* What do their employees receive in the way of benefits? What types of practices exist to respond to their family needs?

About 80 percent of these small businesses provide all the usual statutory benefits: social security, unemployment insurance, worker's compensation. Yet what is astonishing is that almost one fifth do not even do this, despite the requirements of law!

Of particular interest, however, is the contrast between the New York and the New England communities with regard to disability insurance. While some of the statutory specifics vary by state, New York State is one of the five states in the country that require employers to participate in a temporary disability insurance program, either privately or through the state. Although modest, this benefit can be very important for working women employed in small and medium-sized businesses, especially at the time of pregnancy and maternity. In all states with such programs, coverage must be extended even if there is one full-time employee (with some minor exceptions). But some of the smallest employers ignore mandatory statutory benefits in both communities.

Only about 40 percent of these very small employers (36) provide health insurance. On the other hand, among those providing such benefits, most pay for the insurance completely and include coverage for dependents, too, and almost half also provide major medical insurance or something similar.

Three quarters provide paid vacations and holidays. Of these, more than half the Milltown employers (but less than a quarter of those in Waterside) limit the vacation to one week and the holidays to fewer than 10. In Waterside, many employers close for religious holidays, therefore providing more in the way of paid holidays for their employees. About one quarter of the employers in both communities limit both paid vacations and paid holidays to full-time workers only. Even where a two-week vacation is provided, the time is not always flexible. Several of these very small businesses close for one or two weeks so the owners may take a vacation themselves; in these situations, although a paid vacation is provided, employees have no choice about when they may take it. Similarly, whether holidays are paid or not is often a function of how the employer feels about the employee. As one employee told us, "You get paid depending on how the boss feels. You may get paid for the whole day, or only for part. Or if business is slow you won't get paid at all. You couldn't call this a policy about holidays; it depends on the boss."

Not surprisingly, only 10 percent of the employers provide pensions and about 20 percent provide life insurance. Of some interest, all those providing such benefits in Waterside are unionized. They are among the businesses providing the best benefits in the total sample, not just among these very small employers. Furthermore, these are clearly recognized as union-provided benefits and described as such by employers and employees. Milltown, in

Table 5.1. Benefits and Personnel Policies in Milltown and Waterside

	Owner Only (29)		Fewer Than 5 Employees (86)	
	Milltown	Waterside	Milltown	Waterside
Statutory social insurance	13	3	47	22
Health insurance	10	0	27	9
Vacation	8	4	44	20
TDI	0	0	0	7
Paid sick leave	0	0	28[a c]	16[b c]
Pension	4	1	6	3[e]
Life insurance	9	2	13	3
Unpaid time with sick child	0	0	49	24
Paid time with sick child	0	0	23	16
Paid[i] maternity	0	0	5[f]	7
Unpaid sick & maternity leave	0	0	53	29
No.	15	14	57	29

Milltown, N = 127; Waterside, N = 72.

[a] 7 = full time only; 20 = discretionary as to length.
[b] 9 = discretionary.
[c] Maximum length in both places = 5 days.
[d] Half are discretionary as to length.
[e] All unionized.
[f] 3 have one-week sick leave, one has two weeks, one "depends."
[g] Only for full-time workers.
[h] Three employers covered by TDI said nonetheless that their employees would have no right to any kind of paid leave at time of childbirth.
[i] In Milltown this always was sick leave and in Waterside always TDI, except that it could be either in Waterside in 7 enterprises with 10-25 employees.

5-9 Employees (49)		10-25 Employees (22)		More Than 25 Employees (13)	
Milltown	Waterside	Milltown	Waterside	Milltown	Waterside
24	11	11	8	9	4
28	4	9	4	6	3
29	13	9	8	9	4
0	6	0	5	0	4
8[d]	12[d]	7	5	5	3
9	1	2	0	3	1
12	1	2	0	5	3
22	14	13	9	9	4
10	10	7	4	6	3
4[g]	3[h]	5	7	6	4
24	14	6	8	6	4
33	16	13	9	9	4

contrast, has a smaller group of employers providing pensions but a surprisingly large group providing life insurance (almost 25 percent); in half of these businesses, employees share in the costs of the life insurance. We speculate that local cultural differences may be at work in some of the smaller communities.

About half of the employers in both communities offer paid sick leave to employees away from work because of a brief illness. Even among this group of "generous" employers, however, several limit this benefit to full-time employees. Moreover, at least half of those providing the benefit have no policies as such but make it available to "good workers" or "long-term employees" or say the duration of the paid leave depends on the employee, the circumstances, how business is, and so forth.

The result is often not very different from what prevails in some of the businesses where the employer said he did *not* pay employees when they were out sick, except in "special cases," or "only for my old employees." Even where the benefit is technically available, it often means that an employee may take a day or two off and expect to be paid, but much more than that, and it becomes less likely, or the pay is only partial. In the case of a very serious illness of a long-term employee, two weeks' pay would be defined as very generous. Except for those employees covered by disability insurance benefits, or in union shops with specific contractual arrangements, no employee is entitled as a matter of right to a maximum of more than one week (six days) paid sick leave, except in one business providing two weeks, and most can depend on less. Only one very generous employer has a policy whereby an employee may take off time for up to two physician or dentist visits per month, for the employee or his/her family, without losing pay. This is a bank, part of a major national corporation, and proud of its excellent benefit plan.

Almost half the employers said employees could have an unpaid sick leave or an unpaid maternity leave at the time of childbirth, and they would have their job saved for them, as long as the time was "within reason," or "not too long." When asked about their likely response to an employee out because of illness, or because of maternity, they said that what they did varied, depending on how they felt about the employee. For example, many employers said that they would like to save a job for a good employee but that since they employed only one or two workers, it is impossible to hold a job vacant for long: "The business couldn't stand it." Several add, however, that "a good worker is hard to find" and that given the frequency of turnover and the problems of getting "good help," there would usually be an opportunity to rehire the employee subsequently, even if the job could not be held and guaranteed. Some view situations like illness or childbirth and the lack of guaranteed time off as almost a "window of opportunity" for getting rid of an unsatisfactory worker without too much tension. About 15 percent would permit an unpaid sick leave but not an unpaid maternity leave, a policy that is technically against the law.

There is even less paid protection for maternity than for sickness, but there are differences between the two communities. In Milltown, even though the vast majority of employees in these establishments are female, fewer than 10 percent of the very small employers said they would offer a female employee a paid maternity leave. By this, all that employers meant was that their employees could use sick leave, something that they are legally required to permit regardless! The result would be that in three businesses women could have one week off with pay, in a fourth a woman could have two weeks, and in a fifth, the response was that "it depends"! In contrast, in Waterside, in several businesses in which employees were covered by union contract, employers said that the contract specified the amount of unpaid maternity leave a woman worker could take and how long the job must be saved for her, for example, three months in two cases. More important, about 25 percent provide disability insurance coverage, a benefit that, where it exists, must be made available to women at the time of maternity. Moreover, New York has the fallback position of a mandatory state temporary disability law, as noted; of some interest, most of the employers we spoke with were not aware of this.

In contrast, an overwhelming proportion, 85 percent, would permit an employee to take time off to care for an ill child at home and half would not deduct pay for the time lost, if "within reason." Some would require that the worker make up time lost, but many would not even insist on this. A repeated theme was that "where a child is concerned, the child comes first." "Family is more important than work," said one Waterside employer. "If a child gets sick someone must be home to care for it." As we have already noted, there are many middle-sized and large companies where such policies and sentiments are quite rare. However, several of these small employers said they would only take this approach with their female employees; with their male employees they would expect the wife to take care of such problems, unless, of course, the man were a single parent!

About three quarters of the employers would permit an employee to take time off from work to visit a child's school (if the child were in a play), and more than half said the employee would not lose pay as a consequence.

About two thirds would accept some flexibility in hours for their workers, yet only one third would hire someone specifically on a half-time basis. Of some importance, more than 80 percent of these very small businesses were open at least six days a week, and more than half were open at least nine hours a day.

Finally, five of the Waterside employers with fewer than five employees were union shops. These employers provided state disability insurance in addition to the other standard statutory benefits, health insurance, paid sick leave, vacations, and holidays, and three provided retirement and life insurance benefits through the union.

What is the experience like for those who work for these very small employers? One relevant vignette opened this chapter. Two others follow.

In a local outlet of a national chain of photo-processing stores, the store manager is merely an employee of the larger company. Although he is responsible for supervising one full-time worker and two part-time workers, he has no say in company policy. It is clear, however, that he has some leeway in how he interprets company policy. Here, there are formal personnel policies and practices, and there is a printed brochure on "Your Benefits."

Employees are not entitled to any benefits until they have worked for the company for at least one year. Thus, even the manager, who had been with this business for 10 months when interviewed, would have to wait two more months before being entitled to be paid for any of the holidays that the store was closed. More important, only after his first anniversary would he also be entitled to Blue Cross and Blue Shield, major medical insurance, and dental benefits. Despite these limitations, he believes that the company is a "good" employer, because after one year the benefits are good; there is even a profit-sharing plan.

He can be, and has been, quite flexible where his one full-time worker is concerned. She is a single mother with two children ages five and eight. She has been out twice when the five-year old was ill. She sometimes comes in late because she has to take both children to school. If she were to decide that she wanted to work only half time, it would present no problem for him: "There are always others coming in here asking if I have a part-time job available, and I have someone now who works part time and would like more hours." But this is unlikely to occur, he says, because she needs a full-time job herself.

The owner of a housewares store is president of the local merchant's organization. He has owned the store for almost 20 years and is well known in the community. He has two full-time employees and one part-time worker who is paid "off the books." He thinks of himself as a "good" employer, very fair to his employees, sensitive and responsive to their needs, to the extent that he can be. One employee, who has worked for him for three years, gets a two-week paid vacation, and the other, who has been with him for one and a half years, gets one week. "And they can take their vacations whenever they want to—even during the holiday times, but I'd rather they take it during the summer; that's our slow time." Typically, employees leave after three years, if not sooner. "The kids get older. The women can take a job further away that pays better." He gets his health insurance coverage through his brother-in-law's business. It is too expensive for him to have it for himself, even if his employees wanted to participate in a group plan and pay for it themselves. "My employees are like me; they are covered elsewhere." He has no definite policy about sick leave. "This is too small a business to have a 'policy,'" he says. "If an employee is out sick, she gets paid. I have a very liberal attitude, and I've never been taken advantage of."

If an employee got pregnant, he would let her work as long as she wanted to, although, as he put it, "It can get hard to be on your feet all day." "But I would make every effort to keep the job for her, if she were just going to be out a month or so. I can't hold a job open longer in a business like this. It's a two-man store and I have to have someone else here all the time." He says that he might be able to manage some flexibility in hours, to meet the special needs of an employee, but he could not hire someone who would only work half time. He himself takes off only when the store is closed on a holiday, or when he has to be away to do buying for the store. He takes no vacations himself.

Between 5 and 10 Employees. About one quarter of the employers in these two communities have between 5 and 10 employees. For the most part this means that an establishment has 4 or 5 full-time employees and 2 or 3 part-time workers. About two thirds are single-unit establishments, almost one fifth are local outlets of regional or national chains, and the remainder are one of several establishments owned by an employer. Seventy-five percent are open six days a week or more and at least nine hours a day.

Almost three quarters of these provide the usual statutory benefits, the rest do not. More than half provide health insurance. Although a substantially larger proportion have such coverage in Milltown than in Waterside (73 percent in the latter as against 25 percent in the former), one third of the Milltown employers provide health insurance only to their full-time employees, and several have only one or two full-time employees. On the other hand, of those establishments in both communities providing basic health (hospitalization, mostly) insurance, half also provide major medical insurance or some equivalent.

Eighty-six percent provide paid vacations, about half giving one week and half, two. Almost half provide paid holidays; of these, about half grant less than 10 days each year.

Only 40 percent offer paid sick leaves, and of those doing so, almost half limit them to full-time workers only. For half the employees the length of time permitted for sick leave is discretionary. "It would depend." But none provides more than a maximum of one week (six days in a business that is open for a six-day week). Only one unionized employer in Waterside said his employees are also covered by the union for life insurance and retirement benefits, while more than one third of the Milltown employees are covered for life insurance and more than one quarter by retirement benefits. Half of each group with benefits have them fully paid by their employers.

Almost all of the Waterside employers and two thirds of the Milltown employers would permit employees to take an unpaid sick leave or maternity leave, of a "reasonable length." Less than 15 percent, however, would permit their female employees to have a paid maternity leave. In Milltown this is through use of paid sick leave and limited to full-time employees. This limitation in use exists despite the fact that federal legislation requires that pregnancy and maternity be treated the same as any illness or disability. Although the mandatory, statutory, temporary disability insurance law in New York State applies automatically to maternity, only 40 percent of the firms have coverage, and most of them do not know of the law's application to pregnancy and maternity.

Almost 75 percent of these employers of 5 to 10 workers said they would permit an employee to take time off to care for an ill child at home, and most would not deduct pay or require him or her to make up the time lost. An even larger proportion in Waterside, but only about one third in Milltown, would also permit a worker to take time off to visit a child's school under such circumstances as we described (to see a school play). Several employers responded that, "Each situation is different. It depends on the employee, how business is, and so forth." Others took the position that employees could always exchange shifts with another employee, with the employer's approval, and thus free the needed time. One employer thought this would be all right for his women workers but unacceptable for a man; another talked about how he would approve such a request whether it came from a woman or man. As he put it, "It happens all the time with my male workers who are divorced."

About 60 percent said they would permit some flexibility in hours worked, and about half would permit an employee to work half time for family reasons.

Three of the Waterside businesses were unionized, and these three establishments offered the most extensive benefit coverage.

In a large laundry and dry cleaning establishment in which all the work is done on the premises, the owner manages the store and employs five women, full time. "Accommodation is the name of the game," he says. "I appreciate my workers. I'm happy to have them here. They have hard work to do and it's not a great job, but they work well and they take it seriously. I respect them and they respect me. One has been with me 15 years, one 13, and one 9. There is a lot of camaraderie here. When someone has a problem at home we all know about it. We try to help if we can; at least we can sympathize. This week it's their time; next week it may be ours."

All statutory benefits are provided, but no health insurance. The owner has health insurance coverage for himself and his wife, personally. The workers get a paid vacation, one week for three and two weeks for the two who have worked for him for more than 10 years. They get paid for the six holidays the store is closed. If a "girl" is out sick and is home for a couple of days, she will not lose pay but if it happened too often he would not pay her. If an "old timer" were out longer, as had recently happened, the work would be divided among the other workers, who would help out. He would then divide the pay of the absent one, giving some to the workers helping out as a bonus and the rest to the ill employee. A new employee, maybe for the first year, would not be paid if out ill.

When asked about an unpaid maternity leave, he responded that he hires only "mature women"; he doesn't want to have to worry about such things. Similarly, when asked what he would do if an employee had an ill child at home and needed to take time off, his response is, "I would say OK because I give everyone time off for any logical reason, but again, this is why I hire only mature women. In this business the work has to get done, and it is really very hard and unpleasant work. You think it is easy to work back there with the steam? But we give same-day service, so everyone has to hustle."

In a liquor store employing four full-time workers and five part-time, the store closes for two weeks each August, and all the employees get a paid vacation at that time. The store is also closed for six holidays. Sick leave depends on the worker, how long he has been with the business, and how often it happens. When asked about time off at the time of maternity, the owner said he would have to hire a replacement if it were more than a month or so, but he normally would try to get his part-timers to work a little extra and hold the job open. "We are loyal to our people; we try to do for them what's right." He would let an employee take off time to go to a child's school "as long as they told me in advance. I let my workers take off for graduations, or any special family need. I do the same for myself and try to do right for my workers." Similarly, he would try to accommodate a worker who needed to work slightly different hours or wanted to work half time.

"I try to be fair. Listen, if they wouldn't like how I treat them they would leave or complain. No one ever leaves here. Even the fellow who does our deliveries—he has been with me for 12 years now. If business is good, at the end of the year we give cash bonuses. We care. We are like a family."

Between 10 and 25 Employees. Ten percent of the employers interviewed (22) have between 10 and 25 employees. Most of these are restaurants or large retail stores. Usually, this means that there are between 8 and 12 full-time workers. The remainder, however few or many, are part-timers. In one beauty salon, however, there are 12 part-timers and no full-time workers, and in three other stores there are fewer than 5 full-time employees.

All provide the usual statutory benefits, and more than half the Waterside employers provide disability benefits too; no Milltown employer offers disability insurance. Sixty percent of the total group provide some health insurance coverage; about half of these limit such coverage to full-time employees. Half of the health benefits are contributory for dependents. About one quarter of the establishments provide major medical insurance, or its equivalent, as well.

More than three quarters of these businesses provide paid vacations, usually two weeks in duration, but one third of these limit this benefit to full-time workers only. Only half provide paid holidays; this low number probably reflects the high number of restaurants in the group, and they are likely to be open on the holidays. A little more than half provide a paid sick leave, but none guarantees more than one week for such paid leave and several limit the benefit to full-time workers only. Two, both outlets of a national corporation, provide life insurance and pensions, and both require employee contributions for such coverage.

Almost all these establishments would permit a female worker an unpaid maternity leave at childbirth and would save the worker's job for her or provide something comparable. And all would permit an employee to take time off to care for an ill child or to visit a child's school, but half of these would either deduct pay or expect the time to be made up.

About half of these establishments are restaurants, open 7 days a week for between 13 and 24 hours a day. Here, employees are working different shifts and sometimes staggered days. Thus, there is a flexibility where managers permit full- or part-time workers to select shifts and to vary them. As will be seen later, as much can be said for managers of such enterprises in even the largest national companies.

More Than 25 Employees. Less than 7 percent (13) of the employers interviewed employ more than 25 workers; the largest is a discount department store with 150 employees. More than half in this category are part of large chains (discount stores, supermarkets), or local branches of a large bank, or subsidiaries of a large corporation.

Twenty-five, it will be recalled, is the critical number for ERISA. If there are pensions, there are rules to be followed, and employees have the right to written materials and other benefit protections.

Three of the four Waterside employers in this group are unionized and provide disability insuance, health insurance, paid sick leave, vacations, and holidays. One of these, by union contract, provides as well for a three-month, unpaid, job-protected maternity leave. A second provides for such a leave up to two years—a most unusual guarantee in the United States—and a third provides a six-month paid leave at half pay—more than what most large and "leading" companies pay. Two of the nine Milltown employers with only 25 employees grant a paid maternity leave that goes beyond the usual one-week sick leave: one, a medical laboratory, offers a paid three-month leave; a second has a three-week paid sick leave. But three Milltown employers do not permit even an unpaid maternity leave in which they would guarantee a woman's job on her return.

Three quarters of these "larger" employers in both communities provide basic health insurance coverage (Blue Cross and Blue Shield). More than 60 percent offer paid sick leaves as well, even if only for one week, and all grant paid vacations and holidays, too. All would permit an employee to stay home to care for an ill child, and most would not reduce an employee's pay for this reason; and half would permit an employee to take time off to visit a child's school, also without losing pay. Half would permit some flexibility in scheduling.

We offer two specific illustrations:

A local medical laboratory employs 85 people and is open 6 days a week, all year round, 9 hours a day; however, the laboratory is on call for 24 hours a day, 7 days a week. The man who owns and manages the laboratory defines his personnel as largely professional and technical and is convinced that if he wants a stable work force he must provide a good benefit package. He is competing with other technical employers, including a research organization, a hospital, and several clinics. Employees are entitled to a 2-week vacation after 1 year of employment, 4 weeks after 2 years and 6 after 5. Employees get all the usual legal holidays off, as well as 4 personal days. Workers are also entitled to membership in one of several HMOs in the area. Employees can, by policy, use their own sick leave to care for an ill child and they are entitled to up to 2 weeks a year (10 days) for sick leave. They can use their personal days in connection with school visits or however they wish. They are entitled as well to take time for up to two medical appointments a month for themselves or family members, without losing pay. Women can take a maternity leave of up to 6 months and be paid for 3. This company provided the best benefit package and the most responsive, family-oriented work policies of any of the 200 employers in this group interviewed.

A restaurant, part of a national chain, employs 32 workers, on two shifts, 7 days a week. Most of the employees are part time, working between 20 and 30 hours a week, and most are women. They get 2 weeks' vacation after 1 year and are *required* to take it.

The manager explained that management believes that it is very important for kitchen help and waitresses to take off some time each year. Several of the waitresses object, because they miss their tips, an important part of their income. They are entitled to up to 5 days' paid sick leave, but here, too, most do not take the time, because of the loss of tip income. After 1 year they are entitled to Blue Cross and Blue Shield for themselves; they must pay for a family member to be covered, and few do; they say it's too expensive or that their husband's benefits cover the rest of the family. As restaurants go, this one provides good benefits, we were told. "When I worked for − −(a national chain of coffee shops) you got nothing. Here, at least there are some benefits. But I would like dental insurance. And the single mothers would like family health coverage."

What Makes For Differences?

Unions Make Difference. Surprisingly, even in these very small businesses, being a union shop or a union worker makes a difference. Pressers, bakers, butchers, electricians, supermarket clerks−when working in a union shop−were far better off than similar workers in nonunion establishments.

Nine businesses in Waterside, ranging in size from 2 employees to 50, are unionized. All provide the usual statutory benefits, plus disability insurance. All offer paid vacations, holidays, and sick leave. All permit employees to take time off, without loss of pay, to care for an ill child at home, or to visit a child's school. Three provide more than the minimum disability benefit for maternity: one gives a three-month unpaid leave, a second a two-year unpaid leave, and a third a six-month paid leave at half pay. Only one other employer in the whole sample provides better benefits than these unionized small enterprises. Employers may complain about the costs to them of contributing to the unions' health and welfare funds, but for the employee, clearly, unions make a difference.

Small Establishments, Not Small Businesses. If there is no union, employees are best off if they are working for a local outlet of a large, national company. A benefit package designed to meet the standards of a large company and laid down by corporate headquarters generally means that employees will have at least a minimum basic floor of coverage. Branch banks, local branches of a national chain of stores, even restaurants in a large chain, provide more and better benefits than those small establishments that are individually owned.

All provide basic health insurance coverage, even if it takes one year of work to qualify. All provide a paid vacation, even if modest, and almost all provide paid holidays and sick leave. Several provide paid personal days also. Moreover, in these firms, in typical bureaucratic fashion, policies are enunciated, spelled out, and often made available to employees in printed form. These are benefits as a matter of right, not discretion.

Yet despite the presence of formal policies—perhaps because they are small local establishments, regardless—managers seem remarkably flexible. They make allowances for personal needs and problems and view themselves as having a visible presence in the community and, therefore, having to maintain a positive image. Thus, they, too, would permit an employee—who in many cases resides in the community—to stay home and care for an ill child or to take time off to visit a child's school and somehow, most of the time, it would be without loss of pay, although sometimes it might mean making up lost time.

Legislation and Location. Twenty-two businesses in Waterside, 31 percent of the total number of employers interviewed there, provide disability insurance for their employees. Among the other positive consequences of this benefit, female employees at the time of pregnancy and maternity can take time off from work and receive a cash benefit that partially replaces their wage for six to eight weeks and have their job (or one like it) saved for them when they return to work. This may not seem like very much, but it is far more than all but two employers provide in Milltown, in a sample that was almost double the size of Waterside.

Almost all employers in both communities are willing to permit an unpaid maternity leave, typically for a month or one or two months. Less than 10 percent would permit as much as three months, and only four permit longer unpaid maternity leaves, two by union contract. Most were not specific about the time and said that the length of the leave would depend on how they felt about the employee. If she were a good worker and the employer liked her, anything might be possible—a longer leave, a saved job, a phased-in return, a half-time job. If not, maternity became an opportunity to ease out an employee one wanted to get rid of. "In this type of business it's impossible to save a job," said one employer. "However, if a job opened up later, of course I would favor a good, past employee over an unknown new one. Otherwise, it's a good way to get rid of poor workers." Some employers would be more generous to a sick employee than to one having a baby, viewing the latter as an inevitable source of trouble later.

It is with regard to paid maternity leave that the situation is very different. The vast majority of those who say they provide a paid maternity leave mean that an employee may use her paid sick leave; except for three businesses, this means one week or less. A few working women would be permitted to add on their vacations, but at best this would provide a three week paid leave—still far less than the childbirth leave viewed as a minimum convalescence by physicians, and with no leeway for a woman who might have a medical need to leave work a few weeks before giving birth. Only in two banks, branches of large regional banks, is a formal maternity disability policy specified: 6 to 8 weeks at full salary for those who work 20+ hours per week. The real difference between the two communities is a function of state Temporary Disability Insurance (TDI) now mandated by law in only five states (California, Hawaii, New Jersey, New York, Rhode Island) and Puerto Rico. In New York State, this legislation requires that all employers with one or more employees (four domestics) provide this benefit either through a state insurance plan or a private insurance plan. Not all who are mandated to make such protection available do so, as we have noted, but clearly most do. Many do not understand the benefit, however, and even the disability benefits provided insist that their employees have no entitlement to a paid leave in connection with maternity. Furthermore, several state that they would not save a job for a woman out because of maternity. Indeed, some say openly that they would not hire a woman, or would hire only "mature" women—all clearly against the law. Nonetheless, the existence of a statutory benefit makes a difference, and if it is a benefit legislated by the state, being located in that state makes a difference.

Full-Time, Not Part-Time Jobs. To be eligible for benefits, even when they are provided, it is better to be a full-time worker. Repeatedly, employers qualified their statements about health insurance, sick leave, vacations, and holidays — and about being paid for time off for special or personal reasons — by saying, "Of course this is for my full-time workers only." Often this means that only one quarter of the employees, or one or two out of a group of seven or eight employees, would qualify. A very few employers prorate benefits for part-timers, and a few more provide partial benefits, but in more than half the businesses at least one benefit was limited to full-time workers only. What is more, many employers prefer hiring part-time workers precisely because they are less expensive since no benefits are provided, in addition to their being more flexible and therefore more responsive to the different time pressures of work and business.

The Paternalism of Small Business: The Informal Policy System. Again and again, employers would tell us that the advantage in working for a small business is that "it's like one big family." Employees also make this point, if a bit less frequently.

We're like a family. I'm flexible when problems come up at home. There have been times when I had to fill in to let a worker leave early to deal with a problem at home or an emergency. A child breaks his leg at school. There are school meetings, sports events, plays. There have even been times when this has inconvenienced my private life (gift shop owner).

Any employee can take time off for personal reasons. If she asks in advance, then I plan around it. If it is an emergency, if necessary I would fill in myself (discount store owner).

I've had port-a-cribs in the back room so that my employees could bring their babies to work if something went wrong with their child care. I've always told my workers, if school is closed and the kids are home, don't leave them home alone when they're little. If necessary they can bring them here, as long as they behave.

A small business is an ideal place for a woman with young children to work. She can get time off when she needs it and in an emergency. If there's a school holiday and we are open, she can bring the kid to work. One employee even brought her dog here after an operation, because she had to have medicine. I took time off for my kids when they were growing up—for plays, and band performances and sports. I worked my schedule around those things and I let—I even help—my employees do the same.

Flexibility, personal intimacy, and convenience of location are factors many employers and employees stress when describing the advantages of working for these small businesses.

We're all from the neighborhood so we have no carfare and no travel time. Even though I earn less than at my last job, my schedule is flexible and I can take time off for personal reasons, for an early doctor's appointment, or whatever. And we are friends. We are friends here and we often see one another even outside of work.

All of us live in the neighborhood. While I can't pay high salaries I do think I give young people more time for home and family. You don't get mugged because you don't have to take the subway. You don't spend four hours a day commuting. You don't have to get dressed up. And some of my employees even go home for lunch—that's very important if you have a kid at home.

But the enthusiasm is not uniform. Some employers and employees discuss rights.

America is the cruelest country where benefits are concerned. I would like to do better by my employees, but to buy private insurance for them is too expensive. Other countries do things better. I was born in Europe and worked there. You have health insurance there wherever you work. And you're not so quick to lose your rights. I worked for a steel company for years in this country and then I lost my job; they laid me off. It was just six months before my pension was vested, and I lost everything. I was unemployed and we had no health insurance; my wife got sick. This would not happen in Europe. In Europe, young people can work as apprentices and learn a job; here they are unemployed and on the street.

There is a striking contrast between what the boss will do for you personally and what you can depend on getting as a matter of right. No paid sick leave or vacations, but in an emergency he'll go out of his way to help. The question is, on balance, How do we end up? I'm not sure.

How Interviewees Describe Some Advantages and Disadvantages in Working for a Small Employer.

Advantages

• Get to know customers personally
• Like a family

- Eat when you want
- Feel free
- Feel at home
- More chance for personal friendships among employees
- This question depends on who you work for
- No dictators
- Better chance of discussing problems
- More flexible
- More access to the boss
- More personal environment
- You know everyone in management
- Nice to be in contact with the boss all the time
- No competition about advancing in the business
- Don't have to drive to work
- Not a lot of higher-up people
- More easy going
- More flexible working hours
- Less pressure
- No one stands over you
- If you start with a young company you can grow professionally
- Good rapport with customers
- Everybody here likes what they're doing
- More like being your own boss

Disadvantages

- No benefits
- If you're not family you may not get anywhere
- Other employees more likely to impose—borrow money and such
- Work harder
- Have to work holidays
- No pensions
- No health insurance
- No benefits for part-timers
- Too personal at times
- Lack of advancement within the business
- Only two of us work here and we can't take our vacation together
- Can't get sick because only three people work here
- May be a problem in advancing to be manager or owner
- Can't get sick/no hospitalization/no sick leave
- Employees leave work and manager has to do it

- Everyone has to know how to do every job
- Hard work/low salary/low benefits
- No disadvantages!

On Balance—The Situation of Employees in Small Firms

It is a story of pluses and minuses, and the various employers and employees do their arithmetic following different systems of calculation. There is a diversity of needs and motives.

For those in companies with more than 25 employees, and for those working in local outlets of national companies, the benefit picture may approximate the national trends for larger firms. But for those in the "under 25 employees" companies, there is a considerable deprivation of benefits. To recall what has gone before, only 43 percent of the enterprises offer their employees health insurance coverage and paid sick leaves, and within most of these companies only full-timers are eligible. To this, only an additional 25 percent add paid vacations and some paid holidays, often less than the national norms. Within the "under 25" group in these two communities, as noted, more than one third of the more generous are in fact small establishments, part of large regional or national chains, and one fourth—half of the Waterside employers in this group—are unionized. Together, these two characteristics (national affiliation and/or unionization) appear to determine whether employees working for very small employers will have a minimum foundation of basic benefit protection.

Some workers choose low-benefit, low-pay jobs only because they have no alternatives. They simply lack either the qualifications or skills to go elsewhere, or there is a shortage of better jobs at a given moment. Others have made a more deliberate, positive choice. They have traded benefits and pay for:

- Flexible time and a convenient place
- A family-like, friendly environment
- The chance to collect income "off the books"

It is the employers in the smallest shops who talk most often of their family-like characteristics, but some of the employees do make the same point. They apparently mean working hours and time-off flexibility, the ability to have friendly support in time of trouble and emergency, and a primary-group atmosphere.

Those who accept fewer benefits and lower salaries to be "off the books" apparently believe that they save tax money. It is also alleged that some may also hide welfare benefits, but we did not encounter such instances. In any case, there was relatively free reporting of off-the-books employment in some interviews. Some of the employees affected do save on taxes, but they and others may sacrifice social security, unemployment insurance, worker's compensation, and mandated state temporary disability coverage in the process. Also improperly deprived are the very large numbers of small-enterprise employees who are not given mandated benefits for reasons ranging from ignorance to tax evasion on the employer's part, even though they themselves would want coverage. In short, the desire to be off the books is sometimes a motive of the employer, sometimes of the employee. It is always illegal, and often misguided with reference to personal interests. But it is feasible in these small enterprises and far more difficult in larger establishments.

What remains is the most widely recognized and expressed motive—and the strongest case for giving up the many advantages of the larger company: the local job is geographically convenient—especially for people with dependent care responsibilities; it is more flexible with regard to personal time off, emergencies, and part-time work; and it allows the fullest integration of home and family life. The main positive case may be summed up with the word "flexibililty."

The owner without employees is sometimes an extreme case: flexibility so great that work supersedes family needs. Workers, on the other hand, often do talk about the flexibility, and their employers and managers often illustrate it in impressive detail. To elaborate: many women, especially those with young children, say that they choose to work for a small employer, if the job is near home, because of the likely flexibility regarding time. Working mothers repeatedly describe time pressures as a major work/family problem, so that a job that permits some flexibility in beginning and ending work times and some flexibility around

personal and family (usually child) problems and crises holds
enormous attraction. These women say they are often willing to
trade off salary and even advancement possibilities for flexibility
in time, understanding, and responsiveness to personal/family
needs. Of some interest, day-to-day flexibility often seems to be
even more important than scheduled time off, although clearly
that is important too.

The biggest problem many of these employees mention—and
the biggest cost when opting for a convenient job with a small
employer—is the absence of health insurance. This deserves emphasis and illustration. Again and again it was stressed by
employees and by employers in talking about what their
employees want and the things they would most like to do for
them:

I couldn't pay for health insurance for my employees, but I would have
formed a group if they wanted me to—if they wanted to pay. Some
wanted to, but some didn't; they said they had husbands who covered
them. So I couldn't form the group; there weren't enough workers interested.

Health insurance is what most employees want, in case they get really
sick. I wish I could give it to them. I wish I had it for myself.

Employers are aware, as well, of a significant benefit-wage
trade-off, something present in companies of all sizes but very apparent in low-wage work:

Either you pay benefits and lower wages or higher wages and no benefits.
Most of my workers want the money, because the benefits are expensive,
and they're not so good anyway, and some can get them some other
way—through husbands or family or whatever. One result is that some
workers are off the books and some are on.

It must not be assumed that those who do not provide benefits
or those who must forgo them are always uninformed or un-
concerned. Any number of employees and employers talked to us
about the importance of social security and how its availability
lessened the urgent need for a pension on the job: on the other
hand, the absence of statutory health insurance made private
health insurance coverage at work essential, unless the employee
were covered by another family member.

A final point: Some of the part-time or full-time young people in these small neighborhood establishments view their jobs as temporary—something to work at while at school or a temporary transition between education and a good job. Thus, they do not complain about benefits, are often quite unaware, focus on salary, and appreciate the paternalistic supports where available. The problem is, however, that the same or similar jobs are often filled by adults with family responsibilities and are, in effect, permanent. The positives can be generous paternalism and valued flexibility. The negative can be serious benefit deprivation.

6. Smaller Is Not Always More Beautiful

More than half the labor force works in establishments employing fewer than 150 employees. One large group works for the small employers discussed in the last chapter. Another, far more sizable, group works for large employers, comparable in size to those discussed in chapters 3 and 4, yet different in that the actual place of work is small, usually one of hundreds of separate, individual worksites, often in very different parts of the country. Consider, for example, chains of retail clothing stores, coffee shops or doughnut house chains, record and cassette outlets, muffler installation sites, proprietary day care chains, tax return preparation services, or multiple-location banks. While such small, decentralized worksites may be subject to uniform or relatively uniform sets of employment policies, inevitably, workers' experiences will vary because the individual establishments are discrete and dispersed.

In such companies, management may have a special image or view of what the company is all about and may try to communicate—and may even succeed in communicating—that message throughout the company. It certainly can control formal policies and benefit plans. Despite this, there are variations: states have different laws, communities have different industries and different labor markets, establishments have different managers, and so it goes. Policies, particularly relating to leave, working hours, and use of specific benefits, may be established nationally and uniformly, but they are implemented locally by many different individuals. Inevitably, discretion comes into play. It would appear, in theory at least, that such discretion could be both advantageous and disdvantageous in offering responsiveness to employees' personal needs. As we shall see, it is both.

In this chapter we look at several different companies in several different services industries. We concentrate on three consumer services: a restaurant chain (The Eatery), a super-market chain (FoodStores), and a bank chain, (NortheastBanks). Certain characteristics emerge with some consistency. First, management stresses the importance of a people orientation for the consumer services. Since so much of the business success depends on employees and their interaction with consumers, ex-ecutives in different companies insist that employees' personal needs and wants should be identified and responded to whenever possible. "A happy employee is a more productive worker" is a repeated theme. A disgruntled employee turns off the consumer and loses business. An unhappy worker is an unproductive worker. At the same time, however, such businesses are labor in-tensive, and their concern with labor costs (and, thus, with per-sonnel policies and fringe benefits) colors and constrains whatever management might want or be willing to do.

Women tend to dominate the work force in these industries, especially in the jobs that bring employees into direct and close contact with consumers. Since these jobs often require few technical skills, women with little training or education can fill them. Women are viewed as being better than men at personal in-teraction, and by tradition they work for less money, too. If they prove particularly good, they may move up into management. Many consumer service firms emphasize promotion from within. But thus far, in most cases, men are still overwhelmingly domin-ant in top management.

Because most of these companies are oriented to consumer ser-vice, they are often caught in a bind between customers and employees. Both are affected by the new life-styles we have iden-tified as having a significant impact on the workplace generally: more women working, especially married women with children, but also single mothers and childless wives. But just as they con-stitute a new and distinctive component of the work force, they also constitute a new and distinctive consumer group. They may not be able to shop during the usual 9 A.M.–5 P.M. Monday to Friday hours, and they may want to purchase market substitutes for items once produced at home or once done without. As a consequence, shops and services adjust to meet the needs of the new consumer; they stay open at nights and on weekends. When this happens, there is then need for people to work odd hours to sell or provide the service, too. And so the process is self-generating and reinforcing. The response to the needs of working couples and single mothers generates a labor market response that creates pressure for some family units and offers solutions for others.

These multiple-establishment consumer services and retail outlets may enjoy both the advantages of the large organizations as regards economies of scale where benefits are concerned and, at the same time, may offer to employees many of the advantages of very small employers: convenient locations near home and work, conditions characterized by intimacy and collegiality with co-workers and with the boss or supervisor. In theory, these could be ideal worksites. The story is, however, more complicated.

Heavily dependent on women for their work force, consciously interested in recruiting and retaining housewives as an important and stable part of their labor force, do these consumer-service companies in fact also respond sensitively to the particular needs of their employees? Are these large companies with their multiple small establishments, in which women constitute such a large proportion of their labor force, developing new policies with regard to the personal and familial needs of their work force? We turn to three companies, in three industries: The Eatery, a national chain of restaurants; FoodStores, a regional chain of supermarkets; and NortheastBanks, a regional consumer bank.

The Eatery

Eating and drinking places are the tenth largest industrial source of female employment, and more than 56 percent of the workforce in the industry is female.[1] Almost 3 million women were employed in eating and drinking establishments in the early 1980s. With average hourly earnings of $4.06 for nonmanagerial employees, they rank last among 52 industries in their pay scale for women.[2]

Many of these are small "mom and pop" coffee shops, diners, and "greasy spoons"; pay is likely to be low in such establishments, tips small, and benefits nonexistent. Some of these places were included in our discussion of small employers in the last chapter.

A more fortunate group of women work for large national companies, in full-service restaurants, with pleasant surroundings. Pay may still be low, but some basic benefits may be provided and the tips — an important part of earnings — are better, often ranging from good to excellent. Moreover, there are opportunities for advancement into management jobs. Women who work in these jobs view themselves as fortunate, and indeed they are, relatively, despite some obvious limitations, as we shall see.

Even among the best employers in this industry, in which the labor force is dominated by women, there is no pretense at developing employment policies that are sensitive to or specifically and deliberately responsive to the special needs of employees with family responsibilities. However, and this is important, there is recognition that women with family responsibilities have needs that mesh with, or are complementary to, the special needs of the industry. Indeed this explains a history of successful recruitment and the ability to get by with relatively low wages and benefits.

The Company. The Eatery is a profitable and still expanding national chain of about 1,000 full-service restaurants located in almost every state in the country. Established a few years after the end of World War II, the company was privately owned until the late 1960s. Its real period of growth, however, was the 1970s — the years in which the restaurant industry generally was transformed as most women entered the labor force, family income rose, and many family meals were transferred from home to restaurant.

The company employs about 40,000 workers, including some 1,000 at corporate headquarters. A typical restaurant employs between 25 and 50 workers. Each restaurant unit has 1 manager and 2 assistant managers; the remaining employees are mostly waitresses. There are a few cooks, other kitchen staff, and waiters. The restaurants are moderately priced and heavily family oriented, but they also serve a local business clientele. They are open 24 hours a day, 7 days a week. The standard work week at a restaurant is 35 to 37½ hours a week for full-time workers. Employees who work at least 28 hours a week qualify for benefits, but most benefit-eligible employees work more than 30 hours. In fact, any employee who averages less than 28 hours weekly for a month is given a warning about possible loss of full-time status and, thus, loss of benefits. After a second month of low hours, loss of benefits is automatic unless the unit manager intercedes and claims special extenuating circumstances. That does not happen often.

There are three shifts a day: 7:00 A.M.–3:00 P.M. (usually referred to as the day shift, and the preferred shift for most employees); 3:00 P.M.–11:00 P.M.; 11:00 P.M.–7:00 A.M. The company is not unionized, neither in is field operations (the restaurants) nor at corporate headquarters. In general, of course, consumer service industries, especially those with many part-timers, heavy turnover, and/or many women workers are not heavily unionized. The work force at The Eatery corporate headquarters, including all the support staff and some women in lower and middle management, is a little more than half female. The work force in the field is more than 60 percent female. Half the restaurant employees are part-time workers, and these have no benefits at all. Turnover is very high in the field, about 200 percent a year. However, about 20 percent of the workers are long-term employees and provide an important stable core in the individual restaurants. Some units have much higher turnover, and some have significantly less, but turnover is relatively high throughout. Each unit manager's goal is to stabilize the restaurant's labor force and expand the core of stable workes. This policy goal dominates personnel and benefit practices.

The company is described as a good and fair employer, among the best in the industry. It promotes heavily from within and is viewed as providing an excellent opportunity for upward mobility for young people with limited education, including women and minorities. Only in recent years has the company begun to pay somewhat more attention to formal education and credentials. Regardless, it still places primary stress on experience, attitude,

and manners. A young man or woman, hired as a waiter or waitress, who comes to work regularly and on time, dresses neatly
and carefully, is conscientious, and has a pleasant manner with
customers, will be promoted to assistant manager within six
months to a year. For some, although the promotion means a step
up the administrative hierarchy, it may also mean an initial loss
in income since the raise may not compensate for loss of tips.
Moreover, it may also carry a personal burden, since assistant
managers work the worst hours—evenings or nights.

Indeed, The Eatery and the supermarket chain have many
operating management assignments that are combinations of line
jobs and management. In the former, they are identified with the
management group, but in the latter the meat, appetizer, produce, and similar department managers are unionized and distinguished from supermarket managers and assistants. The bank
manager and assistants are closer to central office management
and have even higher status. These distinctions are important for
benefits and personnel practices, as we shall see, and affect local
management approaches to employees on the line.

At The Eatery, a waitress job is viewed as being especially attractive to and convenient for working mothers, and management
makes a point of recruiting such women rather than teenagers or
young single workers. Working mothers are considered a far
more reliable work force.

Benefits, Services, and Employment Policies. In top management's
view, The Eatery should be "competitive within the industry as
regards benefits, but not state of the art." The industry includes
all major national restaurant chains, such as Burger King, Mac-
Donald's, Wimpey's, and Denny's.

The company provides all the standard categories of benefits:
hospital, physician, and major medical insurance, as well as optional HMOs; profit sharing; life insurance; paid vacations; paid
holidays; paid sick leave; short-term disability; long-term disability; educational aid; medical leave; and personal leave.

The benefit specifics are of course most important. Many employees consider the health insurance payment schedule to be too
low, especially in states where medical care is costly. Health in-

surance coverage for dependents is included for employees at corporate headquarters and for managers in the field, but not for the hourly workers. Paying for dependent coverage, many restaurant employees told us, presents a big financial burden, especially for single mothers working for low wages. There is no dental insurance for these workers either, a particular concern for many waitresses, who are convinced that a big smile earns more in tips and say that bad teeth constrain their smiles.

The profit-sharing plan is considered to be excellent. It is, however, limited to full-time workers who have been with the company for at least one year and who contribute 3 percent of wages a year to the plan. The company contributes 7 percent to make a total of 10 percent. Since half the work force at the restaurants is part time, they never qualify at all. Many of those who are full time leave before the year is up, or know they are likely to leave before vesting occurs, and so never participate or benefit. Moreover, with such limited income, most cannot afford any deductions from current income; they are living on a hand-to-mouth basis at best.

The sick leave plan is excellent for management, both in the field and at corporate headquarters: 30 days a year at full pay. Nonmanagement employees at corporate headquarters are entitled to only 6 days a year, but they can accumulate unused sick leave up to 60 days. In contrast, hourly workers in the restaurants have no entitlement to any paid sick leave. Short-term disability coverage is available only to those employees working in restaurants located in one of the five states mandating such benefits. Long-term disability insurance, which is voluntary and contributory, is available only to corporate staff and managers in the field. Hourly workers in the restaurants cannot qualify.

Paid holidays are available to corporate staff but not to restaurant employees.

The vacation pattern at corporate headquarters is two weeks after one year, and three after five. Restaurant managers do better; they qualify for a three-week vacation after three years. As usual, hourly workers are the worst off. They get only one week after one year, two weeks after two years, and three after five.

Unpaid medical leaves of up to six months and personal leaves of up to four months, with full job protection (the same or comparable job on return), are available equally to headquarters and field staff.

Although educational aid is technically available to all employees for job-related courses, the work schedules preclude most field staff from qualifying, as does the very strict definition of job-relatedness applied by management.

Finally, managers qualify for benefits within 30 days after beginning work, and nonmanagement staff at headquarters qualify within three months, but nonmanagement restaurant employees, the hourly workers, qualify only after six months. Many hourly workers thus define these first six months as a probationary period. Only when they have remained on the job for six months and qualify for benefits do they think of themselves as really working at The Eatery. Management, on the other hand, views this work force as so unstable that earlier coverage would not warrant the added expense. However, even this stringent qualification period may vary, as when a new restaurant opens, especially in a community with a low unemployment rate and a tight labor market. Under such circumstances the local district manager may request permission from senior management to reduce the qualifying period in order to recruit workers or even to pay for dependents' coverage under health insurance.

Although managers have a demnding work schedule, they are treated well with regard to benefits and paid time off, indeed, better than their peers at headquarters. On the other hand, the full-time hourly workers in the field get the proverbial short end of the stick. To sum up: hourly workers have no paid sick leave and no right to long-term disability insurance—both, as we will see, essential if women employees in these jobs are to have any paid maternity leaves. They have very limited vacation entitlements, less than the national standard. Moreover, they do not qualify for health insurance until they have worked for six months, a major problem for those who have family responsibilities. Needless to say, few find themselves in a position to take advantage of the profit-sharing plan, even if it is a good one. And part-time workers, half the labor force in the field, get no benefits at all.

Despite all this, benefit costs for The Eatery are 35 percent of salaries and wages. They are higher than they are at any other company in the industry. However, this figure must be placed in the context of a low-wage industry in which waitresses' earnings are at the level of the minimum wage. Thirty-five percent of that does not buy a rich benefit package.

Family Responsiveness? Nowhere, either in the statements of the company's philosophy or in discussion with senior management, is there any indication that responsiveness to the personal or family responsibilities of employees is an explicit concern of management. No policies are so described, and clearly, given the limitations on what is available to the part of the company's work force most likely to carry direct family responsibilities, none are implemented. Where there is any indication of awareness of family needs, it is either happenstance—a matter of meeting the requirements of legislation—or an individual, discretionary response by a restaurant manager. The latter can be quite significant.

Families with two low-pay wage earners may, for example, manage medical care needs because both have coverage, even though neither policy is generous. Several married employees talked about the advantages of both husbands' and wives' having health insurance coverage. Instead of viewing it as wasteful, duplicative coverage (as it is often described in medical cost-control discussions), they experienced it as protective; the overlap assured them of: first-dollar coverage and supplementary coverage when the company plan reimbursed them at a level much lower than their actual medical costs.

Ann Grover (a pseudonym), a clerk in the accounting department at headquarters, gave us a picture of how this works. Having just returned to work two months after she gave birth, she was full of details concerning her pregnancy and delivery and of both hospital and physician's costs. In no uncertain terms she told us,

Without my husband's policy we would have been in terrible trouble. For example, when the baby was born, my obstetrician's bill was $950, but the company plan pays only $577. My husband's insurance will pay the difference. My plan covers 80 percent of a semiprivate room up to $150 per day, but the hospital charges $250. Here too, my husband's plan will pay the difference. But my husband has good insurance, so between us we're O.K. I hear some women worrying how they'll manage because their husbands have no insurance, and The Eatery plan just doesn't cover basic costs.

A young, single mother, a waitress, talked about how relieved she was when she finally qualified for health insurance benefits. "Health insurance is by far the most important benefit the company provides," she said.

They should redo their fee scale, but even though the fees are set unrealistically low, it provides basic coverage. I was working at [another restaurant chain] when my baby was born, and I got nothing—no health insurance, no pay, no nothing. My husband wasn't working at the time; all we had was his unemployment benefits. And they wanted to know why I didn't come back when I was ready to go back to work! We're still paying off the bills from that. I was worried sick the first six months here. I tried to buy health insurance myself, but it was too expensive. Do you know how much a private policy costs? Now, at least I know I have some insurance, and since my husband's working now, his benefits cover him and the baby.

Marie S., an attractive, 26-year-old black woman, an assistant manager, married to another Eatery manager, talked about her own experience. She has a 6-year-old daughter from a former marriage and is expecting a baby in three months. She began working at The Eatery four years ago as a waitress, working part time while completing college, with a major in business administration. She took the job because the hours could be adjusted to her college schedule, and the tips meant a good income for a part-time job. She had worked earlier as a teller in a bank but left because the pay was so poor, and she decided she had to finish college if she was to get a better job. She was working at the bank when her first child was born. Her former husband was in a training program at the time and was not earning much either. With no maternity or disability income and with little other income coming into the household, she could not take much time off and was back at work by the time her baby was six weeks old. She is convinced that she returned to work too soon, did not take enough time to develop the right kind of relationship with her daughter, and does not want that to happen again.

After working as a waitress for a year, she was accepted into the company's management training program. She almost had to drop out of college because of the demanding work schedule but somehow managed to complete her degree. She was made an assistant manager soon after.

Marie S. plans to work until the end of her pregnancy and does not expect to take any time off before giving birth. She wants to save whatever time she has for after the child's birth. She would like very much to be able to stay home for six months after this baby is born. As a manager she qualifies for voluntary participation in the company's long-term disability insurance plan. However, although that plan will replace more of her salary and covers her for a longer period of time, it still covers her only for the period she is disabled—perhaps three months, since she will have a caesarean. However, she and her current husband, a manager at another Eatery nearby, have discussed what she will do after childbirth and have agreed that they could manage even if she took another six months off without salary.

I could only take six weeks when my daughter was born and it wasn't enough. We never really have been close and I often wonder how much of that is because I couldn't stay home with her when she was born. Actually, I'm trying to work something out so that I can come back for a while on a part-time basis. There's another woman, an assistant manager at another unit near here, who is due to give birth about the same time I am. We're hoping to convince management to let us share a job—at least for a while.

Several waitresses talked of using vacation time for maternity. For some, this meant having two weeks' paid leave but then having no vacation time for another year. Some talked about the unavailability of long-term disability insurance following complicated pregnancies and deliveries. Others at corporate headquarters who qualified for it and said they would have paid for it complained of inadequate information about its availability, value, and use, and inadequate information about pregnancy-related policies and benefits generally. Some insisted they had not known that they would lose one day of vacation time for each month out on maternity (personal) leave and that they would be excluded from consideration for promotion and pay raises, too.

Child care is perhaps the most important family-related issue these women talk about. This reflects their ages, stages in life, and social backgrounds. It is not a need for which the company has developed any formal response, though the mothers have clearly been inventive and the local managers sometimes cooperative. A middle-level personnel executive, a woman who herself had just recently returned from a three-month maternity leave, described The Eatery management's philosophy concerning child care:

If we do anything about child care for our employees it will be very limited. The company philosophy is to avoid any semblance of paternalism, to stay out of people's personal problems and to avoid any appearance of intervening in individual or family privacy. The company might be concerned if there are work-related consequences such as high absenteeism or repeated lateness. But even then, the concept would be to help employees locate reliable child care—not to pay for it or help pay for it and certainly not to provide it directly. So if we do anything it might be to offer a child care information and referral service.

When asked how the waitresses manage when a child is home from school or sick, a woman restaurant manager responded,

Sometimes, when a child is home from school on holiday, a woman may take a day off, a vacation day. When a child suddenly gets sick at school or gets seriously sick at a family day care home, the woman comes to me and says, "My child is sick and I have to go home." Employees at headquarters can use one or two days of their own sick leave to cope with family illness, but hourly workers in the field cannot. They have no problem if they want to take a day off, however. It's easy to cover for them. But they lose out financially and for most that's a serious problem. Usually, what they do is they change days with someone. That happens often and as long as they let me know it's fine.

Dana, another waitress, described a complicated child care package for her two children aged 2 and 8. She goes to work at 6:30 A.M. and works four days a week. Three of those days her husband does not have to leave until 11:00 A.M., so he gets the children up and dressed and takes the baby to a private preschool program and the 8-year-old child to school. The baby is picked up by a family day care mother when she picks up her own child at the school. The 8-year-old boy goes home with a friend for one hour until Dana can pick him up. On the day her husband has to leave early too, she brings the children to her sister's house, and then her sister takes them to school with her own children. During the summer, she has a teenager three days a week to take care of the children, and part of the summer they visit her parents.

Tracy, who has worked as a waitress at The Eatery for six years, works full time, 40 hours a week, 5 days a week, Wednesday through Sunday, from 6 A.M. to 2 P.M. Although she has enough seniority to not work on weekends, she continues to do so by choice because the weekends are good for tips. In addition, she moonlights in a coffee shop three days a week from 3:00 P.M. to 9:30 P.M. She has been married for six years. Her husband works at The Eatery as a cook. They have a two-year-old son. She worked while pregnant until the middle of her ninth month and returned to work when her son was 6 weeks old. She was out for 8 weeks and received state temporary disability insurance during that time. For the first month after she returned to work, her mother took care of the baby. After that, a younger brother who was living at home shared the care with her mother. When the baby was 6 months old, she placed him with a licensed family day care mother who cares for 6 children aged 2 weeks to 6 years.

She is quite happy with the child care arrangement, which she has now used for one and a half years. She drives to work and drops her son off at this woman's home at 5:30 in the morning and picks him up between 3:00 and 4:00 in the afternoon. On the days she moonlights, she takes him to a sister-in-law's home, where he has dinner and stays until her husband picks him up. She pays $70 a week to the family day care mother and $25 a week to her sister-in-law for the supplementary care. If the boy were to get sick during the day, the day care mother has a "nurse" on duty and a separate room where an ill child can rest quietly and be cared for. He has not been ill except once, briefly, with a cold. Her son is very happy, loves the woman who cares for him, and likes being with the other children. Although entitled to three weeks of vacation, she rarely uses the full amount and takes off occasional days instead. She has never been out ill. She is very concerned about not losing any income.

A woman restaurant manager mentioned that she had four waitresses out on maternity leave, sequentially:

One worked until she was 7½ months pregnant and returned when her baby was 3 months old. The second worked until she was 5 months pregnant and did not return. The third worked until she was 8 months pregnant, returned on a part-time, 2-day-week basis when her baby was 2 months old and full time when the baby was 6 months old. The fourth worked until her 8th month and returned full time when her child was 2 months old.

It was something of a problem for the manager, because all worked the same shift, and all were very good workers. When asked how she managed, her response was:

One can always hire temporaries. Some part-timers are always ready to work extra hours. And then there is always turnover. The problem is not bodies but rather the quality of the body. It was tough, though. In fact, when I came here to open this unit last year, I told my new hires, "Whatever you do, don't get pregnant this year! I need a year off." I was kidding, but then I found that some took me seriously. A woman got pregnant and was afraid to tell me. The reality is she's a good worker, and I'll always have a job for a good worker.

Although some managers, in some locations, stated that waitresses are entitled to a six-month unpaid medical leave at the time of childbirth, others said that apart from a temporary disability leave, usually up to four weeks before childbirth and six weeks after, waitresses, like all other employees, could take up to four months of personal leave. Regardless, such women could have close to six months' leave after childbirth, but few took that much time off, and by far most return to their job after childbirth within that time.

Few of the waitresses who have children ever call in saying that they are sick—or that a child is sick—and that they have to take a day off. A manager said,

Even when a kid is sick these women come in. They are more reliable than the young, single kids who work here. Many have relatives who care for the children regularly, sick or well, and others have relatives who can help out in an emergency. Or if they have a regular sitter [or some kind of family day care arrangement], she can take care of a sick child, unless it's really serious. Then the woman takes off.

In his experience very few women take time off if they can help it, because losing tips income is a serious financial problem, and they cannot afford it. This is what creates the pressure to work no matter what, not any company policy.

Work schedules are another important aspect of employment policies for employees with family responsibilities. Several waitresses described waitressing as "a good job for a single mother," because of the flexibility of work schedules.

"You can usually work your hours out so that you work mornings and early afternoons, and some women like to work evenings so their husbands are home with the kids," we were told. In many restaurants, the waitresses work a 10-hour day, four days a week. The managers say this is a much better arrangement, because the women come back refreshed after three days home, and it is easier to fill in if one is out sick. Many waitresses prefer it, too, especially those with children. They say it is easy to work out the longer child care arrangements, and it leaves them with an extra day at home.

The situation is very different for managers, however. A restaurant manager said that her regular schedule is 7:00 A.M. to 5:00 P.M., but she often comes back in the evenings to make sure there are no problems. Moreover, when business is hectic—on weekends and holidays—she may come back and help out for a couple of hours. She herself is single and commented that she does not know how someone with a family manages "unless they are married to another Eatery manager!"

To sum up: when one discusses the work and family connection with them, most of the waitresses describe the need for medical coverage, child care help, and maternity leaves. This company has modest medical benefits for the full-timers, fairly typical (which means very limited) maternity benefits, and nothing in child care. But they stay on for the good pay and work-schedule flexibility. And local-manager responsiveness on an ad hoc and individual basis is often what makes it all work.

Management's Views. A senior human resource executive said that most restaurant employees think that The Eatery's benefits are very good. The company is very competitive and uses other major national chains as a standard against which to compare what they do. "All national restaurant chains' benefits are very similar," he said.

The major differences have to do with the waiting time following initial hire before qualifying for benefits. The usual pattern at The Eatery is that new employees must wait six months before qualifying, unless a new restaurant is opening up in an area with a tight labor market. When that happens, recruitment incentives may be established, such as reducing the qualifying period, providing dependents' coverage under health insurance, or improving life insurance coverage. Such modifications are not made casually; they are very expensive. You have to understand, the restaurant industry is not generous where benefits are concerned, and we here are not cutting edge in the industry. This is a labor-intensive industry, and top management is constantly watching labor costs. A big part of labor costs are benefits costs.

Where hourly workers are concerned, their primary interest is in wages. Many of our employees are very young—18 to 24—and they are very transient. They don't expect to stay long. They just want their money. These jobs are not career jobs, yet, for not very well educated young people they can do well, but many don't realize it. The tips are good, however, for those who work hard, and that is what they depend on. But most stay only briefly. The turnover is very high, and even a good unit may experience a turnover of 150 percent while a bad unit may have two or three times that! Some units are very stable, but they are unusual. Limiting turnover is a constant goal for unit managers.

Part-timers don't qualify for benefits; and half our field workforce is part-time. Moreover, since it takes six months to qualify for benefits and turnover is so high, only a minority of workers are covered by benefits at any one time. Basically, it's the stable core at each unit who qualify. Women—working mothers—are a big proportion of that group. They depend on tip income and often do not even want to take vacations for fear of losing income.

Benefits make a difference to employees with family responsibilities, but the difference is only a modest one, and most of our employees are not affected. If asked to rank their benefits, health insurance is the top priority, and hourly workers wish we'd pay for dependents' coverage. Sick leave is important to employees at headquarters, but the absence of sick leave doesn't seem to bother the hourly workers. Their wages are low. It's losing their tip income that matters, and a paid sick leave wouldn't replace this. Dental care would be an important addition, and some would like more vacation.

A somewhat different situation exists for restaurant managers and assistant managers. These are "working" managers who may be found in the kitchen, at the cash register, seating customers, paying bills, or working on the schedule at a given moment. Given the fact that the restaurants are open 24 hours a day and 7 days a week, all year long, the job is a difficult one for managers, especially if they have families. Managers work the day shift while assistant managers work nights, and all work weekends. Managers can't limit themselves to a 40-hour week. In fact, the standard work week for them is 50 hours, and most work 55 to 60 hours a week, even if they stick to a 5-day week. These long days, plus the night, weekend, and holiday hours, often place a strain on family lives and on personal and familial relationships. These jobs, managers say, do offer opportunities for career advancement, but they are demanding. Most are filled by relatively young adults. Assistant managers tend to be in their early twenties and managers in their early thirties, prime years for marriage and child responsibilities. One third are women, and the jobs are particularly difficult for women with family responsibilities, for obvious reasons.

Although the turnover rate among unit managers and assistant managers is nowhere near what it is among hourly workers, it is still far higher than what corporate management would like. "At 42 percent, it is better than average in the industry but not as good as it should be," we were told. According to a senior human resource executive, the major reasons for continuing high turnover among unit managers are:

The hours worked. In addition to long hours they often have to fill in during peak times or when employees do not show up.

The work schedule. Assistant managers have to work nights, and all must work holidays. This is very difficult for young adults, especially those with families.

Money. Although the pay is good for what it is, if they have to work many 55- to 60-hour weeks, it doesn't look quite as good.

Supervision. The relationship between the assistant manager and the manager or betweeen the manager and the district manager is very important. When the relationship is good, all is fine, but when it is bad, it is enough to overwhelm everything else.

With all this, benefits and other employment policies make very little difference. "Unit managers actually have the best benefits of all our employees, but it means little to them," according to the senior human resource executive.

In effect, managers have good pay and good benefits but such a demanding work schedule that it is bound to impinge on any family life. "Just getting Christmas and Thanksgiving off would make a tremendous difference," one said. In contrast, the hourly workers' schedules may be more convenient, and the tips are good, but the benefits are poor, and if they get sick they can have a financial crisis.

A district manager talked about some of the reasons for high turnover at all levels in the field.

There are big differences in how employees are treated and what they receive, and sometimes that creates a problem. There is a distinction between managers and hourly workers, and there's a distinction between full-time and part-time workers. Managers have longer vacations; they qualify for health insurance in one month instead of six; if they get sick they don't lose any income and they can get long-term disability. And part-time workers get no benefits at all. The work is hard. It's the good manager that can make the employees feel as if they are part of a team. But it's not easy. And where the waitresses are concerned, often they come with unreal expectations of tips and quit when they discover they can't earn the kind of money they thought they could. Or they have too many problems at home, so they quit.

Employees' Views of the Company as Employer. Most waitresses think The Eatery is a good place to work. Compared with many other waitressing jobs, "you get health insurance"—the benefit that is most important to them. Most do not count their paid vacation time as important because their pay—minimum wage for the hours worked—does not cover the tips they lose, and tips are the main part of their income. They seem to regard child care as a private concern and maternity as something with which one gets limited help. One real concern often expressed here is the lack of dependents' benefits under health insurance. For hourly workers to pay this themselves is difficult. Very few do so, and most define this as the most important additional benefit they would like to have. Single mothers are the workers most likely to pay for the coverage themselves. Married women often say their husband's benefits cover their children, and perhaps that is so.

Some waitresses recognize that there are good opportunities for advancement, but most see it just as a stable job for a woman with no skills and little education. And most enjoy the collegiality. The part-timers complain about the lack of benefit coverage, but the turnover is so high that most who begin as part-time workers can become full time if and when they want to. Other hourly workers, such as kitchen help, cooks, and so forth, get much better base pay.

Income insecurity and variations in income are a common concern. There are slow times, even on the day shift, and there are slow periods during the year. When business is slow the manager may suggest that some employees may want to go home. Since their income is so dependent on tips, when business is slow, most would just as soon leave. If this happens often, their hours will fall below the 28 hours a week monthly average they need to retain their benefits. Managers say this rarely happens to the "good" workers, and exceptions can be made for unusual circumstances, but the waitresses worry, nevertheless.

A waitress told how she had worked at this restaurant for a different chain, for nine years. Then that company was taken over by The Eatery and she lost all her benefits and all her seniority. She had health insurance, dependents' coverage, paid sick leave, three weeks' vacation, a paid pension plan, and a credit union, and all this was lost when the company was taken over by The Eatery. "I was within a year of having a vested pension and it's all gone now," she said regretfully. "It will be six months before I get benefits here, and to get them for my children, I will have to pay. It will be a year before I get even one week vacation and before I can join the profit sharing plan, if I can manage the money." Although regretful, she was remarkably stoic in her acceptance of the fact that she had worked for nine years for one employer—most unusual in this industry known for its high turnover—had built up all sorts of entitlements, and had lost them all. In interviews in many states one discovers, with shock, how little people in the low-pay part of the labor force are protected and how little many expect. She was grateful, in fact, for a sensitive and sympathetic manager who let her have the work schedule she needed to manage child care.

"When a new restaurant is opened," a waitress told us, "the policy is to hire two or three times as many staff as needed on the assumption that there will be a shakeout and the best workers will remain. It may make sense to management, but to employees it is terrible. Most view the six months as a probationary period and never really think of themselves as permanent until after six months." A manager insisted that although the policy seems harsh, it works out fairly for the "good worker": "Even if it happens that after the shakedown period there are more good workers than needed, there are always nearby units with open-ings, and a good worker who wants to remain at the unit she started with would be given priority for a transfer as soon as an opening occurred."

On Balance. The Eatery has some of the flexible elements of the small neighborhood business and some of the benefit advantages of the national company. But it reminds one as well of the limita-tions of low-wage work and of the service occupations whose ebb and flow of business over any 24-hour period makes employment of part-timers economically desirable. The latter need of business may coincide exactly with the employment objectives of some workers, especially of parents of young children. But it may leave others without adequate income or essential benefits.

As we have seen, unlike the small, unaffiliated neighborhood shops and services, The Eatery is able to offer full-time employees a core of basic benefits. But the core is very modest compared with most medium and big companies, and the gaps be-tween managers, albeit local working managers, and line staff (especially waitresses) is very considerable. As much can be said about the headquarters/restaurant gap and the full-time/part-time discrepancy.

Part of the reason for this is the nature of the work force. Many young workers, especially the young singles, come and go in these jobs as transitory employees. They do not ask about benefits and do not complain. Circumstances are very different for the con-tinuing core, especially the single and married waitresses and their young children and the cooks. Often only success in achiev-ing upgrading to assistant manager or manager provides a viable benefit package.

Job security and better pay are the bottom line, before atten-tion can be paid to benefits; indeed, job security is a necessary if not sufficient condition for keeping decent benefits. And because these are small locations where people can be known, managerial discretion with regard to schedules, leaves, and rehiring after long unpaid leaves are often enough to hold people who may be willing to trade these advantages against others. The flexibility is a major plus for the hourly workers, but the long and irregular hours often present a problem for managers in their own personal lives.

Hierarchical tensions may also become a problem, when there are significant differences between corporate headquarters staff and field staff, between management and nonmanagement, and between full- and part-time workers.

Explicit family responsiveness is never considered an issue here as it seldom is anywhere. Management notes the demographic changes in the labor force, but all that this means is that there are more women available for waitress jobs. In addition, because of legislative and social change, there are more women managers. But these are very demanding jobs for people with family responsibilities. In effect, as indicated earlier, the very aspect of social change affecting the labor force is also affecting the market—24-hour-a-day, 7-day-a-week restaurants—in response to the changes in the family and the household. Workers get caught between their own family needs and the family needs of others. There is both a new work force and a new consumer group made up of workers who need market services to substitute for or supplement their own household services. The Eatery caters to both.

FoodStores

Food stores are 15th among 52 industries in the proportion that women constitute of their labor force. Women are almost half the labor force in this industry as a whole but well over half in the retail food establishments.

More than 1 million women work in local retail food stores, earning on average $7.25 an hour. Average wages rank well above those in eating and drinking places (which have the lowest ranking of all), yet still are 35th among the 52 industries listed.

The Company. FoodStores is a large regional supermarket chain with 3,000 employees of its own working for a nonprofit cooperative organization that handles purchasing and distribution for the chain and for supermarkets with about 30,000 employees. Established in the early 1950s, the company expanded substantially during the 1960s and early 1970s. Here, too, we see the same combination of a large organization with small establishments that we saw at The Eatery, although these stores are larger establishments than the restaurants. An average supermarket has about 150 employees, with 1 manager and 3 assistant managers; about half of these are part-time employees.

Headquarters staff are not unionized, but the stores are about 90 percent unionized except for the managers and assistant managers but including department managers (produce, meat, appetizers, etc.). Twenty-three unions are involved, most locals of the United Food and Commercial Workers. The work force at corporate headquarters is about half exempt employees, almost all full time, and about 50 percent female. About 10 percent of the headquarters work force is management, largely male.

The work force at the stores is about 80 percent female, but the (unionized) department managers and overall assistant managers and managers, are almost completely male. The work force is also heavily part time; about one third of the stores have more than half their work force part time. Moreover, the proportion of employees who are part-timers is increasing. In contrast to The Eatery, part-timers at FoodStores are entitled to benefits. But the pay rate for part-timers is lower than for full-timers, and the benefits provided are not the equivalent of those received by full-timers.

Management prefers part-time workers because (as in The Eatery) they can be used more flexibly, to respond to the demands of consumer buying patterns, and they are cheaper. At the same time, both married and single mothers and college students find these part-time jobs convenient. The work can be fitted around their own personal needs and schedules. No complex skills are needed; the jobs are located near their homes; they can adjust their work schedules to fit child care requirements; and they can take care of personal and family emergencies when these arise. Most women work the 9:00 A.M. to 3:00 P.M. shift. Youths work the 3:00 P.M. to 11:00 P.M. shift, and adult men, the 11:00 P.M. to 9:00 A.M. shift, in stores that are open 24 hours. Part-timers work an average of 16 hours a week but can range up to 30 hours. If an employee works 40 hours a week for 7 weeks, she becomes a full-time worker, so managers monitor employees' hours carefully to be sure that this does not happen except by design.

Benefits polices have been influenced largely by the pressures from the unions. Union contracts set the standard for unionized employees and, indirectly, for the nonunionized, too. Management monitors these developments closely and tries to anticipate developments when setting policies for nonunion and management personnel. The union contracts are fairly uniform across different locals, but policies may be implemented differently, depending on the local, the union representative, and the store manager.

Industry competitiveness, management style, and the corporate culture play an important role in shaping benefits policies, too. Management is paternalist, in the best sense of the term. The company is described as "competitive with regard to salary and wages, but leading edge with regard to benefits."

"People shouldn't be distracted from doing good work because of personal problems and concerns," a human resource executive said. "The company should do all it can in the way of employment policies to make this a good place to work. That's management's philosophy."

Despite this obviously sincere point of view, here, too, there is no explicit discussion about family responsiveness or about labor market changes affecting employment policies. Women are the major source of employees for the stores, but the vast majority are in low-level jobs, mainly part time. Very few are in management, either in the stores or at corporate headquarters. Social changes have affected how supermarkets operate (7 days a week, 16-24 hours a day) and what they stock (more take-out meals and prepared dinners) but not specifically or explicitly how they are managed or what types of employee policies are put in place.

Benefits, Services, and Work Schedules. FoodStores' benefits are excellent, comparatively, both for management and nonmanagement staff, for unionized and nonunionized employees, and for full-time and part-time hourly workers. The availability of benefits for part-timers merits exploration. In a labor-intensive industry with low mark-ups, profits depend on efficient use of personnel. It is important not to be overstaffed at any given moment but to have enough cashiers at the checkout counters and clerks to restock the shelves in those hours when supermarkets are jammed. Part-timers are the answer, and this explains the heavy use of housewives and students on certain shifts. In many spots, the part-timers are the majority of the work force. Unions could not forgo organizing this work force if they wanted to be effective in the industry. Nor could they ignore the issue of benefits for part-timers.

FoodStores is a source of evidence that part-timers need not be without any fringe benefits at all. On the other hand, as we shall see, it is the interests of the full-timers that dominate the bargaining picture. Those part-timers who consider themselves as permanent employees and who work close to a full-time schedule (and would prefer enough hours to be full time) find this inadequate and unfair. The after-school students who come and go are frequently not terribly concerned. That is why the part-timers cannot create the critical mass to have greater impact on union bargaining decisions.

The benefit package includes:

- Health insurance (hospital, physician, major medical, prescriptions, health maintenance organizations), including dependents' benefits. Part-timers have similar benefits except for 80 percent rather than 100 percent coverage of medical costs, no dependents' benefits, and no prescription coverage. (Employees qualify for benefits after three months' employment.)
- Dental insurance
- Vision care
- Group life insurance
- Pensions
- Vacations: two weeks after one year, three after five. (Employees qualify for vacation after one year but can draw on their entitlement in advance after six months. Part-timers get a prorated vacation.)
- 12 paid holidays (prorated for part-timers)
- 3 paid personal days (prorated for part-timers)
- 10 paid sick days (prorated for part-timers). These can be cashed out, if not used. In addition, an extra vacation day or day's

pay is provided for each quarter in which no sick time is used. (If an employee loses no time for one year and comes to work promptly, he or she earns the equivalent of an additional week of vacation, one day for each quarter and a bonus day for the whole year.)

- Legal services (for union members only)
- Long-term disability insurance (contributory and voluntary, for exempt employees only)
- Educational aid (tuition reimbursement up to $1,500)

Finally, if a full-time employee dies, the family remains covered by health insurance and related benefits for one year.

An annual personalized statement of benefits entitlements and their monetary value is provided in a computer printout for non-union employees, underscoring the value of the benefits provided by management. The unionized workers view their benefits as from the union, and some services are directly delivered through union contracts under the negotiated plans. The union provides explanatory booklets and copies of the contract.

Here, too, our interviews disclose that new, young employees are usually not interested in benefits and ask no questions about them. Awareness of benefits is negligible until employees have a family. For the most part, female employees seem much more aware of benefits than men. Medical care, dental care, and vision care are all especially important to single mothers. In contrast, the young, single workers value education aid more, while all value vacations and other types of paid time off.

A department manager in a store commented that "the bottom line is the money. But some people care only about the money while others care about the benefits, too—the married people especially, not the young singles." Another manager said that "Maybe 10 percent of new hires ask anything about benefits. The remainder either take them for granted, expecting that they will have good standard benefits, or they don't care. The only time questions come up is when there is a problem—someone gets sick and goes into the hospital."

Management is now exploring several possible additional benefits, including retirement counseling, wellness programs, cafeteria (flexible) benefits or flexible spending plans (see chapter 7), adoption benefits (see chapter 7), and merit scholarships for employees' dependents.

The costs for this current benefit package equal 34 percent of salaries and wages, about 35 percent for the unionized employees and management and about 30 percent for the others.

Family Responsiveness? The richness of the standard benefit package is appreciated by the many working mothers employed by FoodStores. Even when there are two earners in a family with medical coverage on their jobs, the duplicative benefit coverage assures part-timers that they will have first-dollar coverage. The fee schedules here are set far more generously than at The Eatery, and employees do not complain that their insurance has left them with large bills to pay. On the contrary, a repeated theme is the report of astonishment and relief on realizing that all the costs of a medical emergency would be covered. Perhaps the only complaints concerning health insurance are the lack of dependents' benefits for the part-timers and the absence of well-baby coverage for full-time workers.

One young mother of three said: "All regular checkups for children, from the time they are born, must be paid for personally, and that is a big and growing expense for those of us with kids." Here we have a most dramatic illustration of the fact that workplace fringe benefits have not explicitly sought family responsiveness. The well-baby routine checkup is a standard family concern and a routine expense, yet it does not typically appear in fringe benefit plans. In our interviews with mothers in low-pay jobs—people too well off to qualify for Medicaid and other health programs available to those in poverty but nonetheless just managing money from paycheck to paycheck—the possibility of a benefit that might meet the cost of health checkups for children was frequently included near the top of the wish list.

FoodStores headquarters are located in one of the five states that mandate temporary disability insurance. As a consequence, pregnant women employees are permitted to go on disability leave approximately four weeks before they are due to give birth, unless their physician certifies a medical reason for an earlier or later leave. The standard disability leave after childbirth is six weeks, allowing them 10 weeks in all. During that time they collect a maximum of $184 from the state (in 1985), and FoodStores supplements this up to 75 percent of their wage. FoodStores permits employees to take up to one month of unpaid personal leave after the end of their disability leave, substantially less than is permitted by The Eatery, however. Although it is an unpaid leave, all benefits are continued for that month. Most women return to work at the end of their disability leave and certainly within two months after delivery. Wage loss and benefit loss are strong disincentives against remaining out longer. In the states without TDI, the union agreement requires short-term disability coverage.

Flexibility of scheduling in this type of workplace is an important advantage for many women employees. They say again and again that the jobs at checkout counters or in various other capacities enable them to cope with child and family responsibilities while still earning income. And to many, their hourly wages while in a flexible workplace seem remarkable. Often more than $9.00 an hour for women with no skills and little education, it is far more than many ever thought they would earn, and they can manage it within family routines!

By contrast, managerial personnel at several levels find the work hours demanding and hard on family and personal lives. One is reminded of the restaurant managers and assistant managers of The Eatery. Even though managers work only a five-day week, the responsibility and possible problems cover the whole time the store is open, often the whole week, and the daily hours are long. All work at least one weekend day and many holidays. Assistant managers often have to work evenings and sometimes nights. Long and irregular hours conflict inevitably with family life. Nonetheless, none of those interviewed seemed to think the demands unusual, unreasonable, or not worth the personal price.

How do staff, full time and part time, arrange their personal responsibilities in such a setting? A cashier described her situation as fairly typical. She is 33, has been married for 12 years, works 24 hours a week between 9 A.M. and 3 P.M., any days of the week, but on an irregular, changing schedule. She has three children aged 10, 8, and 6 and worked up until her 7th or 8th month in each pregnancy, returning each time when the child was 2 months old. For child care, she has her mother who lives one block from her and does not work. Until they entered primary school, she brought her children to her mother's each morning and they would stay there for the day. Now, she takes the children directly to school and picks them up when school ends. If a child is sick, her mother comes to her house to care for the child, and on school holidays she brings them to her mother for the day.

A male grocery clerk, married to a nurse, described how they manage caring for their three-year-old daughter. He works days and his wife works evenings. They do not believe in using sitters, he explained. The child is now in a part-day preschool. When she is ready for a full-day program, his wife will change her schedule and work the day shift, which ends at 3:00 P.M. He will then take his daughter to school in the morning.

A woman computer information specialist had an 18-month-old son when she first came to the company, four years ago, following a divorce. Her child care arrangements were "one sitter a year," by which she meant that she used family day care, generally changing each year because, as she put it, "most women only do such work temporarily, rarely for more than one year. They stop either because they have a new baby themselves, or decide to get a 'real' job." Now that her daughter is five she is in kindergarten, but the mother has had to make afternoon and holiday care arrangements with still another family day care mother.

Several women also talked of problems concerning the care of older parents:

My mother had a stroke last year. We took her in to live with us because it was clear she wouldn't recover fully. She can only walk with the help of a walker. I don't like to leave her alone for a whole day because I worry about her. During the week a neighbor helps out on a voluntary basis, checking mother several times a day. Weekends are a problem, however. If I have to work weekends I have to hire someone to stay with mother. Just to have someone reliable come to the house, not even to do much for her, costs me $35.00 a day.

Management's View of Its Wages and Benefits. In discussing the relationship between benefits and wages in the overall compensation package, a senior executive said there is no theory or rationale for the balance between wages and benefits.

Historically, benefits began in response to what unions negotiated. Then, we certainly had to do as well for management personnel. Ultimately, what the union managed to negotiate became the standard for employees generally, because for reasons of equity, if not self-protection, management had to do as well for its nonunion as for its unionized workers.

Management's philosophy is that the company should be competitive within the industry regarding salaries and wages generally but at the forefront of the industry where benefits are concerned. Although the stress these days is on maintaining wages, benefits developments are monitored so that the company does not fall behind. The results of a recent food industry survey of the 20 leading national supermarket chains confirmed FoodStores' leading benefit position. On a benefit-by-benefit basis, Food-Stores had either the best coverage or was among the best. Its overall package is clearly among the best in the industry.

New benefit initiatives come from top management or from union negotiations. Senior human resource staff continually monitor developments throughout the industry, by reviewing the results of special surveys, participating in professional meetings, talking to their peers in other companies, or getting advice from benefit consultants. When contracts are up for renegotiation, union representatives will often suggest a new benefit. If it is accepted it is soon extended to nonunion employees.

In general, as a senior executive suggested,

Employers are more willing to increase their benefit package than to raise wages and salaries. It's cheaper to do this. If they provide salary increases they are also increasing their total wage package because of overtime costs. When only the benefits package is increased, the total compensation costs do not increase as much. In addition, the unions prefer an emphasis on benefits because they have a more visible and richer package to use to demonstrate their achievements to their members. Even during a recession it is likely that the company will improve the benefit package, but not by very much.

Another trade-off between benefits and salary has been in relation to part-time employees. Part-timers have benefits because of union pressures, but the reality is that part-timers would be paid higher salaries if they didn't get benefits. On balance, the unions stress benefits as a way of demonstrating to part-time employees the union's accomplishments and therefore keeping the whole work force organized. On the other hand, for store owners, part-time workers are, increasingly, a preferred work force. The availability of these part-time jobs with convenient hours is good for the women who take the jobs and good for employers who want a flexible and, therefore, less expensive work force.

Employee's Views of Benefits and Conditions. In an internal company survey carried out recently, most employees praised the company's benefits. However, one respondent, expressing views held by several others, said: "Benefits are extremely beneficial to older employees with families. However, to young, single employees they are virtually useless. Even a partial cash reimbursement would be more advantageous than $4000 worth of benefits to a young employee. It could also save the company money." (This is, of course, the concept underlying flexible benefits, as we saw in chapter 4.)

Part-time store employees, the majority of the work force in many stores and likely to be even more so in the future, bring another perspective to bear. Most important, many of them want to work full time but cannot get a full-time job with FoodStores. A manager acknowledged that the problem was a real one and serious for single mothers, in particular:

The company limits the numbers of full-time workers because they are very expensive. Many women come on as part-timers through they want a full-time job. They put their names on the list, but it can be years before a full-time job opens up. It is especially hard for single mothers. They are often in desperate need of the better pay and also feel the absence of the additional benefits. Although 65 to 70 percent of the work force are part-timers, they get less than 25 percent of what the full-timers get in benefits. Most work over 25 hours a week but are not organized enough to have the union give their needs higher priority.

Part-timers are a growing proportion of the labor force at Food-Stores as in the industry generally. Management wants it this way because it is a cheaper and more flexible way to respond to the variations in consumer shopping patterns. The union has addressed the problems of part-timers to the extent that contracts cover them, but obviously not to the same extent as full-time workers. And the unions pay no attention to the problems of access to full-time jobs. Some women prefer to work part time, even if it means sacrificing something in pay and benefits to do so. But most women part-timers want to work full time or at least know that a full-time job is available when they are ready to take one. And that is not the case now.

The part-time problem is a problem largely for women with children and families. The young, single part-timers, both males and females, are largely satisfied with their jobs. They might want higher wages, but neither benefits nor full-time jobs are an immediate concern.

One reason the problems of part-timers may not be getting more serious attention is that women as such are not discussed much. They are not very visible at the level of policymaking: not in the union, nor in FoodStores, nor in the supermarket industry generally. The growth of numbers of women in the labor force may have had an impact on consumer buying patterns but not much on corporate management. There has been a large increase in the numbers of women among hourly workers and a small increase in lower management, but no significant growth in the numbers of women in middle management and certainly none in upper management. One reason is that no women were in management at all until after the legislative developments in the early 1970s placed pressure on companies to hire women. However, the real period of supermarket growth was the 1960s and early 1970s. Since the mid-1970s there has been little growth in the industry, and this is when affirmative action policies first took hold. As a consequence, women entering lower management positions have not had the opportunity to move up the management ladder. Moreover, in the last five years the pattern has been to decrease the number of stores and therefore to have fewer store managers. Thus, the likelihood of women becoming store managers is even less than it was. These trends, coupled with the trend toward part-time rather than full-time hourly workers, are likely to constrain women's opportunities to move into management. Thus, the needs of women workers as a large group of employees carrying heavy family responsibilities are not very visible to management and certainly not something for which management thinks it has any responsibility.

With neither the union nor management paying specific attention to the issue of employees' family responsibilities, it is unlikely to get attention in the near future. Benefits will be protected and may be improved because that is management's philosophy generally, and good benefits are important to families. But it is unlikely that any particular, new responses to labor force demographic changes will emerge, in part because the only change that has occurred in the labor market in this industry has left women as "second-class workers," better off in this company than they are in most of the industry but locked largely into part-time hourly employment. For some women this is sufficient; for others it is not.

The overview of FoodStores enables us to introduce yet another question, to be addressed below: What is part-time? Here, by union contract, full-time hourly wage rates and benefits come into play above 30 hours weekly. If a part-timer should work 40 hours for 7 weeks, she or he has earned full-time status automatically. This means that, depending on the supermarket's particular needs, a person may be working 35 or 40 hours for much of the time, with somebody monitoring it to avoid the full-time commitment. In effect, then, here is unwilling part-time work, contrived with a view to pay rates and benefit costs. It is not uncommon. It is quite different from the high school student hired to work 16 hours weekly at a checkout counter and who can manage no more. The 16 hours may be more typical at FoodStores than the 30 or the 40, but the latter is not uncommon and suggests an issue requiring some exploration if benefits are deemed significant and become to a degree a price paid by the employee to earn the flexibility advantages of a part-timer.

NortheastBanks

Banking ranks third among 52 industries in the proportion of women in its work force. Seventy percent of the labor force in the banking industry are women, earning on average $5.80 an hour, and ranking 46th in wage levels among the 52 industries listed. In commercial, full-service banks like NortheastBanks, the proportion of women in the work force is likely to be even higher than the industry average.

The Company. NortheastBanks is a regional full-service bank, with about 200 branches, all relatively small establishments, with an average of fewer than 25 employees at each branch. It is heavily oriented to consumer service. Its work force is 70 percent female, although management is heavily male. Forty percent of the work force is very young (under 25) and largely single. Like the industry generally, it is not unionized. Turnover is high, close to 100 percent throughout the bank, but it varies substantially by branch; the average employee has been with the bank for less than four years. Pay is very low, even lower than in local large retail establishments, but not as low as in the eating and drinking places industry. Although the benefits are considered very good, they are openly acknowledged by many as not compensating for inadequate pay.

There is no identifiable corporate culture except for a strong desire to maintain good service to consumers and to remain competitive in the industry. There is growing concern about the high turnover in the branches and the impact this has on providing good-quality consumer service. The major turnover problem is in the large urban areas; it is lower in suburban branches.

In an effort at reducing turnover, stabilizing the work force, and improving consumer service, management has introduced a special "Worklife" program with extremely flexible work schedules for part-time work. Benefit coverage for part-time work is provided, too. The Worklife program was designed to be attractive to women with family responsibilities. It has had a limited success.

NortheastBanks' innovative program is an illustration of the limits to trading off time and money. Flexibility is valued by employees and is important, but income, like job security, is still an essential foundation.

Benefits, Services, and Work Schedules. The benefits at NortheastBanks are generally described as good and standard; they have been relatively fixed for 15 years. They include:

- *Health insurance* (hospital, physician, major medical, and health maintenance organizations). Dependent benefits are contributory and optional. Half the work force chooses HMOs. Most workers choose individual coverage, saying that they are part of a two-earner family and therefore do not need family coverage; or they are young and have no dependents.
- *Pensions* (including stock purchase and profit sharing for management)
- *Group life insurance*
- 12 days' *paid sick leave*
- *Short-term disability insurance* (8 weeks for maternity at 60 percent of salary, after sick leave is used up)
- 10 *paid holidays*
- 1 *paid personal day*
- 2 weeks' *vacation (3 weeks after 5 years and 4 after 20 years)*
- *Travel insurance*
- *Tuition remission* (but only for courses closely related to banking)
- A 2-month *sabbatical*, an unpaid, job-protected leave, every year.

A cafeteria benefit plan is being explored but is unlikely to be established in the near future.

All full-time employees and part-timers working 20+ hours a week qualify for prorated benefits. Part-timers working less than half time and temporaries do not. Here, too, we see that where recruitment or work force stability is an issue, the marketplace may respond with benefits and scheduling flexibility for part-time workers also.

Benefits cost 25 percent of salaries and wages, and costs have been stable for some time. As is the case everywhere else, management's concern is with the growing costs of health insurance.

Family Responsiveness?. Women are a major component in the bank's labor force and are a growing component in middle management. More and more women are having children but remaining at work. There has been a 40 percent increase in the numbers of women qualifying for maternity leaves in the last four years, and almost all women in management return to work at the end of their eight-week disability leave.

The Worklife program was in effect for 18 months at the time we visited. The bank's goal is to develop a stable work force and to ensure the presence of personnel on Saturdays and evenings, when consumer demand is high and many employees prefer not working. Management hopes to achieve its goal by permitting some employees to work a more flexible schedule and receive full benefits; the pay scale is still the same.

The Worklife program was specifically designed to help stabilize the work force by attracting women with young children and family responsibilities. The program allows part-time employees who work more than half-time (20+ hours a week) and at least 35 weeks per year to choose their work hours and to qualify for full benefits. However, they must work two Saturdays each month and stay late (after 3:00 P.M.) one day a week, if the bank keeps late hours.

Typical reasons why employees say they prefer the Worklife program include:

- To be home when children leave for school and/or return from school
- To take summers off
- To manage college while working
- To work a schedule that fits a particular life-style and personal or familial needs.

Jane R., a customer service representative with the bank for two years, has three children aged 10, 8, and 6. She is participating in the Worklife program and likes it because it permits her to be home when the children get home from school. However, she sometimes finds it hard to go in on a Saturday. She also objects to the policy whereby she gets a two-week vacation but cannot take the two weeks consecutively. Her concept is that if the program is to be responsive to her needs she should be able to take her vacation when she wants it.

Ellen S. is a teller with the bank for one year and also in the Worklife program. She has three children, too, aged 14, 10, and 6. She likes the arrangement because she could not manage a full-time job but wanted a job with health benefits. Her husband is self-employed and the family is totally dependent on her for benefits. Most jobs she could get would not provide benefits, and paying for individual family coverage is very expensive. She appreciates the flexibility in her work schedule but still says she's very strapped for time. Her husband does help with the children, but with a house, a husband, three children, and a job, she's constantly pressed, nonetheless. She wishes the bank provided a child care subsidy as one of its benefits. "Even though my husband and I each have flexible hours and manage a lot of child care between us, half of my salary now goes to the extra child care we need. But it will get easier as the children get older."

At the bank's computer center, among the 250 employees, 150 are in the Worklife program. Seven of the 12 managers are women, and although they are not in the program, they are permitted a good deal of flexibility because the culture at the center encourages such an approach. Several view this as key in managing their jobs and are enthusiastic about the program for the subordinates.

In contrast, some branch managers have a different perspective on the program. They recognize that the program has solved the difficult problem of Saturday coverage. However, in their view, it is difficult to assure adequate task coverage in a small branch during the week when employees pick their own hours. One woman manager said she would prefer to have the right to juggle her employees' hours herself, in relation to the particular pattern in her bank, and not to have the mandated pattern of flexibility. In effect, she would prefer The Eatery arrangement to administratively structured flexibility.

Clearly, the possibility of a flexible work schedule and full benefit coverage for part-time work is important to women employees. Most also stress that the health insurance coverage is critical, and it attracts them to part-time work. Much lower down in their ranking come vacations, profit sharing, and opportunity for advancement. Regardless, salary remains the first priority, and the salaries at the bank are low. The Worklife program is a creative, innovative idea. Whether it can accomplish management's objectives remains to be seen. Many women who appreciate the flexibility and the benefit coverage know they are paying for it.

It is unlikely that the Worklife program, any more than good benefits alone, can compensate for low salaries, at least once these women find they have options, if they do have options. Management is convinced that they have limited options at best. Thus, for example, in exploring the possibility of a child care benefit, a senior human resource executive said, "There's no need for employers to do anything about child care because people are glad to get good jobs like those at the bank. Child care would be expensive and not worth whatever negligible payoff there might be."

The Tradeoff

These three case studies suggest the following:

1. Market forces do not necessarily ensure family-responsive policies. Often it is the particular nature of the work and the work force that is determining.
2. In small-establishment companies one may find the same type of tradeoff between benefit inadequacy and family-supportive work scheduling that we noted in the very small business. Indeed, many people accept part-time jobs for this reason even though they need full-time work.
3. Often the personal responsiveness of a supervisor and manager substitutes for formal policy responsiveness. It seems at times as though a local assistant manager or a manager in a small establishment like a coffee shop achieves subordinate loyalty and operational control by trading in considerateness.

Although all the companies described in this chapter have been shaped by the social changes affecting their markets and their consumers and all are recruiting among married and single mothers for their work force, it is startling how little effort there has been by the top management of any company to become more specifically family responsive in employment policies. We have come to conclude that marketplace dynamics will not yield family-oriented policy of an explicit and more comprehensive sort. The specific company does what its pattern of operations and worksite require or permit: part-time jobs, convenient schedules that may fit the needs and preferences of students or housewives, flexibility around child or personal emergencies. If recruitment or retention difficulties persist, or if the union demands it, there will also be fringe benefits for part-timers, especially the much-valued health coverage.

Some of the most imaginative and helpful responses are ad hoc on the part of the managers of the local establishments, the local sites where company meets consumers. These managers, often overworked, very pressured in their own daily lives, balance two types of pressure: central office expects performance and results; line workers cannot function if there is excessive rigidity and an unwillingness to adapt. The arrangements do not find expression in formal policies and are hardly uniform, but "street-level management" can be quite inventive. The companies tolerate this, do not press too hard, and gain in the process.

For some workers, this is not a problem. The temporary employee-student may not want much more. The young mother who intends shortly to seek another kind of job will settle for this temporarily. The company must then be willing to accept the constant large turnover.

For there is a tradeoff at each side of the equation. The employer, constantly concerned about the quality of the response to the all-important consumer, must accept the coming and going of front-line workers: waitresses, checkout counter clerks, tellers. In some instances there is also an ongoing training and orientation expense.

The employees weigh costs and benefits, too. They take these service jobs—and we write especially of women because they constitute 60 to 80 percent of the work force in these companies—because the work requires no or few skills; the job locations are convenient and often near home; the hours are good (often coterminous with the school day or flexible), permitting adjustment to personal and family emergencies; and they can work part time. Sometimes they can even obtain the basic fringe benefits that characterize "good" jobs. These women may find the jobs rewarding personally, in many ways, even occasionally paying more than they expected, given the flexibility. Ultimately, however, they face the price. They earn far less per hour than the full-timers; they may work almost as many hours but without the full-time status. The benefits, however welcome, are far less than adequate. The opportunities for advancement are limited. Thus the years of work while the child is young are in a sense "wasted" or partially lost. They must plan to move on and do, unless the mobility comes too late in a lifetime. If they do move, as most must, they add to the turnover numbers.

One inevitably wonders if there are other possibilities.

7. New Needs, New Responses: Child Care and Employee Counseling Services

Business, labor and government should encourage and implement employment opportunities and personnel policies that enable persons to hold jobs while maintaining a strong family life. Family-oriented personnel policies can result in reduced absenteeism, greater productivity and decreased stress. Toward such desirable ends, there is need for creative development of such work arrangements as flexitime, flexible leave policies for both sexes, job sharing programs, dependent care options and part-time jobs with pro-rated pay and benefits. Additionally, employers should recognize the possible adverse effects of relocation of families so that they may provide support and options.[1]

This was the priority recommendation of the 1980 White House Conference on Families. Regardless of ideology, across the spectrum from feminist and liberal to traditionalist and conservative, Conference participants overwhelmingly agreed on issues that related to the workplace; more than 92 percent of the delegates recommended that business initiate family-oriented personnel policies.

This theme of the family responsiveness of employee benefits and services and of employment policies and practices is one that has been repeated in hundreds of conferences, articles, books, and media presentations since then. The Conference itself may have been relatively unimportant; it certainly had no impact on public policies. However, it was the first national platform on which the theme was developed and this agenda announced.[2]

The theme emerged increasingly as a national issue in the 1980s. Given the political bent of the decade toward privatization and away from a strong governmental role in social provision, the stress on an expanded role for employers could be supported across the political spectrum. Not only have women's organizations and women's magazines advocated change at the workplace but so also have various corporate leadership groups, such as the Conference Board, an independent, nonprofit, business research organization; Work in America, a similar organization focused on issues related to work and productivity; the Employee Benefits Research Institute; and newspapers like *The Wall Street Journal*.

The theme that recurs in these groups and the media is the need for employers to respond to a *new* group of needs that are now experienced by a growing proportion of the labor force, in particular, women with children, and to a lesser extent, men with children but also men with working wives. In contrast to the more fundamental types of benefits such as health insurance and pensions, or even paid vacations and holidays, the focus of these discussions is largely on those benefits and policies that facilitate employees' management of home and family responsibilities simultaneously with job responsibilities. Here the focus is on quality of life issues rather than on those benefits that constitute a central component of an employee's standard of living and a significant part of one's total wage packet or compensation package. Unlike efforts and initiatives related to participatory management and quality circles, the concern is with the quality of the employee's *personal* life, not his or her *work* life.

Among the specific types of policy areas identified as particularly important are the following: alternative ways of organizing work and work schedules; employer-sponsored child care services; personal and parental leave policies, both paid and unpaid; information, advice, and counseling services; and relocation policies. Some of these policies began to receive attention in the 1970s. All have had far more attention in the 1980s and are likely to become even more visible as the pressure from working women and some working men becomes greater. It is the acknowledgment that today's labor force is different from that of even a decade ago, and certainly different from what it was two decades ago, that is creating the pressure. And responsive federal legislation, in particular tax legislation, has created new incentives and opportunities for employers to act. What is happening? Who is doing what, for whom, and with what known effects?

In this chapter, we examine what employers are providing in the way of supportive services for employees. In chapter 8, we look at how employers are addressing employees' problems concerning time—constraints on family time and the rigidities of time at the workplace.

The range of services at or provided through the workplace now includes legal assistance, diverse educational programs, investment counseling, recreational services, personal and family counseling, and even some child care services.[3] It is the last two categories of services—*child care* and *counseling services*—that have been stressed by those urging more responsiveness by employers to the personal and family needs of employees.[4]

Much of the literature on these services is largely anecdotal, hortatory, or descriptive and program specific.[5] There has been no systematic study of the quantity or quality of services provided, employees' attitudes toward them, or the effects of such services. The interest and enthusiasm with which these programs have been greeted seem astonishing, given the suspicion and resentment expressed by workers and professionals between the 1920s and the 1940s regarding similar types of services. A few people, in fact, have raised questions of paternalism, possible value conflicts, control of workers, and so forth.[6] Others have warned of the potential for generating dependency, in words like those used to describe the dependency allegedly engendered by the use of government benefits.[7] The available picture unfortunately is fragmented and incomplete.

Child Care

Few services that employers may provide or support are or could be as directly responsive to the family needs of employees as child care services. Indeed, working mothers continue to define child care as the number one problem they face in combining work and family life.

A 1980 report, issued by the Women's Bureau of the U.S. Department of Labor, began as follows:[8]

> As more and more mothers of preschool children in this country enter the labor market, the need for child care is increasing. Employers and labor representatives are recognizing the child care need as a major concern of employees and are exploring ways to alleviate it.

In 1960 only 19 percent of married mothers with preschool-aged children were in the labor force. In 1970, the rate was 27 percent; in 1980, 45 percent; and in 1986, 54 percent. Half of all children under age 6 had working mothers by the mid 1980s. (See tables 1.3, 1.4, 1.5, 1.6.)

With minor variations, this is the context in which hundreds of articles have appeared in the 1980s, stressing the theme of the inadequate supply of child care services in the face of growing female labor force participation and leading up to a statement concerning the need for employers to respond to this urgent and growing demand. Thus, for example, in *Personnel*, a professional journal for those in the personnel and human resources field, an article titled "Employer-Sponsored Child Care Comes of Age" begins similarly but continues: "Finding reliable and convenient child care has always been a problem for working mothers, but only recently have employers recognized this problem and its impact on the organization and looked for ways to alleviate it." [9]

Child care supported, sponsored, or provided by employers is certainly not a new development. Although it was never extensive, mention is made of company day nurseries, nursery schools, and infant schools in several histories of nineteenth-century American welfare capitalism. During World War II, companies such as W. J. Kaiser set up nurseries to provide care for the children of their women employees. As soon as the war ended the centers were closed. The concept was that with the return of the men from the war, women workers would no longer be needed, and therefore there would be no need for day care services.

A comprehensive 1979 survey of employer-sponsored child care services, updated in 1981, documents its rarity even at the beginning of the 1980s. The survey found only 19 day care centers sponsored by industry, 7 sponsored by labor unions with funds from employers of the members, 14 sponsored by government agencies, and 75 sponsored by hospitals. In addition, there were 200 centers sponsored by the military. The extremely limited involvement of private industry was particularly notable; in fact, the number of industry-sponsored centers actually declined between 1970 and 1980.[10]

A 1982 survey identified 415 civilian employers who were supporting some child-care-related activity. About half of these were hospitals. Among those programs supported by private industry, only 42 were on-site child care services, 10 were voucher programs, 20 were information and referral services, and 78 involved some form of support to community services, usually in the form of a modest financial contribution.[11]

By 1986 somewhere between 2,000 and 3,000 employers nationally were estimated to be sponsoring child care services in some form or providing some form of child care assistance.[12] The figures are not precise and reflect much of the public relations atmosphere surrounding developments in this field. The sponsorship or assistance involved actually ranges from a very limited number of employers operating or contracting for the operation of worksite child care services to those holding occasional seminars to inform parents about how to choose a child care service or helping employees to segregate some of their wage and salary income before taxes to pay for child care services.

The types of child care services currently supported by some employers thus include the following:[13]

- *Employer-owned and employer-operated child care services at or near the worksite.* In this type, and the type described below, employers usually pay all start-up costs and partially subsidize fees or operating costs, albeit modestly.
- *Employer-contracted-for child care services provided by an independent operator located at or near the worksite.*
- *Child care services owned and operated by an independent private child care provider and located at one or more sites in the communities where employees reside.* Through a contractual arrangement with the employer, these services are offered

employees at a modest discount (5% to 10% off the fee for each child) as long as the employer guarantees that a specified minimum number of children will be enrolled.

- *An off-site child care center established by a consortium of employers who are located reasonably close to one another.* The companies usually provide seed money for initial construction or remodeling of a facility and may underwrite some of the operating costs of the facility or provide a partial subsidy of tuition costs for children of employees.
- *A vendor program in which the employer purchases a number of "slots" or child care places in one or more centers or family day homes and makes these available to employees at a partially reduced rate.*
- *A voucher program in which employers provide a coupon to the employee worth a specified amount toward the purchase of child care from any licensed provider.* The employer may either fully fund the cost of service or subsidize the child care cost on the basis of the income and/or family size of the employee, and the employee may choose among all available licensed providers.
- *Employer-provided child care information and referral services.* The employer hires an employee specifically to provide this service, among others, or the employer assigns an employee responsibility for this task.
- *An independent information and referral service. A child care consultant or organization provides the service to employees through a contractual arrangement with the employer.*
- *Child care as a fringe benefit.* This benefit is included in a flexible benefit plan, so that employees may choose a small subsidy for child care as one of their fringe benefits. The employer either pays a small amount toward the employees' costs of child care or reimburses employees for part of the costs.
- *A salary reduction plan that includes child care as one of the benefits.* If this course is followed, employees may allocate a portion of pretax salary to pay for child care each year. (This is a benefit that costs the employer nothing unless the employer chooses to contribute, and most do not, and it provides the employee a subsidy that varies in amount depending on the employee's tax bracket. It is paid for, in effect, by the taxpayer.)
- *A philanthropic contribution by the employer of money or services to a child care center located in the community where the employer is based or where the employer has a facility.*

According to the informal estimates of Dr. Dana Friedman, a nationally respected expert on employer-sponsored child care who is affiliated with the Conference Board, the national picture of almost 3,000 employer-sponsored child care services looked something like this in 1986:[14]

- Approximately 400 hospitals had on- or near-site child care services.
- Approximately 150 corporations (and 30 public agencies) had on-or near-site child care services. Except for those operated directly by the corporation or a subsidiary, almost all were contracted out to private independent providers and operated by them.
- About 300 employers had contracts with one of the large proprietary child care chains that offer a modest discount to employees' children; and about 50 of these employers actually contribute as well. (Dr. Friedman estimated that about half of these were with one large child care service chain.)
- About 500 companies were either operating child care information and referral services themselves or had contracts with another organization to do so.
- About 150 firms had cafeteria-style or flexible benefit plans, and half of these included child care as an optional benefit.
- About 800 firms had flexible benefit or salary reduction plans, but only about 10 percent of these included child care.
- About 25 firms had voucher plans.
- About 20 firms had sick-child care initiatives.
- About 75 companies were involved in some way in after-school child care.
- In addition, about 200 employers made some form of contribution to local child care centers and about the same number had held parenting seminars and workshops to which outside speakers are invited to discuss various aspects of parenting problems ranging from child care for infants to the substance abuse problems of adolescents.

These numbers represent the maximum estimates of employer involvement in child care in 1986. We discuss below and describe some of the most important of the different models of employer-sponsored child care.

On-Site Child Care Services. Initially, when employer sponsorship of child care services was first discussed, the most frequent proposal was for a child care center located at the workplace and operated directly by the corporation, operated as a separate subsidiary corporation but responsible to the parent corporation, or operated by others but under contract to the corporation.

An obvious way to provide care for children whose parent (or parents) is employed, so the discussion would go, is to bring the children to work. While the parents work, the children can be cared for in some group arrangement. With this proximity, parents have the opportunity to see their children at certain times during the day, regularly check on their progress, and be readily available for any emergency. Nursing is possible. It is an arrangement that seemingly can reduce the typical disjunction between work and family life. Other possible advantages for families include the convenience of not having to commute to another location in order to drop off and pick up children.

Certain disadvantages of worksite child care, documented in earlier U.S. experience, were largely ignored in these discussions. Most notably, for example, was the experience of American Telephone and Telegraph, the company that was the country's largest employer of women until 1984 (when it carried out the court-ordered divestiture plan, spinning off seven regional operating companies and thereby becoming a far smaller company than previously). For three years, from 1971 to 1974, AT&T operated day care centers at two of its locations, Washington, D.C., and Columbus, Ohio. Given the company's large female labor force, working at thousands of locations across the country, in particular in heavily urban areas, the argument was that "If Bell could demonstrate the viability of industry-run day care centers in large urban settings, a powerful impetus could be given to this type of child care."[15]

Despite great expectations and much publicity, the Washington center, with a capacity for 110 children, opened with only 16 children, and the Columbus center, with a capacity for 50, opened with 22. The occupancy rate averaged 65 to 70 percent at both locations and never exceeded 80 percent for any sustained period of time. By mid-1974 the company closed both centers.

In evaluating the experience, the company conducted a longitudinal study of an experimental group (working parents using one of the two centers) and a matched control group of nonusers. The major findings were as follows.

1. Lateness was reduced in the experimental group as compared with the control group. However, reducing lateness had not been a major objective in establishing the centers.
2. Absenteeism, which was a major company concern, was *higher* among parents using the center, because when their children became ill, parents had no readily available home-based or near-home support and therefore had to stay home to care for the child.
3. Turnover, another company concern, was no lower among those in the experimental group than among those in the control group.
4. The evidence was not adequate to indicate whether the centers proved a recruitment device, because the company's own hiring policies changed during the period the centers were operating.
5. Far fewer employees were interested in the service than was expected.

Although the labor force situation is clearly very different now, more than one decade later, and the same problems, successes and failures may not necessarily hold true today, the findings of this unusually rigorous effort at evaluating an on-site child care center do suggest that this approach is certainly not the definitive answer to employees' child care problems. Nor should it be employers' preferred option in responding to these problems. Indeed, these and other findings raise serious questions about onsite care and employee responses to this type of care. Of equal interest, however, the results suggest how important it is that employers carefully monitor and study whatever approach they choose, if they have specific goals in mind when developing a child care policy.

Some companies that established on- or near-site child care centers in recent years have been very satisfied with them, but usually the success of the arrangement has to do with factors that may be unique to the particular company involved. Several of the companies that view their experience with on-site child care centers positively are located in communities that resemble company towns, where they are the primary employer or a major employer and where few alternative child care arrangements are available. A large group among the employers who have on-site child care services are hospitals or medical complexes of some sort. These organizations, employing a large number of professional women (nurses) and nonprofessional cleaning and support staff, largely female, and open 24 hours a day, 365 days a year, face special problems in recruiting and retaining staff and have unusual work schedules; on-site child care services may be highly attractive and appropriate for their personnel.

A precise figure on the number of nonhospital worksite child care centers is still not available, but estimates range from 42[16] to 80[17] to 150.[18] Even among these relatively few programs, there are substantial differences. Thus, for example, those at Wang Laboratories and Hoffmann-La Roche are completely in-house operations where center staff are considered corporate employees. Intermedics operates its child care center as a wholly owned subsidiary. Corning Glass, through its corporate foundation, provided start-up funds and some ongoing support for the establishment of an autonomous, nonprofit child care center. Other companies with on-site centers include Connecticut General Life Insurance Company, Stride-Rite Shoe Corp., and Zale Corp. Several governmental agencies have also established on-site child care centers, including one in Albany, one in Boston, and several in Washington, D.C.

Another approach to providing child care at or near the work site is to contract with one of the large child care chains to offer employees a discount on their child care fees. Sometimes the employer provides a small subsidy to the employee, but usually the discount is offered by the provider for the assurance of a guaranteed minimum enrollment of employees' children. At Disney World, the center is operated by Kinder-Care, a private, commercial (for profit) child care company on contract with Disney. A similar pattern exists at Allendale Insurance Company in Rhode Island and Union Mutual Life Insurance Company in Portland, Maine, where Living and Learning, another large commercial child care chain, leases space from the insurance companies. The companies guarantee a certain minimum enrollment, and Living and Learning provides a 10 percent discount to employees.

Except for those centers operated on a contractual basis by an independent child care organization—often a commercial child care chain—employers typically bear start-up costs. In almost all these centers, the fees for employee-parents are partially subsidized, usually very modestly. In several, the center serves children from the community whose parents are not company employees as well, although employees' children do have priority if space if tight. Often community children are needed to make adequate use of the space and available staff.

Many in senior management in other companies that considered the development of an on-site center but rejected it have commented about the earlier negative experiences. Among the reasons that management in many companies have decided against on-site child care are the following:

- The costs of establishing and operating a center
- The complexities of a business that is new and unfamiliar and the regulatory maze involved in starting and operating a center
- The difficulties in monitoring the quality of service provided and the potential problems of liability if accidents occur
- Siting and transportation problems
- The unreliability of employees' actual use of such centers despite expressions of positive interest (sometimes the issue is convenience, sometimes cost, often preferences about programs)

Labor unions have also been involved with the development of child care centers near where their members work.[19] The Amalgamated Clothing and Textile Workers Union (ACTWU) has been the most active union where child care is concerned. In 1981 there were six ACTWU child care centers, five located in the east and one in Chicago. Most are operated out of the ACTWU health and welfare fund, to which management contributes as part of a collective bargaining agreement; in Baltimore, however, there is a special child care fund under joint control of the union and management. In all these centers, fees are heavily subsidized; indeed, in Chicago, until 1978, child care was free for union members.

Of some interest, given the negative attitudes of many in management about operating a worksite based child care service, is the increasingly similar attitude expressed by union officials. Several of the ACTWU centers have closed in the last few years, including the Chicago center. The Baltimore center in 1983 had only three members' children! As one senior union official said:

> We would not establish day care centers again. Day care centers are expensive facilities and need permanent financing. The labor force changes in a plant. Members get older. The communities where plants are located change, and the members with young children move to different neighborhoods. Plants move. Parents want child care near where they live, not near where they work.

An illustration of an unusual combination of a union-sponsored, government- and management-financed, worksite- and community-based child care center is one in New York City's Chinatown, under the auspices of the City's child care agency and the ILGWU. Here, in a unique situation, federal child care funds, city and state child care funds, private foundation funds, and funds from management are supporting a community-based child care center for the children of the low-earning Chinese employees—union members who qualify for publicly subsidized child care. Management's contribution enabled the center to serve almost twice as many children (70 instead of 40) as it would have if only public financing was available. In effect, this is a publicly funded center in which supplementary funds are provided by local employers in order to increase the numbers of employees' children—who would qualify for public child care if it were available—that can be served. It is very small and meets special circumstances. Moreover, by 1986 employer funding had ended (the commitment was for the start-up and phasing-in periods only), and the program became a totally philanthropically and publicly funded program.

Additional objections by parents to worksite child care, in part documented in earlier and more extensive experiences in European countries (which are increasingly eliminating such services), have been supported by the findings of parent surveys in the

United States too. These objections include the potential for disrupting a child care arrangement if they wish to change jobs; the problems of transporting children long distances during peak commuter hours, often on mass transportation; the lack of neighborhood friends when a child's relationships are limited to the children of other employees; and preferences for neighborhood-based care.[20]

More important, there are a variety of other potentially very attractive options whereby employers can support, facilitate, and subsidize child care services for employees, and these options, often far less expensive than on-site child care, are receiving increasing attention. Among them are several types described earlier:

- Organizing a consortium supporting community-based services
- Providing a voucher covering a full or partial reimbursement to employees for the costs of child care
- Subsidizing a number of slots in various community-based facilities near employees' places of residence
- Contributing to the support of one or more existing child care centers located near where employees work
- Including child care within a flexible benefit plan

Child Care Consortia. In theory, at least, among the most feasible models for small or medium-sized employers is a consortium. As one report suggests:

... one of the least used, but perhaps the most feasible for the majority of companies, is a consortium. In a consortium, employers can join efforts by sharing resources, liabilities, and costs and by pooling their populations of parents and children. . .[21]

For the most part, what is needed to start a consortium is a group of employers located relatively close to one another geographically or at least drawing their work force from a common residential community or communities. Centers can be started in industrial parks or complexes or even in shopping malls. Some have been started by employers in the same or related industry.

One child care consortium was begun as a collaborative effort by employees and employers, a university, and the National

Academy of Television Arts and Sciences, Inc. This center, the Broadcasters' Child Development Center, was started by four television and two radio stations and serves the children of local television and radio station personnel at all levels.[22]

Another consortium was established in the early 1970s by a group of Minneapolis companies under the leadership of Control Data. This consortium, supporting the Northside Child Development Center, included such companies as Dayton-Hudson, Pillsbury, Northwestern Bell Telephone Company, Northern States Power, Minnesota Federal Reserve Bank, and Farmers & Mechanics Savings and Loan. Over the years, participation by employees declined and participation by community residents who were not employed by the sponsoring companies increased. The center became increasingly dependent on government funds for survival. By the late 1970s the center had essentially become a community child care facility. Of the 120 children in the center, recently only 12 were reported to be the children or grandchildren of employees.[23] In commenting about the changes over time, the center director said, "The work force at the plant [Control Data] has remained relatively stable over the last decade. As a result, few of the employees have children young enough to enroll in the center."[24] Her statement sounds remarkably similar in context to a statement made to us by the President of the Amalgamated Clothing and Textile Workers' Union. Although Control Data continues to provide financial assistance and in-kind services to the child care center, the company no longer offers child care benefits within its fringe benefit package to its employees. In effect this is a consortium that was; it is no longer operating as such.

Still another consortium was established by six high-tech companies in the Silicon Valley. The city of Sunnyvale approached four subsidiaries of TRW and several other companies, including Hewlett-Packard, about the possibility of joining together to support the establishment of a local child care service. The local companies were very enthusiastic about the possibility and agreed to provide some funding to get the center launched. Some were so enthusiastic that they tried to get some additional funds from their parent company but were unsuccessful. Management in the local high-tech companies were convinced of the need for additional child care services and saw this as a way to encourage the development of more services and provide some aid to their female employees without getting to the costly and complicated effort of actually operating a program. The companies make a financial contribution to the center, and in return, employees are entitled to a 5 percent discount off the regular fee and are given priority for places when space is tight.

The human resource manager of one of the participating companies described the consortium as "fairly successful." He said that the center provides very high-quality child care but that it is expensive and beyond the reach of many of the single mothers who are employed as support staff and were originally viewed as the primary consumer group for the center. The subsidy provided by employers is small; it is not adequate for most of their women workers, who tend to earn low or at most modest salaries. Over the years since the center was first established, there has been a decline in the numbers of employees using the center. Thus, for example, in 1984, only about 10 female employees out of a total labor force of 3,000 in two firms in the consortium were using the center. Moreover, not only are the costs of the service a problem, but also, over the intervening years, residential patterns have shifted somewhat. As a result, although the center is located where many young families lived initially, by now most of these firms' employees who might use the center live in a different area; they prefer using a child care program that is nearer where they live. Here too, the situation is somewhat reminiscent of the on-site child care programs. The labor force is dynamic and over time needs change.

Contracting with a Private Provider. In this model, employers identify one or more private providers, usually large corporate child care chains with several facilities in the area, and contract with the provider(s) to offer a small discount to employees on the basis of the employer's guaranteeing a certain minimum enrollment of employees' children. An alternative approach involves an employer's encouraging a provider who has facilities in other communities not too far away, but none in the immediate area of the employer's worksite, to establish a new facility nearby. In neither case does the employer have any financial obligation to the child care provider, nor does the employer provide any subsidy to employees to purchase child care. Employers using this approach merely act as facilitators, and if enough children are enrolled, the employee benefits from a modest discount.

Honeywell in Minneapolis established such an arrangement with Learning Tree (the name under which Children's World operates in Minnesota) at one site that had recently experienced employee relocation. A relatively large number of professionals had been relocated and the company wanted to be responsive to their problems. Child care was viewed as a potentially important problem for employees, in particular because no child care facility was located near the worksite or in the surrounding community. Management initially explored the possibility of an on-site child care center but rejected it for a number of the usual reasons. They then explored the possibility of a local public school operating such a program but dropped that when they discovered that a leading commercial child care chain was in the process of establishing a center near where the plant was. An employee survey had revealed that about half preferred having child care available at a facility located near the worksite while the other half preferred a facility located near home. A contract was negotiated with Children's World whereby Honeywell employees would get a 5 percent discount (later raised to 10 percent when the employee participation rate was higher than anticipated). A similar contract was negotiated with two other commercial providers with facilities located in the nearby communities where employees lived. In 1984, out of approximately 2,500 employees at this location, about 100 parents, with slightly more than 100 children, were participating in this child care discount program located at 30 centers. The fees for care were $60 to $65 a week for preschoolers and $90 to $100 a week for infants. The second child got a 15 percent discount. The company provided no subsidy for employees; in effect, it was a discount based on numbers—the company assured these three providers of at least a certain minimum number of child participants.

Subsidizing "Slots" or Places for Employees' Children. In this model of employer-sponsored child care, employers guarantee payment for a number of places in established child care centers, and these are reserved for employees.

Commercial child care chains such as Kinder-Care, Children's World, and La Petite Academe offer an employer a 20 percent discount for their employees' children, for which the company pays 10 percent and the center absorbs a 10 percent reduction in fees. Equitable Life Assurance had a pilot project with Kinder-Care in Atlanta, Georgia; Albuquerque, New Mexico; and Columbus, Ohio. The project was ended because employee participation was much lower than anticipated, in part because of the inconvenience of the sites. Equitable is now moving in a different direction as regards its child care policy (see below).

An alternative way to subsidize individual places in different child care centers for employees' children is for employers to contribute funds to a nonprofit agency that can then provide vouchers to pay for child care to those who qualify for the service. For the most part, the efforts at doing this have received very limited support and exist on a very modest scale. Among those places in which such a model exists are Austin, Texas; Minneapolis and St. Paul, Minnesota; and San Mateo County, California. A few organizations have obtained small contributions from employers and have used these to leverage public child care funds. The main advantage has been to help communities obtain public funds that they might not have been able to otherwise and to expand the number of places available.

Although anything that expands the availability of reasonably good child care services deserves attention, these programs, which have received a great deal of publicity, thus far provide very little in the way of new child care money for very few, if any, additional children.

Voucher Systems. The term "voucher" is used to describe a subsidy provided by employers and given to employees to purchase child care at any licensed facility, or sometimes, from any licensed family day care provider. Two companies, the Ford Foundation and the Polaroid Corporation, are among the very few employers using this approach to help employees defray a portion of their child care costs.[25] Each had initially considered establishing an on-site child care center and chose instead a system of financial assistance. Polaroid Corporation, in Cambridge, Massachusetts, pays anywhere from 5 percent to more than half of the child care costs of employees whose income is below a certain level. Similarly, the Ford Foundation reimburses employees who qualify for the subsidy for up to 50 percent of their child care costs, to a defined maximum. Both organizations limit the subsidy to employees with incomes under a specified ceiling. Polaroid chose the voucher model because they operate out of many different locations and could establish neither a center at each site nor a center at one site that ignored all the others. The Ford Foundation rejected the concept of an on-site center because they were convinced their employees would not want to bring their young children to a midtown program but would prefer to use a service near their homes. Moreover, both organizations were convinced that child care services were available but that the problem for their employees was being able to afford a good-quality program. They concluded, therefore, that what was needed was a child care subsidy, not a specific place. Polaroid has since found that for its evening shift workers, a subsidy is not enough; there are just not enough services around. Polaroid provides another child care service for employees who do not qualify for financial aid (see below).

Here, too, developments have been very modest; at best, a handful of companies have established this model.

Information and Referral Services. Child care information and referral services are expanding everywhere, in part in response to a growing diversity of programs and to the concomitant problems of parents trying to locate them and be assured of the quality of care provided. One new development is employer sponsorship of these services, either by employing someone on an in-house basis to provide the service or by contracting with an existing child care information and referral service or a child care agency to provide such services for their employees.[26] This is an inexpensive, simple, yet helpful and highly visible way for employers to do something about child care.

Three companies that were among the first to establish in-house information and referral (I&R) counselors are Mountain Bell in Denver, Colorado; Polaroid; and Steelcase, Inc., in Grand Rapids, Michigan. Steelcase, the largest manufacturer of office furniture, is a nonunion, family-owned business with about 7,000 employees at the Grand Rapids plant. According to one report, its human resources department offers a counseling and referral service on a range of issues to company employees seeking help.[27] Employees meet with a counselor to discuss child care needs and the counselor suggests possible alternatives. Parents are told about the characteristics of a good child care program and are helped to develop criteria for choosing a service that will best meet their needs. Counselors are knowledgeable about the resources that exist in the community and make referrals to both center care and family day care providers.

An alternative model, whereby services are provided on a contractual basis, is the approach taken by IBM, beginning in mid-1984. IBM contracted with Work/Family Directions, a Boston-based private organization, to provide child care information and referral services, as well as parent/consumer education, to its employees located throughout the country. The service is delivered through a nationwide network of more than 250 local agencies and individuals with whom Work/Family Directions contracts. Most of these community resources are thus also available to serve other employers, as well as the general public. Work/Family Directions contracted with I&R services where they existed and helped create such services where they were lacking. By 1986, 90 percent of IBM employees were covered by this service through contracts with I&R services in 45 cities, while about 200 contracts in a variety of organizations around the country carried the remaining 10 percent. Of the 240,000 employees covered, 14,000 had used the service.

According to Work/Family Directions, all IBM employees who call the referral service receive child care consultation, referrals to available services, and a parent handbook that describes how to choose a good service. IBM also sponsors training workshops for child care providers as a way of improving the general quality of services available. Early reports are positive, often enthusiastic.

The costs of the information, referral, and parent education services are prepaid by IBM (which has also provided personal computers to many services), but the employees pay for the child care service itself.

The IBM development seems to have constituted something of a breakthrough. Several large employers now seem interested in making I&R services available to their employees, and Work/Family Directions has contracts with MacDonald's, Kraft, Merrill Lynch, and several other large companies. As more employers decide to make this service available to their employees, the IBM model of purchasing the service through a community agency or a national network is likely to become the prevalent information and referral mode.

A variation of this model was developed earlier by Child Care Inc. (CCI) in New York City, currently one of the local agencies under contract with Work/Family Directions to provide services to IBM employees in the New York City area. An experienced and well-established child care information and referral service, CCI developed a relationship with several large corporations interested in providing child care information and referral services to their own employees. On a contract basis, CCI makes this service available at no fee to employees of a corporation, providing information about what is available, the criteria for making choices, and referrals and recommendations to a range of services that seem to meet employee-parent needs and preferences. CCI also initially organized parenting seminars for corporations but later simply facilitated access to specialists. It is presently exploring options in providing sick child care services, too (see below). Among the 25 companies currently contracting with CCI are International Paper, Philip Morris, Time, American Express, Equitable Life, Morgan Guaranty, and Conde Nast.

Among the variety of employer-sponsored child care services, thus far it is these information and referral services that seem to be the most likely to expand. They improve understanding and access and, perhaps, may stimulate supply.

Parent Education. Closely related to the information and referral services described above, and often provided along with these services, are various parent education programs. We include a brief discussion of these as one variety of child care assistance because one type of seminar is designed to educate parents about the characteristics of "good" child care services, about how to differentiate between "good" and "bad" services, and about the criteria to use in choosing among existing services, be they centers, preschools, or family day homes.

Among the most popular of these parenting seminars are the "Noontime" or "Brown Bag Seminars" sponsored by employers and provided at the workplace, usually during the lunch hour. They address a variety of parenting, child care, and work and family issues. Thus, for example, in addition to the child care information needs of working parents, other child and family issues may be discussed, such as coping with work and family responsibilities, surviving divorce, managing as a single parent, dealing with the school system, communicating with adolescent children or with stepchildren, and recognizing substance abuse problems in an adolescent.

A visible indication of employers' interest and concern, these programs, too, are easy to carry out and the most inexpensive of all types of child care assistance to implement. Organizations providing these seminars include the Texas Institute for Families, the Bank Street College "Work and Family Seminars," and the Parents in the Workplace program conducted jointly by the Greater Minneapolis Day Care Association and St. Paul's Resources for Child Caring, Inc. There are also many private consultants offering seminars.

Caring for the Sick Child. When enumerating the problems of managing work and family life, working parents frequently list the difficulties of coping with the need for emergency child care right after talking about their child care problems generally. Many parents, even when they manage to find an affordable, reliable, and satisfactory child care arrangement, still speak with something akin to horror when they describe their fears about a child getting sick on a workday. While most employers permit time off when an employee is ill, very few companies specifically allow the use of those same sick days to care for an ill child. Furthermore, many employees who would return to work after the acute phase of a child's illness is past cannot do so because they are unable to make arrangements for their child to be cared for while convalescing. Sometimes, even if able to take some days off, an employee has to be present at his/her job "for a little while," "for an important meeting or task," and cannot make a care arrangement.

For many parents, an ill child means that whichever parent has the "less important" job, or the more flexible job, or the more sympathetic boss or supervisor will stay home. Needless to say, for single parents, there is no choice. For the parent who has to stay home, this may mean taking off a day or two and losing pay, or if the parent has paid sick leave at work, it may mean the parent/employee lies to her boss (and it's usually *her* boss) and takes time off by saying that she is ill herself. She then runs the risk of eventual job loss for excessive illness and unreliability.

Employers are becoming increasingly convinced that caring for an ill child is one major cause of absenteeism, and employee/parents agree. Among the responsive options, some employers have instituted the following policies:

• Employees may use their own paid sick leave to take care of an ill child, or in some cases, an ill dependent such as an elderly parent.
• Employees may use their paid personal days for personal emergencies, including the illness of a child.
• Employees are allowed a specific number of paid days off, in addition to their own sick leave, to take care of an ill child. (More and more European countries are including such entitlement in their social security systems.)

One alternative or supplementary approach is an in-home sick child care service, a special service that provides a trained caregiver to come to the child's own home in the case of illness. Two such services exist in the Minneapolis-St. Paul area: Child Care Services, Inc., and Control Data Temps. Similar services exist in a few other large cities. These services involve either a babysitter who is trained to care for a mildly ill child or a home health aide who is trained to work with children. In each case the caregiver goes to the child's home on a temporary basis. One major problem with this service is the cost, usually between $35 and $50 a day for the baby-sitting service, and far more than that for a home health aide. Few employees can afford such a service, and not many employers are likely to offer the service or provide a significant subsidy for it.

In Tucson, Arizona, the Sick Child Home Health Care Program is now in its fifth year of operation, staffed by trained and certified health care aides and available to help working parents meet sick child emergencies. A call at 6 A.M. can lead to a dispatch of an aide by 7:00. The aides care for children with common childhood ailments. They may also provide nonspecialized care for children with special needs and terminally ill children. They are available, too, in special instances when a child is not ill, as when the usual caretaker is ill or there are other gaps in child care arrangements.

The minimum service unit in this program is four hours. In 1984 the fees were set on a sliding scale basis between $1.50 and $4.25 per hour. To the extent that parents' fees did not meet the full costs, there was funding from a woman's service organization, a foundation, the City of Tucson, and the United Way. Two electronics firms have contracted to share the costs of the aide with their employees.[28]

Another approach is that of the family day home or center that permits mildly ill children to be brought to child care and has a separate room where the ill child may rest or play quietly, with some supervision. Medicine can be given as needed also.

Still another pattern is found at the Berkeley, California, Children's Service, in its satellite sick child care program, Wheezles and Sneezles. This program was established in 1978 in a three-bedroom apartment adjacent to the child care center. The program is licensed as a family day care home, and the caregivers are familiar to the children because they sometimes staff the regular child care program. All the children have opportunities to visit the sick child care facility so that if they do become ill it is not a strange place. Probably as important, the ill children all come out of the same contagion pool, so children are unlikely to be exposed to new illness while convalescing from the old. A variation on this involves a community medical facility, with a few rooms set aside in a special wing for ill children and staffed by a registered nurse, with a doctor available on an as needed basis.

Thus far there are few such services of a formal kind. One of the newest is "Chicken Soup" in Minneapolis, Minnesota, with room for 20 children in a child care program. It plans summer closings. The San Juan Batista program in San Jose, California, is a year-round, more medical operation.

Other approaches include employers who operate summer camp facilities for the use of employees' children (Fel-Pro Industries, Skokie, Ill.) and employers who have established special loan programs for the construction and renovation of child care facilities (e.g., Bankers Trust Co., Chase Manhattan Bank, and Citibank, all in New York City).

Tax Policies Provide the Spur. The primary factor acting as a spur and catalyst in the development of new forms of employer sponsorship of child care services is the possibility of establishing a "Dependent Care Assistance Plan" (DCAP), legislated as part of the Economic Recovery Tax Act in 1981. Employers have generally ascribed their reluctance to provide child care services for their employees to problems of high costs, possible liability in operating on-site facilities, a concern that such policy would be viewed as a discriminatory benefit by the majority of their employees who do not have very young children or do not need such a service, and a reluctance to appear too paternalistic. One other obstacle, however, has been tax legislation requiring that, unlike many other employee benefits, employer payments for child care assistance be considered as taxable income to the employee. Except in situations where an on-site facility was established, it was easy to identify the specific amount of employer subsidy to be counted. Thus, any increment employers might provide for child care offered no more benefit than a straight wage or salary increase.

Of particular importance, the 1981 legislation establishing these DCAPs (known also as "Section 129 Plans" because of the locus of this tax advantage in Section 129 of the Internal Revenue Code) permits an exclusion from gross income for the value of employer-provided child care services. In addition, the legislation provided an increase in the credit available to taxpayers for child dependent care expenses necessary to their employment and a new depreciation system for employers who improved facilities by creating on-site or nearby child care centers for employees' children.[29] The tax-free status of this benefit and the increase effective 1982 in the child care (dependent care) tax credit are most important in generating these new developments. The employee takes advantage of the child care tax credit at the time of filing an annual tax return. Special employer initiative is needed to establish one of several possible programs subsidizing employee child care in a tax-free fashion.

Child Care and Flexible Benefits or Flexible Spending Plans. Two other approaches to providing child care financial assistance for employees are flexible benefit plans and flexible spending (salary reduction) plans (see below). Both of these involve providing child care assistance as an employee benefit, either with a subsidy from the employer or through the use of employees' pretax income, or both. Providing child care aid this way permits the employer to avoid the issue of a discriminatory benefit—and often even to avoid spending any of its own funds—yet to contribute to a reduction in the out-of-pocket cost to the employee, nevertheless! Several companies have gone this route, including Northern States Power in Minneapolis, which has included child care in its flexible benefit plan, and the nearly 100 other companies that thus far are known to have included child care in a flexible spending plan. The flexible spending plan, created through establishment of a salary reduction plan as permitted by the Internal Revenue Service, allows employees to reduce their salaries by a specific sum and to deposit that amount into a fund from which an employer pays child care bills by using pretax dollars. Another variation on this permits employees to pay for child care directly and then, at the end of the year, apply to their employer for reimbursement from such a fund.

The 1986 tax reforms may decrease the availability or attractiveness of some of these tax-advantaged child care benefits. Dependent care is now limited to a maximum of $5,000 under salary reduction plans, as is employer-provided care.

An Office Furniture Manufacturer Assembles Several Components. Steelcase, the leading office furniture manufacturer, employs 10,000 workers countrywide, 7,300 of them in Grand Rapids, Michigan. Its child care initiatives are embedded in a total program and philosophy expressed as follows in a statement by its vice president for human services:

The Steelcase Family commitment is comprehensive: from an innovative child-care referral program that has gained national publicity ... to a gerontologist-conducted, eight-week pre-retirement program for employees and spouses ... to a Steelcase-sponsored Retirees Club where former employees can maintain their "family ties," participating together in picnics, cruises, and other social events...

That commitment to employees and their families is inherent in the Steelcase corporate philosophy: while change is Steelcase's constant partner, people are Steelcase's constant future. Steelcase's employees, dealers, customers, stockholders and suppliers are partners in profit. Steelcase believes the key to corporate success is three-fold: (1) the identification of the needs of each of these people groups; (2) balancing individual group needs for the mutual satisfaction of all groups; (3) supporting the individual group needs for the collective benefit of all the groups. And so what's good for the employee is good for the company.

The company's strong and committed paternalism involves services, as well as a comparatively generous benefits program and profit sharing. They have not had a work stoppage leading to a labor dispute since 1912. Especially noteworthy, apart from the child care efforts, are family-oriented recreation programs at a large 1,178-acre camping ground (as well as city-based programs), flexitime, many aids to students, a food service, a van transportation service, and a company-operated rehabilitation program.

The child care offerings are quite unusual in national context:

Steelcase also offers employees assistance in obtaining and *paying* for quality care. Steelcase screens prospective child-care providers and makes recommendations to employees seeking individual child care in their own neighborhoods. Steelcase also offers dependent care reimbursement (in tax-free dollars) as part of its flexible benefits program. The referral program is advantageous for both the company and the employee. The company doesn't have to build and staff a central child care facility. The employee has the privilege of individually-tailored child care.

Two full-time, on-site staff members individualize the referral service, visit potential family day care homes to be sure of a good "match," and help upgrade provider services (even lending providers furniture and equipment). The program has been in operation since 1980. Its quality assurance components parallel what a number of other companies are now doing under special contractual arrangements with local information and referral services.

Summary: Child Care Issue and Trends. One female executive, among the very few in senior management in a major company, herself a mother of young children, listed the issues succinctly.

First, management in private sector firms is at best ambivalent about women with children working. Most are men with at-home wives; they are firmly convinced that children should be cared for at home—by their mothers. If the women are working it's not management's responsibility to see to it that their children are cared for.

Second, there is no evidence that any child care developments at the workplace have any positive impact on productivity.

Third, senior management is by far removed from much of the social change occurring in the society at large. The problems experienced by many of their employees are not "their" problems, nor are they "real" problems to them.

Fourth, even for those in management who are aware of the changes that have occurred and see child care as a big problem for some employees, the concept remains that it is a "women's" problem—not a problem for all employees—and largely a problem of low-status female employees.

Fifth, in management, when a woman returns to work after childbirth—that's the end of any special attention. From there on, the expectation of women in management is that they are managers—not mothers.

Sixth, if there is an easy, cheap, visible way for employers to do something about child care—like paying for information and referral services, some progressive employers will do it. But most employers won't even do that.

Another senior official chimed in: "You won't get far if you expect employers to lead the way here. They will only move ahead if they are forced to."

The 1980s can be viewed as the decade in which employer support of child care services has come to the forefront of the child care discussion—and the work and family discussion, generally—in the popular and professional press. Some see employer sponsorship as the answer to the continued shortage of child care services and to the continued interest in reducing public expenditure for social services. More and more employers recognize that their female employees have a child care problem, but relatively few, even now, view solving the problem as their responsibility. Moreover, even those who are willing to "do something" are not yet clear about precisely what they can and should do.

For many years, the only option discussed was child care provided at the workplace: on-site care. A few companies experimented with such programs; most concluded that they were not worthwhile. Some employers in special situations or with special needs, such as hospitals, medical complexes, or employers located in residential areas or where no child care services existed, have established worksite programs and found them satisfactory and appropriate, but the vast majority have rejected this model and have sought alternatives or dropped the idea of doing anything at all.

The majority of employers who now express interest in responding to the child care problems of their employees are experimenting with other options, either providing some form of financial assistance to employees purchasing care, directly or indirectly, or providing information that will enable employee-parents to be more informed and better consumers. Information and referral services offer an inexpensive yet visible service that is clearly helpful to employees. However, such services neither add to the supply of services available nor help employees afford good-quality care, and both of these problems continue to plague employee-parents.

The interest in alternative strategies for providing child care financial assistance has been stimulated by passage of recent tax legislation permitting employers to provide such aid without imposing a tax obligation on their employees. Here, the goals are to increase the affordability of child care services and perhaps to encourage a greater supply by helping employees pay for the service. Several innovations are now being tried out, and it is unclear which will prevail—and why—but much will depend on reactions to the 1986 tax legislation. The main pattern is the provision of financial assistance for child care as a fringe benefit, with employers contributing, at most, a modest financial subsidy or even less, with employers merely facilitating a plan whereby employees can use pretax dollars to pay for child care and thus pay with "cheaper" money. Some employers, in addition, or instead, are influencing providers to offer small discounts to their employees, and others are providing child care information and referral services. Both these options are useful, inexpensive, visible ways for employers to aid employees, especially their female employees, with their child care problems. They are not adequate to aid low-income employees who cannot manage with less take-home pay, taxable or not. For them, the child care tax credit is helpful if limited, but a real subsidy for child care, as an add-on or a supplement, is essential.

Clearly, any help on the part of employers—I&R, financial aid, or direct provision—is worthwhile and valuable to those employees who benefit. But the reality is that relatively few employees, at best, can benefit and even when available, most of the benefits are still quite limited. Even by the most generous estimates, there are fewer than 25,000 children in some form of employer-supported child care, and almost half of these are either at a hospital-based facility or in an arrangement in which the employer acts as the facilitator but provides no direct financial assistance at all.

A 1986 General Accounting Office report estimates that federal employees have about 700,000 preschool children but there are only 28 on-site child care centers. About 1,500 children, 0.2 percent of the total group, are thus served.

Surveying large and medium firms in 1985, the Bureau of Labor Statistics of the U.S. Department of Labor found that only

1 percent of employees worked in firms offering full or partial defrayment of the cost of nursery, day care center, or babysitter costs for employees' children. Typically, only a small sub-group of the eligibles actually use such benefits. Given the 11 million children under age six with working mothers, and the additional millions of primary-school-aged children in need of before-and-after school care, employer-supported child care, however helpful, shows no sign of becoming a significant component in the child care system.

More important, practically all of these illustrations are examples of what large and leading companies can do. In contrast, the majority of the labor force works for small and medium-sized employers. These employers are not likely to offer such benefits because they cannot afford to do so and probably have too few eligible employees to make it an economical approach in any case. Thus a large part of the work force would be excluded if public policy should rely solely or heavily upon employers.

I&R services and even modest financial aid are helpful to those who receive them, but ultimately, employee-parents must confront the reality of a limited supply of good-quality care at a price they can afford. Something more is needed, no matter who the employer is.

Finally, we should not lose sight of the fact that, ultimately, practically all employer subsidies are in significant part publicly subsidized, through tax benefits to the employer and to the employee-parent receiving the benefit. Thus, ultimately, the larger benefits accrue to the better off workers, but the costs are borne by all of us and the impact on the child care service supply is still very modest. We shall return to this issue later.

Employee-Counseling Services

By far the most extensively developed direct service at the workplace is the provision of information, advice, and referral to other resources for help with regard to workplace problems and/or personal and familial problems that may or may not have direct impact on the individual employee's job. These services are generally described as either employee-counseling programs (ECPs) or employee assistance programs (EAPs).

Some employers have established such programs, arguing that business has an obligation to respond to the needs of individual employees and that a counseling program can help workers solve personal problems that may affect job performance. Some employers view counseling programs as meeting their responsibility to their locality or community at a time the private sector is under increasing pressure to fill the gaps left by cutbacks in federal social service funds. Many of these employers would argue, too, that a counseling program can be a valuable tool with which a company can adjust to the changing composition and expectations of its work force. Regardless, for most employers, the value of such a program lies in its potential for reducing the costs of employees' personal problems to them: absenteeism, lateness, excessive medical claims, turnover, accidents, security breaches, damage to equipment, and so forth.[30]

Here, too, there were some predecessor programs during the late nineteenth century. Some modern program activity began as early as 1917 when Northern States Power Company in Minnesota hired a social worker to counsel its employees. Department stores like Macy's in New York and unions like the National Maritime Union had programs in the 1940s. A small number of worksite alcoholism programs were established during the 1940s, 1950s, and 1960s. However, the major modern expansion has occured since 1970 as a consequence of the creation of a federal government agency, the National Institute of Alcoholism and Alcohol Abuse (NIAAA) and the program of grants it established in 1970. The NIAAA Occupational Program Division charts an expansion from 499 grants with some types of occupational program in 1974 to 2,500 in 1977 and 5,000 in 1980.

The exact number of ECPs in industry is unknown, but clearly the number is growing. If the first growth spurt occurred in the early 1970s, when federal policies began to encourage the development of alcoholism programs, many observers are convinced that a second and larger development is occurring now, in response to the major changes that have occurred in the labor force and at the workplace.

In 1980 Donald Godwin, Chief of the Occupational Program Branch of the NIAAA, cited a study estimating there were more than 5,000 employee assistance programs covering approximately 10 million workers.[31] A more recent assessment reported 8,000 such programs.[32] The numbers, by themselves, reveal however, little of the diversity in the types of programs, services, staffing patterns, and problems dealt with or people served.

The overwhelming majority of programs were established after 1970. Those programs established in the early 1970s, or before, tend to be more narrowly focused, usually concentrating on problems of alcohol and drugs. More recently, "broad-brush" programs, dealing with a range of personal problems rather than directed specifically at alcohol and other substance abuse problems, have become the most popular model.

A 1981 survey of a random sample of 1,000 American Society of Personnel Administration members, which drew 504 responses, found that 110 companies had ECPs.[33] Ninety-four percent of these programs said they provided family and marital counseling and that this service was the second most frequently used service after alcoholism treatment. This seems to be a fairly typical pattern.

Services may be provided on site with staff hired by the company (internal programs), or employers may contract with social agencies or with private consultants (external programs). According to one private consultant, there are about 100 private consultants around the country now providing counseling services.[34] Internal programs may be housed in medical departments or in personnel departments. Most internal counseling programs are small and serve only a very small minority of a company's employees (5 to 10 percent). Even among employees who acknowledge they have personal problems, only a very small minority use ECPs. For the most part, employees who seek help are either referred by their supervisor or refer themselves, when, in the view of their supervisor or in their own view, a personal problem has interfered with work performance.

Although in many senses the EAPs with a focus on alcohol and substance abuse and the ECPs with a broad-brush approach are merely at opposite ends of a continuum, they do represent different philosophies, serve different populations, and constitute responses to different problems—or at least different definitions of the problem. The former is often thought of as an effective interventive strategy for employees who have specific problems that are interferring with their job performance and who cannot be reached in any other way. In contrast, the broad-brush programs are often less stigmatized and are described as serving a wider range of employees with more diffuse problems and as providing a wider and more nearly universal range of help. The broad-brush programs are the ones more likely to be included when employers list the new ways in which they are responding to problems of a changing labor force.

Thus for example, the "Where to Turn" program is an information, advice, and referral service provided by General Telephone (Everett, Washington) to employees and their immediate families. It is an internal program with counselors who are employees of the firm. As the brochure describing the service states.

Where to Turn is a "useful tool" that can provide assistance with the complex responsibilities involved with day to day living...

G.T.N.W. is dedicated to the idea that our most important resources are the individuals we employ. We do not want to lose any employee because a personal problem becomes unmanageable. Our Company realizes that none of us is immune to personal problems that can affect our physical and mental health, family situation or work performance. Through Where to Turn, G.T.N.W. can provide practical assistance to individuals with personal situations that may be difficult to manage alone.

Where to Turn is a referral and guidance service that provides assistance to all G.T.N.W. employees and immediate family members who are troubled by personal problems. The problem may be alcohol or drug related. It may be emotional stress, physical illness, legal, financial, family difficulties—or any combination of these.

The service is described as a confidential service, voluntary, free but referring to other services that may require payment that may be covered by company medical insurance, and not carrying any stigma regarding future career directions. For some sense of the distribution of problems for which employees come for help, see table 7.1.

Another illustration, this time of an external program, is the

Table 7.1. Where to Turn Contacts, 1982

	No.	Percent
Alcohol/Drug	42	6.6
Emotional	82	12.9
Marital	30	4.7
Family	48	7.5
Financial	38	6.0
Legal	52	8.2
Job frustration	115	18.0
Miscellaneous and general employment inquiries	109	17.1
Health	79	12.4
Supervisor consultations	42	6.6
Total for year	637	100.0

Source: Material provided by Employee Relations Administrator, G.T.E.N.W.

Xerox Employee Assistance Program (**XEAP**) operated nationally through a contract with the Family Service America (FSA). An employer of more than 60,000 people at many sites around the country, Xerox first signed a one-year contract with FSA in early 1980. This contract was the first such arrangement for providing employee-counseling services between a large national corporation and a national non-profit organization with a network of local agencies serving families. Within one year after the signing of the contract, 120 member FSA agencies had signed agreements with FSA to participate in the Xerox-FSA network.[35] Under the terms of the contract, Xerox pays for up to two diagnostic interviews and for 80 percent of the cost of up to eight outpatient sessions for alcohol- and other drug-related problems. At the end of the first year, about half the problems the agencies were dealing with were related to substance abuse; the other half were marital, family, and personal/emotional problems. Initially, most referrals came through managers and supervisors, but after efforts were made to inform employees about the service (for example, when a leaflet explaining the program was included in all employee pay envelopes), self-referrals increased very substantially.

A third illustration of an ECP or EAP, also an external program, is that of Tektron, a relatively small company, with a work force of about 600 employees.[36] Its employee-counseling program was established in 1983 for both part-time and full-time employees. At Tektron, a high-tech firm located in Silicon Valley, more than 60 percent of the work force are highly educated, skilled professionals. Senior management had become increasingly aware of the high proportion of marital and family problems experienced by personnel and decided to try to make it possible for employees to get help. They contracted with a private, confidential counseling service connected with a local hospital. In the first year that the service was available 9 percent of their employees used the service, an unusually high proportion for the first year of operation. Most of the requests for service were generated by employees themselves; very few were management or supervisor generated. There is equal participation by men and women and about 60 percent of those using the service were professional staff.

The benefit brochure for the company describes the service by stating: "Experienced professional counselors can assist employees in areas such as alcoholism, family counseling, drug abuse, financial, marital and legal problems." For the first year the breakdown in the allocation of presenting problems was:

sociologial, 30%
marital, 23%
family problems, 13%
alcohol, 10%
legal, 10%
vacation, 10%
drugs, 6%
financial, 6%
psychiatric, 3%

Although the classification scheme is not precise, and clearly there is category overlap, it is equally clear that family-related problems constitute more than one third of the presenting prob-

far more than twice the proportion concerned with substance abuse problems.[37]

Still another approach involves contracting with private counseling firms. Brownlee, Dolan, & Stein Association is a national firm based in New York City that provides employee-counseling service to a number of banks, insurance companies, publishing firms, and other businesses. Staff provide services to employees in the organizations with which they have contracted and charge the firm on a per capita fee-for-service basis. The firm recommends a broad-brush approach, accepting self-referrals, as well as those based on job performance. Services are provided on site where practicable, and telephone consultation is available as well.[38]

Some of the programs involve intervention and intensive treatment by on-site or off-site professional staff, confidential in regard to personal details but monitored for follow-through by supervisors concerned about an employee's disruptiveness or unreliability. Others merely offer a brief screening or counseling service, making referrals to a diversity of outside resources, which may, as appropriate, be paid for by health insurance, mental health coverage, or by the employee; or they turn for the service to the range of governmental and community voluntary social service programs.

In general, when asked who uses these services, most professionals in the field and many in management state flatly that only if there is a real commitment by the chief executive officer or other top staff are they used by both managerial and non-managerial staff. Otherwise, it is largely nonmanagement, nonexempt staff who use the services. For the most part, when a service is first established, early referrals tend to be low-level personnel, because they are more likely to be referred by their supervisors and to feel under pressure to go for help; middle management are likely to use the service only when it has achieved some acceptance in the firm generally. There is a difference of opinion about whether the services are used more by men or women, but the general agreements is that for the most part they are used more by nonmanagement personnel.

Most employers offering such internal or external services, including, for example, Illinois Bell, Oldsmobile, Navistar (International Harvester), Utah Power and Light, Steelcase, and AT&T, claim they are cost effective; they report substantial savings as a result of providing these services.[39] Navistar has reported that before entering their ECP, nearly 85 percent of the group were rated as poor or fair in work performance; after the program more than 67 percent were rated as good or excellent. Similarly, Illinois Bell reported that before using their program, 90 percent of program users were rated poor or fair in job performance; after the program, 66 percent were rated as good. Reductions in absenteeism, accidents, sickness, and disability benefits are reported by almost all these companies.[40]

Beech Aircraft completed a two-and-one-half year evaluation of its EAP and also found an overall success rate of 82 percent. In slightly more than four years, the program served 445 employees out of a work force of 6,200, or slightly less than 8 percent. In an examination of absenteeism one year before and one year after referral to the service, the study showed that employees who entered and completed treatment—or even entered the program and then dropped out—had an average of approximately one half day improvement per week in attendance.[41] However, no effort was made to account for any other variables that may have affected attendance.

Precise data on costs and effects do not exist, however, nor do rigorous and systematic evaluations. The cost effectiveness and cost benefit of ECPs are less evident than many company reports would indicate. According to one analysis of four company evaluations of the cost/benefits of their ECPs, one company saved $1,240 for each employee in the year after using its service; another saved about $23 per employee. In contrast, the other two programs increased the costs of these employees: in one program, the cost per employee increased by $71 and in the other the cost increased by $526 per employee! Further, in all four companies, absenteeism was the largest cost to the companies, followed by sickness and accident benefits and workers' compensation. In this study, however, the program showing a $71 increase per client did not have records on absenteeism.

Of some interest, of the 11 programs described in one report only 1 had carried out an actual evaluation study. A second expected to, and a third, in the guise of an evaluation study, merely surveyed employees who had used the service concerning their satisfaction with it.

Summary: Trends and Issues. One employee service that expanded significantly over the last decade and one half is the service variously described as an employee assistance program (EAP) or an employee-counseling program (ECP). Developed initally to deal with alcohol problems of employees that were interfering with job performance, these programs got their first big incentive for development in the early 1970s, when federal alcoholism legislation provided a subsidy for employers to establish such services. Although the growth spurt declined somewhat once the major subsidy was removed, a significant number of firms found the concept useful and the service inexpensive yet sufficiently effective to warrant continuity of support. Many went from alcohol and drug abuse programs to broad-brush offerings. Many employers hope that the availability of these services may lead to reduced use of medical services and, therefore, ultimately, to a reduction in the costs of their health insurance benefits. They are also motivated by concern for work force reliability, stability, and performance. In any case, the numbers of such services have continued to grow, even if at a much slower pace than earlier.

Of some interest, those writing about how employers can become more responsive to the personal and family needs of a changed labor force always include a discussion of different types of counseling services. In contrast, those reviewing employees' wish lists and responses to preference surveys concerning what they would like employers to provide never seem to include these services.[42] One issue may be that these programs are very diverse, some stressing help with alcohol and drug—or substance abuse—problems; some stressing personal, marital, and family counseling; and some stressing response to a broad range of problems. The reality is, however, that where employers are concerned, these programs are established with the specific intention of reducing work-related problems and improving productivity. Only a very few pay attention to the problems employees may have in balancing home and family, on the one hand, and work and job responsibilities, on the other. Furthermore, no employer among those we interviewed even suggested that these services were established for this purpose, nor were they expected to help the typical employee with work and family problems except under circumstances of serious difficulty or in a crisis. These services may be important as alternatives to certain social services in the community, or they may be important as linkages between workers and existing community resources, and they may be an important source of help at the time of a crisis, but as they are now designed and operating, they are not an important component of any package of employer responses to employee needs growing out of the changing demography of the work force.[43]

Worthy of mention is the fact that two *new* types of counseling services are beginning to be developed in a few companies: one is preretirement counseling, a service that many employers suggest will be expanding as the work force ages; a second is relocation counseling, in particular as two-earner families come to dominate the work force even more and as the problems of dealing with a management request for an employee to transfer, or an opportunity for a promotion that requires a transfer, are assessed from different perspectives.

This chapter has dealt with the employees' personal problems, especially those at the interface of jobs and personal family lives or those that impact on job performance, and sometimes with the problems of family members. We turn now to an examination of how employers are responding to the specific problem their employees have in managing personal and family *time* while coping with job responsibilities.

8. New Needs, New Responses: Time Off and Flexibility

"The number one benefit of value in the future for the full-time work force is released time—both paid and unpaid," according to one employee benefits expert.[1] "Next to released time in perceived value are flexible work schedules and a choice of benefits and benefit levels from among a very large benefits pool," he continues.

Changes in family structure and composition and changes in the work force are making time off and flexible work schedules essential for workers trying to manage home and job simultaneously. Despite time-saving household equipment and a large growth in personal and consumer services, there is still no way to manage a household without spending some time at it. And many of the services used to help manage home and family responsibilities are still open only during standard working hours. Flexitime and other alternative work schedules offer one approach to managing by permitting a reallocation of work time to facilitate carrying out personal and family tasks (see below). Here we focus on the essential component of *additional time off, both paid and unpaid.*

Paid Time Off

Vacations and Holidays. In chapter 2 we described the status of paid vacations in the United States today and pointed out that although the 1970s saw a dramatic increase in the availability and length of paid vacations, at best, the standard vacation is two weeks, far less than most European workers receive, and a substantial part of the work force still does not even have that much.

Longer vacations would clearly make a difference to employees with young children. Typical European vacations, lasting five or six weeks, combined with standard European school years that last several weeks longer than in the United States, obviously reduce or eliminate working parents' child care and child supervision problems.

Although employees typically receive ten paid holidays a year, about one day more on average than a decade ago, workers in the retail servics and in the food and restaurant industry do not necessarily benefit; holidays and Sundays are often workdays in these industries. Many other workers keep factories and services operating while others have holidays. On the other hand, some large companies now close the Friday after Thanksgiving, and a few close for the week between Christmas and New Years. Employees in these firms comment repeatedly and enthusiastically about how important this policy is for those with children and other family responsibilities.

In what follows we look at some other developments concerning time off.

Personal Days. In contrast to such specified days off as days off because of a death in the family, marriage, jury duty, medical appointments, and so forth, the kind of personal day off that employees say they need and want is something the Conference Board labels a "personal float"—a day off with pay, chosen by each employee to meet personal needs and preferences. In most companies that provide such personal days, however, management controls the overall scheduling of the days.

There are no national data on paid or unpaid personal days, in particular, days that can be taken off on an as-needed basis without advance planning and notice. The BLS survey reports that in the companies providing personal leave days, the average number permitted is 3.7; more important, however, only one fourth of the employees have such a benefit.[2] The Conference Board reports that about 40 percent of the employers in their survey of large companies provide one or two floating personal days and that this practice is more likely to be in effect for office workers.

Although such paid personal days are a growing policy in many large firms, most employees view them as additional paid holidays, but not as responsive to what employees say they really need: days that can be taken off when there is a personal or family emergency or when something important comes up—a day off that may *not* be able to be planned for in advance. In one large company that prides itself on its excellent benefits, large numbers of interviewed employees complained to us that personal days had to be requested weeks in advance, and although helpful for activities that could be planned ahead, did not meet employees' true "personal" needs. Thus, for example, a supervisor explained that although she knew some of her staff called in sick when a child was ill, they had no alternative; they could not use their personal days for reasons of family illness, because they had to request personal days in writing, several weeks in advance.

Flexible Time Off. One particularly innovative time-off policy was developed at a small electronics systems company located in Silicon Valley. The policy has since spread to several other companies in the area, including Hewlett-Packard. "Paid Personal Time Off" (PPTO) as the benefit is called, is an innovative concept that allows each individual employee to personally manage *all* of his or her time off from the job. How an employee uses this time off—short absences for minor illness, staying home with a sick child, personal business, vacation, medical appointments—is up to the employee. Although where possible employees are expected to give notice of use, an employee can decide at the last moment to take time off and that is acceptable.

A full-time employee receives three full weeks or 120 hours of PPTO annually. After two years of full-time work with the company, an employee accrues an additional bonus day of PPTO for each year of service beyond the first two. This amounts to one extra week after seven years of employment; part-time employees accrue time at half the rate of full-timers. The time can be taken off as individual days or all in one lump.

The program was designed specifically for flexible short-term use; the company has a short-term disability insurance plan for illnesses lasting more than one week. Before the PPTO plan was instituted, a new employee would have two weeks of paid vacation each year and two weeks of paid sick leave. Employees were not permitted to accumulate either vacation time or sick leave. Management discovered that at the end of each year there would be very heavy absenteeism, even among their highly skilled professional staff. Employees who had not needed to use their sick leave days for illness and could not accrue them in case of future illness viewed these as a wasted benefit. As a result, a significant number decided to use their sick leave for personal reasons. Furthermore, in reviewing patterns of use, it was discovered that supervisors and managers adminisered the sick leave policy in very different ways. Some would be very harsh with regard to any laxness or potential abuse in the use of paid sick leave while others were very relaxed and almost implicitly encouraged its use. Some permitted employees to use their own sick leave for family illness and others refused to. In the course of an employee survey concerning benefits and employment policies generally, management learned how angry employees were about the policy and how much resentment existed as a consequence.

Management decided to explore doing something different and examined a variety of policy options used in other companies, including permitting employees to accrue sickness benefits, cashing out unused sick leave, receiving a bonus for not using sick leave, and so forth. Rejecting all these options for a variety of reasons, management decided to invent a "flexible time off" benefit. Initially, it was very controversial and professional employees objected to it particularly strongly. However, since it became operational, it has been viewed as a great success and has been copied by several other firms. In effect, personal leave, vacations, and sick leave have been integrated into one paid leave package of three weeks (for new employees), and employees can use the time as they wish: for vacation, personal illness, family illness, or personal time.

However, paid time off for childbirth is treated strictly as a disability because of the direction the law has taken (see chapter 2). The best that a female employee can expect is the very good short-term disability insurance coverage the firm provides. Women employees can be assured of full job protection only while out on a disability leave. Other than that, there is no right to a job-protected unpaid leave, nor can they add on leave from their PPTO benefit. Of course, as in many firms, there is a discretionary policy whereby particularly desirable employees who want to take supplementary time off may be permitted to do so and will have their jobs saved for them. But for the most part, any woman who is out on maternity disability leave and wants to return to her job at the firm comes back at the end of her disability leave.

This company provides one more indication of how important disability insurance is to women at the time of childbirth, even when a company has a good paid leave plan policy. As we discussed in chapter 2, only when employers provide such benefits do working women really have income protection at the time of childbirth and right after. Where states have legislated short-term or temporary disability insurance, working women have at least a minimum of protection. But for the majority of working women even modest protection is not available. Paid sick leave, even though available more widely than disability benefits, is still not available to all workers and rarely provides more than an absolute minimum of coverage, perhaps enough to cover the time a woman is in the hospital, but certainly not enough to cover a normal period of convalescence. No new benefit innovations have emerged. Thus, maternity—or maternity disability—coverage is very limited at best and often totally unavailable, and paid parenting benefits are nonexistent.

Time off to care for an ill child exists, but only in a handful of companies. Thus, for example, Levi Strauss allows its employees to use their own paid sick leave, as necessary, to care for an ill child at home. Few other employers even permit this as an explicit policy, and none as yet supplements the worker's own sickness benefits by adding on a special additional benefit for sick child care.

Unpaid Time Off

Maternity Disability, Parental and Child Care Leaves. A major accomplishment of the 1970s was that almost all working women are now entitled to at least an unpaid but job-protected leave at the time of maternity. Most of the companies with such policies in place instituted them during the 1970s. Yet there are still some women who do not have such a right. Seventy-two percent of employers in a 1981 national survey indicated that such job-protected leaves are provided and that employees on leave are guaranteed the same or a comparable job on return.[3] Large firms and banking-financial-insurance companies are most likely to provide such leaves and are the most generous in the extensiveness of the leaves. In contrast, small employers and firms in the retail trade and service industries are least likely to provide leaves, or if permitting a leave, to guarantee the job on return.

Policies vary, as well, with regard to when the leave can begin, how long it can last, and what qualifies an employee for such a leave. Almost half the respondents in our 1981 survey report a flexible policy in which the commencement of the leave depends on the woman, her particular job, her medical condition, and her own preference. Another 25 percent of the employers specify four to six weeks before expected childbirth as the time that a leave could begin. A woman may not be required to take a prechildbirth leave unless medically shown to be unable to do her job without endangering her own health or that of the unborn child.

Of those who grant a postchildbirth unpaid leave, few employers responding to the 1981 survey permit more than a six-month maternity leave overall, including the period of disability following childbirth; considerably more than half limit the leave to three months or less; and two to three months is the most common practice. Only 8 percent permit longer than six months. In practice, this seems to mean that women in firms providing a paid disability leave at the time of maternity will be able to take another three to four months off, *maximum*, and usually only about one month if their jobs are to be kept for them.

Many legal experts today are convinced that while establishing a special maternity leave would be against the law, as being discriminatory, a special parental or child care—or personal —leave is not. Thus far, regardless of the label, although some childbirth-related leaves exist, they are clearly of brief duration. In contrast, the pattern in much of Europe is one in which working women, and often working parents, are permitted at least a year of unpaid, job-protected leave, in addition to a statutory paid leave, considerably longer than what is provided in the United States.[4]

A United States Supreme Court decision in 1987 (*California Savings and Loan Association v. Guerra*, No. 85-494) ruled that states may require employers to grant special job protection to employees who are physically unable to work because of pregnancy and childbirth. The Court upheld a California law requiring employers to grant up to four months of unpaid leave to women disabled by pregnancy and childbirth even if similar leaves are not granted for other disabilities. The majority opinion took the position that the California law's preferential treatment of pregnant employees promotes equal opportunity because it allows women, as well as men, to have families without losing their jobs. The decision is likely to spur similar laws in other states. Efforts are now underway to pass federal legislation that would assure job protection at the time of maternity or other disability for at least two months and provide a supplementary parental leave for another four months. Opponents argue that it would be a new precedent if the federal government were thus to mandate conditions of employment (but they seem to ignore the minimum wage).

Summary and Trends. More time off and greater flexibility in using available paid time off is clearly of major importance to dual earner families and to single-parent families who often find themselves "time poor" as a consequence of carrying out both job and home tasks and responsibilities. "There never is enough time" is a constant refrain of working mothers. For employees in some industries such as retail trade, food stores, and restaurants, the conflict beteen family and work time is obvious and often intense and is a problem that is difficult to resolve. The managers and assistant managers of The Eatery and FoodStores who had family responsibilities all described it as a personal problem, in contrast to many of their employees, who chose part-time work schedules to conform to family responsibilities.

Incremental improvements such as longer vacations, the right to a full, job-protected parent leave, paid sick leaves to care for an ill child, and additional personal days constitute one model for some employers. An alternative that is still early in its development is for employers to give employees a large block of paid time off and let them use this time flexibly, whenever they wish, and even accumulate some of it if they prefer to save it up and use it for a longer leave. Still a third model that has been discussed but only now is being tried out is the inclusion of additional paid time off in a flexible benefit plan as one other benefit that workers can "buy" or "exchange" when packaging possible options in a cafeteria or flexible benefit plan (see below). We encountered one company whose operation could manage nicely if mothers were permitted extra-long unpaid summer vacations. Those who could afford to do so took advantage of the opportunity. Instead of additional time off, a fourth model involves a different approach to scheduling work.

Alternative Work Schedules

Conventional work scheduling became the rule at a time when family responsibilities were generally divided along traditional lines; however, such scheduling obviously places great strains on those families in which both parents are in the labor force or in which there is only one parent and that parent is working. Initiatives to enhance the flexibility of work scheduling and make it more compatible with the diverse family lives of workers are high on the list of recommendations of those seeking greater responsiveness of employers and the workplace to the new needs of today's work force. Here we review a range of developments, reporting on the existing evidence of scope and impact of some of the most important among them: flexitime, permanent part-time work, and a variant of it—job sharing. As will be apparent, the lack of much systematic analysis of these developments underscores their relative novelty, even if some experts are convinced that they constitute the beginning of a "new show."[5]

Of some interest as well is the fact that scheduling innovation is not necessarily all altruistic. As already seen in chapters 5 and 6, it is essential to the needs of many businesses, particularly in consumer- and business-related services. One wants heavy staffing only during the hours of greatest consumer activity. Sometimes, even if a bit inefficient in a formal sense, flexibility may pay off in morale, employee response, and as a recruitment attraction. Some experts, looking ahead, argue that new concepts of industrial production will also require greater work-time flexibility (see below).

Flexitime. Essentially, flexitime is work scheduling that permits employees some discretion in determining arrival and departure times. Although the total number of hours in the work week (or month, sometimes) generally remains fixed at the standard full-time level, employees are not locked into a nine-to-five routine.

Although most employees—and to a lesser extent, employers —like the general idea of flexitime, they may not always be talking about the same thing. In actual practice this label refers to a variety of scheduling innovations, incorporating quite different levels of flexibility.[6] Most plans allow daily variation in starting and stopping time, but they differ in their requirements for advanced notice of change. Also, to ensure necessary communication among workers, most require that all employees be present during a specified core period. Each program makes its own determination concerning core period "band width" (number of hours between the earliest starting time and the latest finishing time), and flexible hours (number of hours within which choices about starting and stopping may be made). Some plans allow workers to carry forward a surplus or deficit of hours as long as they work a full week, and a few even allow this banking of hours across weeks. The different forms of flexitime, from the least to the most flexible, include the following:[7]

- Flexitour. Employees choose a starting and ending time, remain with that schedule for a period of time, and work eight hours a day.
- Gliding time. Employees may vary their starting and ending times daily, but they still must work an eight-hour day or however long the company workday is.
- Variable day. Employees can vary the number of hours they work each day as long as they work the weekly required number of hours each week.

- Maxiflex. Employees may vary their daily hours as they wish and are not required to be present for any core period.

Despite the diversity of these plans, the common element is that they give the worker some control over working time that had previously been held by management.

Thus, for example, some companies, such as the Equitable Life Assurance Society, have a number of flexible work schedules in effect. These are available at a manager's discretion, depending on the employee's job and the size of the work unit. Certain features like a "flex" day option are so popular with employees that units that have instituted such a policy are in great demand, and one employee is said to have refused a promotion into another department rather than lose that option.

About 13 million workers, almost 14 percent of all nonfarm wage and salary workers in May 1985, were on flexitime or other schedules that permitted them to vary the time their workdays began and ended. The percentage is about the same for working parents as for employees generally. When we look at full-time workers only, however, the option was more common for fathers than for mothers (13 versus 11 percent), and of particular importance, still more common for fathers of preschool-age children than for mothers of very young children (13 versus 10 percent—table 8.1).[8]

There are also indeterminate numbers of workers on de facto flexitime: managers, many professionals, and the self-employed, as well as many office workers whose bosses wink at informal arrangements rather than force an issue with an employee or go to the trouble of instituting a formal program.[9]

Flexitime first appeared at a West German plant in 1967 and was introduced in the United States by Control Data Corporation in 1972. The German managers who developed and introduced the policy appeared, however, to be motivated primarily by a desire to reduce traffic congestion rather than to accommodate the workers' family responsibilities. Given the relatively brief experience with flexitime, it is perhaps surprising that its use spread as quickly as it did in the 1970s. Between 1974 and 1980, the level of usage doubled, and clearly, it is continuing to increase if only moderately now.[10] Flexitime generally continues to be

Table 8.1. Percentage of All Wage and Salary Workers and All
Full-Time Workers Who Had Flexitime in May, 1985, By Sex,
Presence and Age of Children

Presence and Age of Children	Men		Women	
	All Workers	Full-Time Workers only	All Workers	Full-Time Workers only
Total	13.9	13.1	13.2	11.3
No children under 18	14.4	13.2	13.2	11.6
With children under 18	13.1	13.0	13.3	10.8
With children aged 6-17	13.4	13.3	13.4	11.0
With children under age 6	12.8	12.6	13.1	10.4

Source: Bureau of Labor Statistics, unpublished data provided by Earl F. Mellor.

more widely used in Europe than in the United States. Current estimates in Germany are that 50 percent of all employees are on flexitime. In Switzerland and several other northern European countries, the proportion is about 40 percent.

Flexitime has been adopted in a wide range of work settings. Some nationwide assessments suggest only modest variations in adoption rates based on industry type, sector, and firm size. However, these conclusions must be viewed with considerable caution because of the small size of the sample studied, as well as its unrepresentative industrial distribution.[11] Organizations with flexitime programs seem more likely to be offices (especially banking and insurance companies) than factories, service producers rather than goods producers. It is not that flexitime is incompatible with mass-production technology, but only that it is more complicated to institute and has been tried less frequently. Among the companies that have established flexitime policies are J. C. Penney, half of whose white-collar workers chose flexitime when first given the option in 1977; Hewlett-Packard; IBM;

Prudential Insurance; and TRW. Innumerable other companies have implemented flexitime in all or part of their operations.

The willingness of some employers to make the necessary adaptations is undoubtedly spurred by a widespread perception that flexitime has the direct economic benefit of enhancing productivity, as well as the indirect benefit of improving employee morale—all for a relatively slight expenditure of managerial energy and direct costs. Many of the studies evaluating the impact of flexitime, it is true, rely on rather soft data, such as unvalidated managerial and employee reports on productivity impacts, and worker opinion polls; nevertheless, in a number of different types of work settings, flexitime is reported consistently as reducing tardiness, absenteeism, sick leave, and overtime.[12] Furthermore, in the general absence of any negative consequences, the consistent finding of employee appreciation for flexitime creates an added impetus for its adoption. Even though the studies on which these conclusions are based were generally unsophisticated in design, the overwhelming evidence suggests the potential values of wider adoption.

In contrast to these workplace-related rationales for employers to introduce a flexitime policy, it is also appealing to a much wider constituency because it is supposed to improve family life. Any number of proponents have advocated flexitime as a way to help workers mesh their work and home lives.[13] Among the potential benefits described are the following: parents can coordinate their work schedules more closely with available child care arrangements or the school day, and others may come home at an earlier time to enjoy some recreational activity with family members or to prepare a family meal. Perhaps because the benefits are assumed so readily to be present, there is hardly any systematic analysis of how flexitime actually affects family life.

In one of the very few rigorous U.S. studies of the impact of flexitime on family life, the participants were office workers in two large federal agencies.[14] In both agencies the workers on flexitime spent more time in the evenings with their families than they had before its adoption. However, the fact that even the more flexible of the plans allowed a band width of only two hours greater than the standard day limited any increase in family time.

The time allotted to family activities among those working on flexitime in this agency increased from about three hours to four-and-a-quarter hours. In addition, the participants on flexitime reported less difficulty in a number of specific aspects of family life, including spending time with their spouses during the week; seeing friends during the week; pursuing education, recreation, and hobbies; and having relaxed evenings.

In contrast, another study of flexitime among a different group of federal employees is notably less supportive of its benefits for family life.[15] This study compared the family experiences of employees in two matched federal agencies—one on standard time and one on flexitime. They found no differences in time spent on home chores and child rearing, no difference in the equity in the division of family responsibilities between parents, and only very minor differences in scores on an index of stress.

Despite these limitations, employees in firms with flexitime in place are extraordinarily enthusiastic about it. Innumerable working mothers in companies with flexitime in place described it to us as: a "lifesaver," "the only thing that has made it possible to manage," "without it I would have had to quit and take a job nearer home." There were many other very positive comments. Women, in particular, seemed enthusiastic about flexitime, not because it permitted *more* time to be with family, but because it permitted better allocation of time.

As described in chapters 3 and 4, employees who have the right to flex their work schedules often do so to make it possible to drop children off at a child care facility or school and to pick them up or to share responsibilities with their spouses. Coming in to work an hour later may mean the difference between depending on someone else to take the children to school—or being constantly harrassed and often late—and managing by oneself, without stress. Similarly, beginning early, perhaps because a spouse can take the child to school, and quitting an hour and a half earlier may mean being able to pick up one's child at school and therefore managing without an after-school child care program.

In one company, flexitime covers the range of hours between 6:00 A.M. and 6:00 P.M., around a core time of 8:30 A.M. to 3:30 P.M., and the hours can be changed daily. However, the usual pattern is for employees to pick a schedule that fits their needs and keep to it, with only very minor modifications. "The benefit of flexitime," as one worker whose company established the policy two years ago said, "is that now I can organize my workday to mesh with the more rigid time demands of children, school, and my husband's job." Or, as another worker said, "Flexitime makes it possible for my wife and me to share delivering and picking up our child at his preschool. Before, either my wife did both, or she asked a friend to take the boy. But it was a hassle until flexitime made it possible for us to manage ourselves."

Despite these enthusiasms, the research literature on the family effects of flexitime is extremely limited and hardly conclusive. The extent to which flexitime affects various aspects of the family lives of different kinds of workers in diverse settings is simply unknown. The lack of knowledge is particularly pronounced with regard to the impact of flexitime on the social-psychological aspects of family life. Thus, Stanley Nollen's cautionary note seems well worth heeding:

Realistically, flexitime is a fairly minor alteration of the work environment and not that potent in the face of ingrained family practices. Unless both parents have liberal flexitime programs and are ready to alter family roles as well as work hours, the kids will still be mother's responsibility and child care will still be needed.[16]

Flexitime is a simple device. It is neither difficult to establish nor costly. Certainly, it does not create extra time for family and home life. However, what it does do is permit employees to rearrange their work hours to fit better with their personal and familial needs. As modest as this is, it can be very helpful and important to employees, in particular those with children. Although researchers, policymakers, and families themselves should not expect flexitime to be a panacea for the conflicts between work and home life, since gains through it in quality of family life will likely be modest, it is no less worth promoting for that reason.

Part-Time Employment. Part-time employment is an umbrella term that includes all work less than full time. Full-time work is defined in U.S. Department of Labor statistics as 35 hours or more per week, so part-time could mean anything between 1 and 34 hours![17] Countries differ in this definition; therefore, comparisons must be made with caution.

About 20 percent of the labor force worked part time in 1985; of these, 14 percent did so out of choice and 6 percent did so involuntarily. One labor economist, Audrey Freedman of the Conference Board, has suggested the term "contingent workers," defined to include both these part-timers as well as almost 800,000 temporary workers, and added numbers of self-employed. The total could be close to 30 million in a labor force of 110 million.[18]

We cited voluntary part-time work in both The Eatery and FoodStores in chapter 3 and in our two chapter 5 community studies. The pattern met employee preferences and family needs in many instances. It was not, however, all voluntary, and many so-called part-timers at FoodStores were allowed to work almost full time but not quite enough to gain the status, the salaries, and the benefits that go with a 40-hour week. On the other hand, FoodStores had prorated (or better) fringe benefits for part-timers, something missing in most places.

Although for both men and women full-time employment is the predominant pattern, women are twice as likely as men to be working part time. Women accounted for 70 percent of all those working part time involuntarily but only 40 percent of all those on full-time schedules in 1982. Furthermore, although about half of all men working part time do so voluntarily, three quarters of the women working part time do so by choice. Among married workers, the gender difference is dramatic: only 3 percent of married men but 24 percent of married women work part time; in contrast, where single adults are concerned, about the same proportion of men and women work part time.

One major factor leading to the growth in part-time jobs has been the long-term shift in the pattern of job growth from the goods-producing industries to the service industries. Four service industries in particular have contributed especially to the growth in part-time jobs—retail trade, health care (including hospitals), business services, and personal services (including hair salons, dry cleaners). There are economic advantages for labor-intensive business to stagger the work force in accord with consumer patterns. Indeed, the strongest growth has occurred in retail trade and in personal services—the leading sources of part-time jobs for women. Almost two thirds of all women on voluntary part-time schedules are in white-collar occupations—clerical and sales jobs—while only about 40 percent of men are in such jobs. Finally, most part-time jobs are nonmanagerial and nonprofessional.

Until the early 1970s, most of the actual growth in part-time employment had been among persons working part time by choice. However, since then, the numbers of those working part time involuntarily, because they cannot obtain full-time jobs and have no alternative, have grown more rapidly. In the 1981-1982 recession, the number of involuntary part-timers rose to an all-time high of more than 6 million. Of some interest, only the Scandinavian countries have a larger proportion of part-time workers than the United States, and this group is even more heavily female than in this country.

In short, according to one BLS expert, the picture of the part-time worker in the United States today is *"Committed, Reliable, Flexible, Largely Female, White Collar, Retail Trade and Service Concentrated, Underpaid."*[19]

Many employees have indicated that part-time work with full-time benefits would contribute a great deal to alleviating work/family stress.[20] At present, however, most employers still do not provide prorated benefits for their part-time employees, let alone full benefits. Particularly when there is no second earner with health coverage, the benefit deprivation cools the attraction of scheduling flexibility, even if it is possible to tolerate the limited earnings.

Some working women have suggested that they would like to work part time for some time when returning to work after childbirth. Some fathers have indicated they would like part-time work to be available to them, too, at this time. Swedish legislation guarantees employees (male and female) the right to work a 30-hour week until their child is age eight. There are no data on the numbers and types of U.S. employers who permit a phased return to work for mothers after childbirth. Fathers do not, of course, have such rights.

Although permanent part-time work is now frequently advocated as a way to help individuals, especially women, to reconcile work and family responsibilities, there is, of course, little that is novel or rare about part-time work per se. What is new, though perhaps not readily definable, is an expanded concept of permanent part-time work, connoting some kind of career relatedness with potential for upward mobility.[21] The notion is that an option of a career-type part-time job would appeal to a young mother who wants to spend more time in child care and child rearing than a full-time job permits but who also wants some income and does not want to withdraw totally from the labor market.

There is little evidence, thus far, that many employers have responded in this way. The scale of demand also is unknown. With regard to the concept of part-time permanency, it is relevant to note that in recent years only slightly more than one third of all part-time workers have worked all year, and this is about the same percentage that has prevailed for more than a decade.

As previously suggested, part-time workers generally remain excluded from managerial and professional ranks. Only about 10 percent of all managers and professionals work part time on a voluntary basis (most in the latter category hold jobs without administrative responsibilities). The percentage of managers in part-time positions has remained essentially unchanged since the 1960s, while the percentage of professionals and technical and kindred workers has grown slightly since that time.[22]

Besides the poor pay, which also characterizes most permanent part-time work, even the privileged part-time jobs frequently do not have the benefits package that most people consider essential. Since most benefits surveys pay little attention to coverage of part-timers, precise data are not available. Nevertheless, two surveys of mostly large private enterprises suggest that permanent part-time workers are only about half as likely as their full-time counterparts to receive such key benefits as health insurance, sick pay, and life insurance. They fare slightly better in pension benefits and are most likely to be eligible for a prorated paid vacation.[23]

Employer worries about an expanding part-time work force appear to coalesce around the issue of fringe benefits. The concern stems from the following: social security and unemployment compensation may cost proportionately more for part-timers; health insurance is not readily prorated, although most other benefits are; and the Employee Retirement Income Security Act of 1974 (ERISA) regulations relating to pensions create proportionately higher administrative costs for part-timers. However, with fairly minor changes in policy, firms can institute fringe benefit packages for part-timers that are both considerably more equitable than existing packages and only proportionately costly.[24]

We would emphasize here that, obviously, part-time work is unlikely to provide a solution for single-parent working families, which need the income from a full-time job. Furthermore, on the basis of limited availability, experience, and data, the extent to which a part-time employment policy could attract two-parent working families willing to trade some income for more time at home remains to be seen. What many working parents, especially mothers, do seem to want is the opportunity to work part time for a while, if they wish it. Thus, either as a transitional experience after childbirth, or while children are very young, some parents might choose this work style, if it were available and if they were not to lose basic benefits, at the very least, and for some, if they were not to lose too much with regard to career development. This interest hardly appears unreasonable and the objective need not be unattainable.

As we saw in our discussion of FoodStores and Northeast-Banks, the preference for part-time work varies enormously even among those workers usually viewed as most interested—mothers of young children. Some working women talked enthusiastically about such jobs; others, in the same company, wanted full-time jobs and resented being limited to part-time work. Some, even among the very fortunate few who had part-time jobs and full-time benefits—those in NortheastBanks—appreciated their special situation, while others in the very same situation were convinced that they were exploited and paid very low salaries to compensate for the benefit privilege. Clearly, what is wanted is choice and flexibility, in particular at certain times and life cycle stages.

According to one labor economist, current trends regarding part-time work suggest that

there is going to be continued pressure to treat part-time workers like other human beings in the work force, to provide legal protection that other workers have, to provide the kind of job security that other workers have, to try to provide the kind of fringe benefits that other workers have, and to provide the kind of self-actualization or professional development that other workers have.[25]

While not often recognized, what is now developing is a working hours continuum, replacing the old sharp dichotomy between full time and part time with some obviously part time jobs (16-20 hours), many that are defined arbitrarily (25-40 hours), and some clearly full time in the traditional sense. At the same time and as part of this process, there is a move to a shorter week generally. Already, in the service sector, this is a visible trend. Many full-time positions are now 30-32 hours a week. If the standard workday should eventually become a 6-hour day, and the standard workweek 30 hours, many of the problems now associated with a time crunch will be reduced. Some workers would still want to work even fewer hours, but for many, if not most, the time problem would be greatly relieved. Until such time, however, workers will need to seek out other solutions, and the issue of fringe benefits for part-timers, however defined, will remain.

Job Sharing. Various initiatives that may be gathered under the rubric of job sharing represent some of the more innovative attempts to accommodate the frequent desire for part-time careers. The term "job sharing" is usually used to mean "an arrangement whereby two employees hold a position together, whether they are as a team jointly responsible for the whole or separately for each half."[26] Shared jobs involve the restructuring of positions generally designated as full time for one person. For example, two teachers are jointly responsible for a fifth-grade class, one in the mornings, one in the afternoons; or two clerks together hold a position in a county medical office, with alternate days of work and some informal division of tasks so that they can concentrate on those that best fit their particular skills and interests. In effect, the job is full time, but the job holders are part-time.[27]

For many workers seeking a part-time commitment to work, the fact that the job sharer holds part of a full-time position is likely to be appealing. As noted above, most existing part-time jobs are low-status, low-paying jobs with very limited career prospects. By contrast, shared jobs, being sufficiently important to have previously warranted full-time workers, frequently could offer a level of responsibility and pay that surpasses the typical part-time job. (The full-time salary is split between the job sharers.) The job sharer can thus have a part-time *career*, although perhaps one with relatively limited prospects for advancement.

Although it is easy to imagine a widespread desire for such arrangements, particularly among parents who want time with their children, as well as some involvement in a career, very few workers actually share a job. Most discussions of job sharing in the literature are largely anecdotal or are case studies and small exploratory studies. The same stories recur. When one explores developments with employers, even among the most progressive, the numbers of job sharers found are few and far between. And the types of jobs that are shared in fact are usually low-level or at best mid-level jobs.

Teachers are the professionals who appear to have taken the lead in job sharing. Among other professionals who seem likely to participate in job sharing opportunities are counselors, social workers, and psychologists. Although there is little evidence of job sharing among either high-income workers (management and the elite professions) or blue-collar workers, a few individual cases do exist.

For the most part the major limited initiatives have occurred in public and voluntary, not-for-profit organizations. Private industry has clearly lagged in trying out job-sharing arrangements, and the relatively few instances seem to have been initiated on an

ad hoc basis. And as might be expected from the nature of the occupations involved in job sharing (and women's relative inclina-
tion to trade off income for more leisure), the overwhelming
number of job sharers are women.

While there are no systematic studies showing the effects of job
sharing on family life—any more than there are of part-time
jobs—the pioneers of job sharing generally tend to view it
favorably, claiming that it offers the opportunity to balance work
and family life sensibly and with far less tension than otherwise.
There obviously are no systematic studies showing the effects of
job sharing on productivity, but anecdotal reports suggest that
absenteeism and lateness may be reduced.

Relocation[28]

Although corporate relocation policies affect far fewer families
than some of what has been discussed, they may be critical to the
family lives of transferred workers, especially middle- and upper-
level managers. For some years, American corporations followed
the policy of transferring executives from location to location in
order to meet the perceived managerial needs of the company.
For transferred executives, the move from one community to
another obviously entails considerable costs — the direct costs of
moving a household, as well as the varied psychic costs that the
executives and their families may bear because of the disruption
in their lives.[29]

In recognition of the substantial direct costs, large corporations generally have instituted relocation policies that reimburse
the transferred executive for many of the expenses of the move.[30]
Since the mid-1960s, large corporations typically have picked up
such costs as shipping of household goods, trips for house hunt-
ing, and temporary living expenses at the new location. Also, with
the emergence of a highly inflated housing market and difficult
financing conditions, corporations have instituted a variety of
policies to ease the sale and purchase of a home.

Increasingly, however, executives' concerns for their families'
welfare have introduced new considerations into the design of
relocation policies. Many companies report greater difficulty in

convincing executives to move. Many executives appear to favor stability in their own and their families' lives over the promise of career advancement. Even more, this growing concern may reflect the increasing numbers of two-career families among the executive ranks.

One author expresses what seems to be a prevalent view in much of the personnel literature:

The two-salaried family, a growing fact in the United States, can make it difficult for organizations to recruit or transfer high-potential managers to new areas. A wife who moves automatically when the husband is transferred is a thing of the past. Numerous executives will not move because of family reasons, even though they receive substantial offers elsewhere.[31]

Whereas many human resource professionals have stressed the need for corporations to respond both to the psychic concerns of family members and to the career interests of spouses, the actual implementation of such responsive policies has not been common.[32] Moreover, a 1983 survey of a sample of leading companies suggests that even many human resource officers are still unrealistic in their understanding of the growth of two-career families, underestimating the actual numbers and inaccurately projecting little impact on corporate relocation policies.[33] A few companies offer workshops and counseling for executives and their families about the practical and emotional implications of making a move, but such policies are still in the vanguard. Among the few who have developed initiatives, most still focus on traditional one-earner families and not on dual-career families.[34]

In general, although many corporations report that acceptance of transfer is less critical to career advancement than it used to be, they show few signs of cutting back on their policy of transferring many executives and do little to attenuate the problems of a working spouse.

Flexible Benefits (Cafeteria Plans)

At the cutting edge of benefits plans today are the cafeteria-style flexible benefit plans.[35] Many observers, including staff at the U.S. Chamber of Commerce and the Conference Board, view these plans as the wave of the future, given the current trends in labor force composition. In chapter 4, we described one such plan in some detail. Here we discuss flexibility in benefit plans more broadly.

Although specific benefits vary among companies, almost all now design their benefits systems as if every employee were part of a one-worker family with spouse and children at home. Thus, a male worker may be given health insurance for himself and his dependents, even though his wife has equally good coverage from her employer for herself and her dependents. It is a system, then, that has not caught up with the reality of many two-earner families.

The employee benefits system also appears predicated on the assumption that all employees have similar needs and that these needs are largely the same through all stages of the life cycle. Yet plainly some workers would attach great value to, say, a paid parenting leave or paid child care service while postponing attention to retirement benefits, and they would be willing to forgo some of the latter for a while to ensure more generous provision of the former. By the same token, others would surely find child care and maternity-related benefits irrelevant and gladly forgo them for higher retirement payments or better health coverage. Indeed, in one company that offered a flexible plan, single mothers selected more vacation time, health and life insurance coverage, and lower pension coverage than the standard package provided.[36]

Nevertheless, advocates for such flexible systems continue to outnumber actual users by far. Despite much publicity, only a relatively small number of companies had instituted a cafeteria-like, flexible benefit system by the mid-1980s; beginning then, however, the approach seemed to take hold, especially in large companies.

In part, only when the concept of a flexible benefit plan was expanded to include what are known as flexible spending plans did the model finally begin to be adopted by many companies. Estimates in 1984 suggested that only about 100 firms had cafeteria-type, flexible benefit plans in effect while more than 1,000 had instituted salary reduction, flexible spending plans. The difference betweeen the two is explained below.

Cafeteria-type, flexible benefit plans are permitted by Section 125 of the Internal Revenue Code. The term "cafeteria" is used to describe a plan in which employees can choose from among a variety of different items in making up an individualized and personalized benefit plan, much as an individual might put together different food items in selecting the meal preferred. Cafeteria plans give employees the opportunity to put together a personalized benefit package by choosing the combination of available employee benefits that best suits their needs. Such plans must offer at least one taxable benefit (such as cash or vacation time) and at least one benefit that is designated by statute as being nontaxable (such as group term life insurance, coverage under an accident or health insurance plan, coverage under a qualified group legal services plan, educational assistance, or coverage under a dependent care assistance program).

In the cafeteria or flexible benefit plan, a core of usual benefits is provided (health insurance, pensions, disability insurance, life insurance), but the employer may offer employees choices within the core items, as well as certain additional options based on modifications in the basic benefits. The employee can choose among more or less generous benefits in each of several categories, by trading off among the possible choices, adding pretax dollars to pay for an additional supplement, or taking in cash the difference between a more expensive benefit and the cheaper one that is selected. Although there are a range of choices permitted in such plans, usually a specified minimum must be taken in any case, as a form of protection for the employee and for the employer. Not every benefit must be included in a cafeteria-style benefits plan; the plan may have some standard benefits with no options and others for which the employee has a choice.

A flexible spending plan, in contrast, involves the assignment of pretax dollars to an account administered by the employer, through which the employee may pay for a variety of benefits or services, particularly medical care and dependent care services. In its simplest and most common form, the employee is given a choice between a certain portion of his/her salary and one or more nontaxable benefits. In one illustration, an employee with a $20,000 salary could trade $1,000 of her salary for nontaxable dependent care services, meaning that she would be taxed as if she had only $19,000 of income. With the remaining $1,000. the employer might give her $1,000 worth of on-site child care services, or $1,000 worth of vouchers for certain child care services, or $1,000 of reimbursement for the worker's own child care provider—all depending on the type of dependent care assistance program that the employer has set up and is making available under the flexible spending plan.[37]

Frequently, the employer does not contribute at all, but the employee designates a portion of earnings to be placed in a flexible spending account and to be paid out by the employer, as instructed, for certain permitted purposes: health coverage premiums, dependent care fees, dental or vision coverage, other types of insurance, and so forth. There are regulations that affect the maximum amounts permitted and limit discrimination among classes of employees. The amount that the employee deposits for such purposes is not taxed as earnings. Unspent money may not be carried over or refunded to the employee.

In addition to "pure" salary reduction plans such as the one just described in which the plan depended totally on voluntary contributions from the employee, flexible spending plans may operate partially or entirely on the basis of funds that are contributed by the employer and not derived from voluntary reduction of salary by the employee. They may also allow the option of taking taxable cash in place of contributions to specific benefits.

Employees at New York's Chemical Bank received a total of $267,000 in tax-free reimbursement for dependent care, including child care, in 1983, through Chemical's Employee Spending Account (ESA), an innovative feature of the bank's new flexible benefits program effective since January 1, 1983. The dependent care option is described as a significant move by Chemical Bank to address the special needs of working parents. However, support of child care is only one very small part of what this plan offers. Of the 80,000 claims filed for ESA reimbursement in the program's first year, only 852 were for dependent care. The vast majority were for such benefits as noncovered medical expenses (eyeglasses, preventive medical care), deductibles, coinsurance, and so forth.

To fund this plan, Chemical Bank deposits an annual contribution of $300 into the ESA of each eligible employee (18,000 at the time). In addition, an employee may contribute additional pretax dollars either from a profit-sharing plan or, of particular importance, through a Salary Redirection Program, which allows eligible employees to contribute up to $5,000 of gross salary to an ESA through payroll deductions. The ESA acts as a supplement to the comprehensive benefits program the bank provides to employees, which covers the basic benefits such as group life insurance, accidental death, dependent life insurance, long-term disability, health insurance, HMOs, dental assistance, pensions, profit-sharing, and more. The ESA may be used to pay for the variety of out-of-pocket expenses not covered under this plan (such as deductibles and coinsurance), but especially important, it can cover services that are not provided in the plan, such as legal services, and all types of dependent care both for children and for the elderly or handicapped.

Chemical Bank is among those companies that explored the establishment of on-site child care service for employees but rejected it because it was viewed as too expensive, as well as a potentially discriminatory benefit (only a small minority of employees could benefit from it). Since the bank was concerned about benefits costs generally, as well as about responding to requests from some employees for different types of benefits, it brought in a well-known firm of benefits consultants to assess employee preferences and suggest an alternative plan. The flexible benefits plan, incorporating within it the ESA, is seen as an ideal solution by both management and employees.[38]

Chemical Bank's flexible benefits plan is described by management as flexible, simple to administer, easy for workers to understand, and tax effective. Although only a relatively small number of employees used their ESAs for child or dependent care, 65 percent of employees put some of their own money into an ESA.

Flexible benefits plans are attractive to employers because they can enhance employee satisfaction while at the same time introducing cost sharing; thus these plans are both cost effective and pleasing to employees, an ideal combination. Moreover, when a pure salary reduction plan is used, it costs the employer nothing (except modest administrative costs) and actually saves the employer social security and unemployment insurance taxes, which are not paid on the portion of salary that has been traded for nontaxable benefits. Employees benefit from these plans because they can select the benefits they need and, by paying certain of their expenses out of pretax dollars, reduce their income taxes. Since the employee is paying out of pretax dollars, the benefits/services purchased through the account cost the employee less than if they were purchased by him/her directly. Although this is most advantageous to taxpayers in the highest brackets (lower-paid workers may be better off using the dependent care tax credit for as much of their dependent care expenses as possible), most taxpayers can benefit to some extent. Workers can reduce their social security taxes through salary reduction, too, but this may result in reduced social security benefits in the future. Despite this, most analysts suggest that on balance the trade-off is advantageous.

In a late 1984 report the consultant firm Peat Marwick Mitchell noted that of 1,067 employers surveyed, 40 percent had implemented or were implementing a flexible benefits program and another 50 percent had it under consideration. Almost all these employers (91 percent) said that the motivation was to better address changing employee needs: "Benefit plans designed for an 'average' employee are not adequate to meet the needs of a work force comprised of 'nonaverage' people."

Of some interest, 83 percent of respondents to the Peat Marwick survey also reported that containment of benefit costs was a significant reason for moving toward flexible plans. It is in the nature of cafeteria plans and flexible spending accounts that employee understanding of benefits is enhanced, there is better targeting, and an element of increased cost sharing is introduced.[39] Specific data from Pepsico and American Can show significantly less increase in health care costs among the "flex" group during the medical inflation. We reported similar findings in chapter 4 from a Hi-tek evaluation.

The Peat Marwick survey also noted specific recruitment advantages to flexible plans, as reported by employers.

Given recent IRS rulings concerning both flexible benefits plans and flexible spending plans, and the enthusiasm with which benefits consulting firms have greeted these plans, it is likely that there will be significant increases in the numbers of companies with such plans within the next few years. The greatest applicability will be to health options suited to individual needs, dependent care, and choice among and with other benefits and between benefits and taxable cash, in a fashion suited to different income levels, varied family structures, and diverse circumstances. Tax legislation passed in mid-1986 will both limit the amount of money employees can put in a salary reduction plan (a constraint affecting only a small number of employees) and reduce the advantages of a tax-free benefit. Nonetheless, these still represent the most innovative and flexible approaches to benefit plan development that have emerged thus far.

Conclusion

Increasing time off is a high-priority goal for most workers. Yet little attention has been paid to any aspect of this issue in recent years. Vacations remain brief in the United States as compared with other Western industrialized countries. Flexitime, although useful and liked by employees generally where available, is too modest a policy to make a major difference in daily life, and still affects only a small minority of the work force. Paid parenting leaves are practically nonexistent; only a minority of working women qualify for full disability leaves at the time of childbirth. Unpaid leaves are more available, but parenting leaves with full job protection, for example, for six months after childbirth, are still very rare; at best, two months might be granted, and the issue of full job protection is still not resolved. Part-time work is growing; but many who now work part-time would prefer full-time jobs, while some who are not now working say they would work part-time if only those jobs were available. Most part-time jobs still provide only limited benefits at best, and little if any opportunity for advancement.

A few new developments seem to be particularly responsive to the diversity of the workforce and therefore to the value of employee choice and flexibility. These are benefits plans and employment policies and practices that stress the following flexibilities:

- Of work schedules
- Of benefits
- Of time off
- Of workplace

Presented here from the perspective of family concerns, some developments—particularly the use of part-time and temporary workers—are in fact based on employer interests. Indeed, there are those who argue that we have seen only a beginning. Choate and Linger see the future of American competitiveness as requiring *The High-Flex Society*.[40] The Organization for Economic Cooperation and Development, looking at all the leading industrial societies, states:

Flexibility of working time. Patterns of working time are also changing because of changes in the pattern of production. Industrial production has typically been accompanied by standard production methods, repetitive tasks, and highly structured man-machine relationships. The continued shift to services has already altered the work environment. And the growing importance in small-batch production in manufacturing, together with changes of work organization required for the effective application of new technologies, are reinforcing this tendency. Flexibility of work-time arrangements is needed to support this development. There is a case for public policy and collective bargaining practices to remove barriers which prevent enterprises and individuals from opting for flexible working-time schedules.[41]

Obviously, even if these predictions prove correct, they do not guarantee full and easy meshing of employer and employee interests in *particular* flexibilities, for particular individuals and locations. A complex process of change lies ahead. Who will be the main players? These are the questions for chapters 9 and 10.

9. What Shapes Developments?

We have described many kinds of companies. Some, discussed in chapter 3, may have high benefit costs but are limited to good provision within the traditional package and have not been fully responsive to the needs of many current employees and their families. Others, as chapter 4 illustrates, are leaders in innovation and responsiveness. Most are in between, sometimes trading off some benefits for flexibility, salaries for responsiveness, often doing some things that their employees find helpful but not others. Some companies deal more adequately with the requirements of some employees in some places than with others.

Sometimes (chapter 5), the enterprise does what it can afford, and that may mean some desirable things (flexibility) and some unattractive (poor salaries and benefits). Quite often, as seen in chapter 3 in particular but also in other parts of the discussion, the failures come not from an unwillingness to spend money, but from defects in implementation or administration. Most frequently, the issue is the benefits themselves and the company's benefits policy. These have not adapted to social change.

High-level participants in the very same company often perceive of the decision process involving benefit initiatives differently. In one instance, the top West Coast benefit person for a multinational firm had one version of what occurred and the top East Coast person had another. Each believed that his operation had set the company pattern.

To the West Coaster, ideas came from three sources: union bargaining initiatives, reports and surveys of trends among big companies, and leads generated personally out of experience and analyses by himself and his boss. They explored and tested all of this with peers, and then, when agreed, he and his boss took a package to the executive committee. In addition, the top management people sometimes added their own ideas.

The East Coaster said that the West Coast forgot where most of the workers were and exaggerated its importance. A series of corporate directors for compensation, benefits, training, equal opportunity, and employee relations in the enormous East Coast division report to the corporate vice president for employee relations. All the above-named directors have counterparts in the other major geographic divisions and at headquarters. There is much phoning, meeting, and consulting in the division, and ideas on which they agree move up to a management committee in the division. That committee, in turn, moves ideas to the corporate level and the CEO. Often people from different divisions discover shared interests and meet with their counterparts before making recommendations.

Central to initiatives and choices in this executive's view is the presence of a well-articulated corporate philosophy: the quality of experience of the company's consumers in this service industry is affected by the quality of employee experience. Therefore company leadership must seek constantly to enhance employee experience if the corporation is to be successful. Continuous employee opinion polling is now built in and regarded as essential. Indeed, it is carefully targeted polling because there is interest in continuity in some categories of employees and turnover in others.

A third observer in this company sees it all very differently. He stressed the large number of unions and the significance of collective bargaining in this company. He expressed astonishment that the other executives had downplayed this factor.

The financial limitations of marginal businesses apart, why do these differences in policy occur across companies and variations in explanation within them? What are the forces that shape these developments? What must be understood by those who would change things for the future? How does one learn from all this, if learning is needed to achieve greater responsiveness in the future?

An Ecology of Games

This is a field with many players, an ecology of complex and intertwined games. The variables that appear in the discussions in

earlier chapters are on on several different levels and refer to
several different aspects:

- Incentives or constraints in the economy and the labor market
  at a given time and the state of the specific industry
- Company and enterprise size and geographic location
- What company management decides it wants to do or not do
  (the social policy of the firm)
- Factors that make a company actually decide on, or agree to
  pursue, a given policy or to adopt a particular policy or
  program or benefit
- What occurs on an operational level within the company as a
  whole or some of its units after policy or program choices have
  been made
- Where relevant ideas come from and how they are carried from
  place to place
- What is said about all this internally, publicly, and in professional contexts

At various times one, or another, or all of the above can be relevant, even important. Our conclusions in regard to strategic intervention points are most readily summed up under the series of
topics that follow. It should be recognized both that there is a
degree of overlap and only intensive local study would enable one
to assign weights to a given factor at a given moment, and that
these weights would cease to be valid as soon as something
significant in the "ecology" or "system" began to shift.

The following do or could shape developments:

1. *Company policy and industry pressures* (staking out a specific
   niche in its industry or region; the need to attract or hold
   scarce, qualified personnel; a desire to reduce turnover; concern for the morale of employees who deal with the public,
   face to face; cost containment or cost shifting)
2. *Company culture, leadership, and commitment* (paternalism,
   responsiveness, and ideology)
3. *Unions* (the collective bargaining process, the desire to avoid
   unionization)
4. *Public policy* (mandated benefits, tax changes, and regulations)
5. *Consultants and the active organizations*

Company Policy

Perhaps the key dynamic is the desire to attract and retain person-nel. Both individual qualifications and labor market conditions affect this dynamic, depending on time and place. Neither individuals nor unions can bargain very hard for benefits when unemployment is high unless they happen to be in the lucky sub-categories of the occupational structure or in fortunate geographic regions.

We have found, in short, despite all the conference reports or resolutions, that paternalism, altruism, and a concern for families or children are relatively weak forces in determining what occurs, as compared with labor market conditions. Only those who argue for a more "social" market (not optimizing pro-fits in the light of social concerns) hold otherwise. The more acceptable and popular argument is: "Paying attention to employee personal and family needs is part of social investment in human resources; successful firms are those which make this invest-ment." This reduces itself, however, to recruitment and retention strategies; wages and benefits are part of personnel policies with a payoff.

Thus, the slogans and conceptual formulations and rationales vary, even reflecting the current favorite "buzz words" of business magazines, the other media, or newly published and publicized reports, but the "bottom line" is personnel attraction and reten-tion. Companies compete for good personnel within their in-dustry or geographic area. Where that is not a conscious concern, the company "coasts." (Were we not concentrating on the private sector, we also could cite the efforts of the United States armed forces in this country and abroad to develop an elaborate family service, support, and benefit program to aid in recruitment and retention.)

There are, however, important differences in how this objective is interpreted. Other variables enter. Atlantic Utility, we reported, seeks to be among the top 25 percent of the Fortune 1000 companies. Benefits are negotiated with strong unions, but this objective is the point of departure as negotiations begin. A major, national, entertainment business regards its employees in several divisions as constantly "on stage" in dealing with the public: the way they look, talk, appear to feel is critical to the company business. This company consciously cultivates its reputation for paternalism and an orientation to family values and must consider whether its policies are consistent with such public perception. To attract and hold a needed labor force as it developed a major site in an unsettled area, this company was willing to facilitate the development of residential areas and essential amenities that are attractive and effective.

In a historically low-wage, poor-benefit industry, a midsize farming and packing company, employing what was once a migrant labor force, is concerned with labor force stability and reliability. Better than average wages and still better, albeit modest, benefits, as well as facilitation of access to statutory benefits, achieve effective results with a deprived population.

Other variations may be cited: NortheastBanks is working hard to ensure a stable work force and Saturday coverage. FoodStores and The Eatery developed some degree of flexibility and responsiveness in their policies because of management consciousness of the importance of employee morale in services in which the quality of daily interaction with customers may make or break a business—all this even though personnel are not generally hard to find. Two smaller high-tech companies and Hi-Tek itself also reflect the consequences of a decision to create a sense of peer equality, informality, work time and workplace flexibility. These are largely (and especially in the two smaller companies) custom-designed operations. Creativity is at a premium. A collegial, relaxed environment is deemed necessary. When highly skilled and scarce personnel are found and become useful, one does not want to lose them. As we have seen, such a company becomes an exemplar of flexibility in all domains and at all levels. Hi-Tek is by now very large and inevitably quite bureaucratized, but its employee services, flexible benefit plan, and personnel policies remain in marked contrast to the more traditional old-line companies.

Company policies can be motivated by a wish to maintain a public image. A leading national pharamaceuticals and health care company is determined to have the best health insurance package in its field because of its visibility and the possible impact on its public reputation. It surveys leading companies annually and sets a generous pattern in developing benefits for its salaried workers. The unions, which represent 40 percent of all its employees, mostly salaried, are content to follow the pattern.

The most typical company motive as expressed *is the need "to be competitive in the industry."* One does not need to lead, but one should not lag too much. The Green drug chain in several East Coast states finds this difficult because supermarket drug services are more prosperous. It therefore competes for personnel only with the free-standing companies. A major oil company told us that they simply determine and maintain the industry standard so as not to be at a disadvantage in personnel recruitment and retention. They keep up by informal exchanges with responsible officials in similar companies. It is understood in the industry that ARCO and Exxon are in a position to set the pace. While wages, salaries, and benefit packages are very generous, they never become a big problem to the oil company, because wages are not determining in this industry. Exempt and nonexempt employees, unionized or not, fare quite similarly. Labor-intensive industries like restaurants and supermarkets are in a very different situation.

Having chosen their niches, companies work at keeping informed. Sometimes it is the unions that provide the needed information, as indicated below. The entertainment company mentioned has staff assigned to monitoring wage and benefit trends. Hi-tek staff provide elaborate analyses to management, locating themselves with regard to each specific benefit element. FoodStores follows a similar practice but on a less elaborate and less costly basis. There are consultants to carry the story, and there are industry-wide studies, company-initiated studies, journalistic reports, journals from the professional associations, task force recommendations from national trade and public interest groups, and government surveys. The goal is to remain competitive within an industry, a particular part of an industry, or a geographic region in order to recruit and retain personnel.

Company Culture—Leadership and Commitment

Analyses of any given company's benefit policies tend to converge on the items summarized above as determining, yet when business leaders were assembled in several major top level meetings in which we took part they added another ingredient: *The new benefit, the innovative program, the unusual company response—and they meant family responsive policies—also require a high-level champion, an executive who for one reason or another may make it his/her special priority.* Bureaucracies do not often create major departures. Routine processes do not sustain controversial and risky innovations. Unions (see next section) are not often creative in the sense here suggested. This is not the place to probe concepts of leadership or theories of how industry produces leaders, but there are enough specific illustrations available to suggest that this is certainly one of the important patterns, if not the only one. Nor do we discount the evidence that wives, daughters-in-law, and personal family experiences can matter as a CEO makes up his mind or directs his attention.

Hi-tek (chapter 4) in many ways is the prototypical illustration of management-initiated major innovation in a leading company. Given its industry, its large proportion of highly skilled personnel at all levels, and a constant concern with successful recruitment and retention of engineers, computer specialists, many types of scientists, mathematicians, and other scarce personnel, management constantly watches the competition and ensures that it is comparable in most compensation and benefit areas, ahead in some, and offering amenities and workplace attractions to keep it competitive. The overall package should be competitive, not necessarily each element.

In FoodStores (chapter 6), company leadership, both the president and the vice president for organizational development, say that they are guided by a philosophy that is supported by many of the supermarket owners, who come from a paternalistic ethnic tradition: be competitive with regard to wages but a leading company with regard to benefits; "people should not be distracted from doing good work because of personal concerns."

Sometimes, the presence or absence of women in middle or top management may be determining. There are women managers who succeeded in an utterly unresponsive and inconsiderate environment who expect those who follow them to overcome similar obstacles. Other women managers are convinced that women should prove that they can succeed on the same basis that men do—with no special allowances. On the other hand, some women supervisors and middle-level managers who experienced personally the burden that simultaneous job and family responsibilities can constitute are often inventive and flexible, just because they can identify with workers' problems. There were many situations in which the inability of top company management to move at all yielded the comment: "We probably need to wait until there are some women in senior management."

Company leadership, nonetheless, continues to operate within the framework of a formal organizational decision structure or a bargaining tradition that usually is determining unless a high-level executive stakes out a major initiative. Even a company that is known to be innovative may not always sustain its leadership role if top management is uninterested. The story of Hi-tek and child care is instructive. We asked why this responsive, innovative company, which was a pioneer with its benefit plan, had done nothing as yet about child care. While Hi-tek sounds quite special when we review the flexible benefits story, it sounds like many companies if one discusses child care. Many professional women employees, as well as secretarial-clerical workers, saw the need (although most female professionals are childless). A women's task force in the company was raising the question. Our query went to benefits administrators and planners at intermediate and top levels, to several company grass-roots leaders on women's issues, and to the responsible divisional senior vice president. The consensus was that nothing was likely to occur soon. Nobody made all the following points, but each person repeated one or two:

- Child care would be expensive as a flexible benefit; including it in the plan would preempt the innovation money for the year.
- This is not a time for adding new benefits; the time will come, and then something new might be considered.

- Most of those who have the problem are the secretaries and clerks; they don't influence policy.
- Perhaps the really objectionable development would be on-site child care; an information and referral service or financial aid could be helpful and supportive, like other benefits, and will probably be developed.
- There is ideological opposition in senior management; it is "paternalistic" to pay attention to personal and familial problems like child care.
- Nobody high in management has come forward to champion this cause.

New causes, it is agreed, need influential champions.

In the small local shops, managers and owners, in daily personal interactions with employees, sometimes shape considerate policies and helpful benefits. Historically, the paternalistic company attempted to do as much on a larger scale. There are records both of success and of cynical misrepresentation. It is of some interest that one still finds currently and previously family-owned firms that are determined to be considerate of and helpful to employees and to share the fruits of joint success. Such companies tend to concern themselves with the kinds of responsive and flexible benefits and policies that are of interest here. Steelcase and Levi Strauss are examples. There are also companies with no tradition of paternalism at all in which current presidents, board chairmen, chief executive officers, and others, for reasons of principle—which, they attest to their stockholders, is also good business—become committed to an ideology and program of reform. They may talk of "social responsibility," "social policy," "affirmative action," "concern for the intersection of work and family life," "concern for the community"; the result sometimes is serious attention to benefits and personnel issues that matter to families. This occurs in both unionized and unorganized companies.

Of course, the company leader's personal beliefs may not be supportive of the benefit departures we have been discussing. Some "libertarians" favor flexible benefit plans as more protective of autonomy than set packages, but others want to meet their obligations by paying cash, implementing mandated government benefits, and "not interfering with employee lives." One top officer saw provision of child care services as taking over family prerogatives.

Inevitably, company size, industry, age, and leadership style shape these matters. Complex national and multinational companies require staff at different levels and coordinate them in different ways. There are "bottom up" and "top down" processes. There are hierarchical and matrix organizations. Major departures are sometimes assigned to special working groups or task forces. Only one obvious generalization has emerged thus far: these high- and intermediate-level structures sometimes correct in modest ways for limitations at the top, and they may also defeat half-hearted efforts of company leaders to do new things. However, the problems we have highlighted cannot be solved by these specialists and administrators alone. Ultimately, too much is at stake. At the least, there must be assent at the top. For important progress there must be commitment and active leadership.

None of this should be taken to mean that everything is done, even with a coherent management philosophy and given a commitment to responsiveness and to recognition of the new demography of the labor force, or that it is all easy, or that costs do not matter. There are lean years and years of substantial benefit growth.

Unions

With only some 19 percent of the labor force organized in 1985, we were surprised to be told again and again by management, as well as the union representatives, how important unions are in setting benefit standards. It was particularly startling since our study was carried out in a period of general union decline in power, economic troubles, and contraction in those manufacturing smokestack industries in which unions have traditionally been strong for decades. The business upturn came in the service occupations, where unions have very weak representation (under 11 percent) and where women, who are traditionally more difficult to organize, constitute important labor force components.

Companies may know what niche they seek, but the specific

substance that defines wages and benefits must come from somewhere: how is the compensation pot to be divided between cash and benefits? Which are the priority benefits and the cutting edge attractions? How do we decide if something is important to do? Union demands often—apparently very often—provide the cues both in industries that are heavily organized and those where unions may be weaker. They often shape the benefits for nonunionized cadres, and even managers in unionized firms. Others not at all involved with the unions also apparently quite frequently observe from afar and interpret what they see as signaling employee preferences.

A group of international presidents of major unions whom we interviewed, most of them unions with significant numbers of female employees, were aware of this union role and proud of it. They saw it as part of their larger historical contribution to American workers.

FoodStores provides an illustration. Benefits are always preferred by management to higher hourly wages, because they do not add to the overtime costs. The union cooperates, preferring to have a visible, rich benefits package to deliver to a membership constantly asking about the returns on their monthly dues. But the dynamics are even more complex. Union leaders clearly use benefit negotiations and administration to consolidate power; they cultivate with their members the notion that benefits come solely from the union. Management, on the other hand, while believing in generous benefits, also knows that in the labor-intensive supermarket business, markups are very small, so the compensation package spells the difference between profits and losses. Management's objective is to keep as many personnel as possible in a part-time status, responding to the variable consumer demands and at the same time preserving lower wages and fewer benefits.

A tradition has developed of adding one new benefit with each new contract, usually every three years. As far as benefit developments are concerned, surveys tell the FoodStores leadership what their competitors for labor are doing. Union personnel hear of new benefits from their associates elsewhere in the industry. Each side also follows the media and consultant initiatives. Trends are spotted, issues highlighted, innovations lauded. The vice presidents for human relations and organizational development and the benefits administrator are the company's benefits planning committee. They have the advice of a cross-section of managers one level below. The board and president get their recommendations, and the board's executive committee is the decision-making body. (In many other firms it is rare to get as much executive committee attention to benefits; some executive committees do little more than ratify, except where there are major departures or special financial problems.)

FoodStores is careful to keep up in its nonunion fringes with what the negotiations grant to union members. It also tries to ensure its nonunion personnel an advantage, at the present time an attractive educational package. They want to make unionization unnecessary for their employees in their nonunionized divisions. In this firm as in many others, lower levels of management staff also monitor union bargaining carefully, because their fringes reflect what the union has obtained for nonmanagement personnel.

The perception of union influence is not merely impressionistic and anecdotal. In their 1984 volume, *What Do Unions Do?*, Freeman and Medoff assemble the impressive research evidence that union-represented workers earn higher salaries and wages. The effect is greater for some categories of workers than for others; the effects also vary by markets and time periods. Larger and more impressive, however, is the substantial union effect on fringe benefits. In the 1974-77 period, workers in union plants received 18 percent of their compensation in voluntary fringe benefits while those in nonunion plants received 12 percent of compensation in this form. The former were also more highly paid.[1]

This much learned, we were also surprised at how little the work-family issues were at the forefront of attention as we explored a group of the major unions, many with large female memberships, which might have been concerned. They all were agreed about member priorities, as reflected in surveys, conventions, conferences, and instructions to bargaining teams: (1) wages/salaries, (2) health benefits, (3) pensions. We were told by a top union official that when the time came for the auto workers to negotiate the essential and inevitable "give back" package with Chrysler, officials were constrained because under no circumstances would the employees ratify any health benefit give backs. Many similar illustrations were provided.

We were told, as well, that unions are embattled—attempting to protect earlier wage/salary gains, pensions, and health benefits in the face of the health-cost escalation and the poor state of the labor market. Innovation is thus not feasible.

Moreover, a longer time perspective still did not yield a record of significant union emphasis on maternity or parental benefits, child care, personal or emergency time, time for sick-child care, well-baby coverage, or any of the components of policy flexibility or innovation that could sustain family routines or help with responsibility for child care or the care of dependent elderly parents. In company after company, top officials said, for example, that child care could become an important item on the bargaining table if unions were to elevate it. Union officers and staff said that perhaps they might elevate it if their members did. At the moment, there were other priorities. And the Freeman and Medoff data for 1974-77 showed that while, *in general,* union plant workers received more fringe benefits than the unorganized, the impact on fringe benefit expenditure was for benefits favored by employees with seniority. Unionism actually reduced expenditures on three fringes not favored by senior workers and subject to employee discretion: sick leave, paid maternity leave, and paid vacations. Unions had the capacity to increase fringes, but at that time, at least, had not focused on some of the benefits that are important to parents of young children.[2]

As in the instance of management, specific, dedicated leadership taking on a benefit cause can also make the difference in a union. A low-pay union in manufacturing, for example, saw two local leaders create out of their own conviction and sense of mission health centers, housing, and child care service programs. A national leader inspired a college scholarship program. Indeed there are those who argue that spontaneous requests or demands from the ranks never engender major union benefit initiatives. Unions, however, have done many things that very few of their members asked for and that most members learned about only after negotiations were concluded. Democracies—whether governmental or organizational—expect leadership, as long as the consent of the governed is sought and their prerogative guarded. Therefore, if there is now no strong movement for some of the types of benefits we have discussed, it is also because no union leaders have decided it is time to take them on. The lack of member demand, in this view, is excuse, not cause.

Unions, in short, have helped shape and specify what is in place. They could be important factors in the shaping of future workplace responsiveness. They could even help define company initiatives, it is held.

The case is even stronger. Some industries, or companies, are heavily unionized, some partially so. Some are unionized for hourly workers, not for salaried—yet often companies negotiate a contract and then apply the terms to the others. There are exceptions. One of the largest of clothing manufacturers begins with salaried nonunion personnel, and the union bargainers, speaking for half of a multistate work force, then take their cues from that pattern.

The intertwining is even more complex and more important in some places. In Atlantic Utility, FoodStores, and Fantasy, management personnel watch the progress of negotiations with mixed feelings. On the one hand, they have certain loyalties to the company's stockholders and its profit margins. On the other hand, in each instance, and others could be cited, the union settlement predicts the management fringe benefit adjustments as well.

Part of the explanation is the lack of precision in these categories. What is "management"? Atlantic Utility has a proportionately very large management cadre, consisting of many people from foremen through a range of supervisory roles (classified as management, some say, to keep the company operating during work stoppages). The true managers are only one fourth of this group of 20,000. In any case, the union does set the pattern, and the "managers," who feed information to senior management and to company negotiators, could have a conflict of interest before the contract is finally settled.

FoodStores is different. Here the supermarket department chiefs ("managers") and assistants actually have their own specialized unions, and they bargain for the best packages in the company.

The entertainment company, Fantasy, has a story that perplexes some inside and outside observers. Yes, the multiunion bargaining sets the pattern for all except the very top management (33 unions, nationally, in three basic groups, representing half of all employees, with almost constant bargaining as a result). However, as already reported, some management personnel do not understand the absence of a proactive thrust from the top. They are convinced that the company's objectives should be a supportive, even paternalistic, and popular benefits package. This could probably be enhanced and win even greater employee gratitude and loyalty if management were to initiate more and plan systematically.

Unions do not concern themselves centrally and in a major way with family responsiveness and related issues. It is not that there are no union leaders who talk about such things. Yes, there are more and more "women's issues" conferences within major unions, too. A Coalition of Labor Union Women (CLUW) has developed. The major slogans are equal pay, affirmative action, equal rights, and comparable worth. The other items on the responsiveness agenda—child care, flexible benefits, flexible hours and schedules, emergency time off, and so forth—are known, sometimes discussed, but not yet given real priority, however, by leadership in the major unions.

Industry and union leaders are accurate in their observation that even unions that have large female memberships have as yet not taken on a major women's or family responsiveness agenda. Some ascribe it to the times, difficult times for unions to do any more than hold their own, others to a desire to prove that women can be the same kinds of workers and union members as men and not need a different agenda. Still others note that although eventually most women workers are wives, give birth, and have children to care for, at any given moment the maternity benefits and the child care constituencies are too small to create a critical mass in many places.

A number of other elements help shape what occurs. First, there are subgroups within the employee groups with different stakes. In several of the companies looked at intensively, there were large groups of young workers for whom the particular job was expected to be brief, not the main source of lifetime work. These might be part-timers, temporaries, brief-time workers, seasonals, or after-school students in the supermarkets, entertainment company, restaurants, and banks. For one reason or another many did not care about or need fringe benefits; they wanted and needed a maximum amount of cash at once. Some were in companies in which part-timers who worked at least 16 or 20 hours a week did have prorated benefits, occasionally generous ones, but such personnel never had their rightful weight in setting union priorities in relation to their proportions in the work force; their very part-timeness meant that they were not present at crucial meeting times or properly represented in the decision process. Ultimately, their interests were different and lost out. Or the part-time and full-time groups had such divergent interests that the union leadership initiatives were crucial (and could be missing).

There is, too, a historic union benefit device that has not been productive with regard to family-supportive benefits. Many of the unions we explored bargain, not for specifically defined benefits and programs, but rather, for certain sums (a supplement for each hour of work, for example) to be contributed to a welfare fund to be administered by a joint union-management board. These boards work in many different ways. They are often union dominated and led. Sometimes the payments are assigned to a fund to be union administered. Nothing precludes use of these funds for the new initiatives here explored. That this seldom occurs suggests that, as in the instance of government agencies, it is rare for program operators (trustees) to innovate in dramatic ways without strong pressures or very new mandates. The required mandates are lacking.

In the instance of Atlantic Utility Company, there is yet another variant. The main bargaining and agreements have been national. However, a specific subsum is left for local bargaining and to meet local needs. There are no instances of major innovation here. It is the small local issues as defined by local union officials that set the agenda. We can conclude only that members have not insisted that it be otherwise.

During the explorations, one encounters other interpretations as well, although it is difficult to assign weighting to their importance. Thus, one experienced union official, with many years of intimate acquaintance with the decision processes, notes that decisions about benefits are complex matters. Careful choices should be based on analytic capacity, data bases, and computer programs to calculate the potential outcomes of alternative options. Many of the national unions—represented by people who have come up from the ranks through a political process—arrive at bargaining sessions not backed by substantial analytic work. Whether by choice, style, or necessity, the positions taken on new benefits may be intuitive or based on their prior rationales. Or they, too, turn to outside consultant firms. Very few unions invest in policy staff and computers to do the needed, ongoing analytic work. Currently, in a few spots, small, new, think tanks are attempting to service unions as they meet a new milieu.

Some of the reluctance to call for child care benefits is, of course, based on experience: the negotiated center that in a few years had no employee children because of the changing age composition of the membership; the health center no longer attractive to members now living over a wide geographic area or not relevant to people with medical insurance; and so forth.

A number of the union leaders oppose the move to cafeteria benefits and flexible benefit plans out of organizing strategies. They see value to unions in delivering specific benefit programs either administered by the union or attributable to it. Under the flexible plans each member shapes a unique package, which perforce is management-arranged and demands constant interaction with company counselors or administrative staff.

Several union representatives also expressed what is now widely characterized by others as a paternalistic and overprotective view, often heard from the management side: the union should negotiate a specific package because the employee with many health, pension, and flexible spending options can make serious mistakes and be left with inadequate protection against the risks of a lifetime in the labor force.

We met only one major international union president who said of flexible benefit plans what others had said about many other potential benefits: When his members ask for flexible benefits he will negotiate them. He is not selling the idea. This is, however, a recognized strong leader who has sold other program initiatives!

Leadership in low-pay unions express yet another perspective. They must limit their bargaining demands to the wage package and an essential core of health and retirement protections. All else must be forgone as unrealistic or as infringing inappropriately on what they see as inadequate take-home pay. They have turned their energies and resources, instead, to acquainting their members with community health and welfare resources, both public and private, and to assuring their members that it is appropriate for them as tax-paying citizens to use these facilities. At the same time these unions become active both in public social policy advocacy and in local community activity to ensure the availability of adequate and responsive programs.

What of the future? Should the trade union movement be expected to move American industry toward greater responsiveness, variability, and flexibility in fringe benefits and personnel policies, as well as in the provision of services? Early in 1985 the *New York Times* compared union membership in 1980 and 1984 and then spoke of "slippage in the ranks."[3] Unions have traditionally been stronger in manufacturing, but that work force is declining; the service work force grows and employs many women but is not yet successfully organized. The union membership rate of 18.8 percent in the labor force breaks down into 35.7 percent of government workers and 15.3 percent of private sector workers. (In 1986, the overall rate was 17.5 percent.)

The trade union movement is gearing itself for innovation, change, and major organizational drives in the services, especially among women, who accounted for half of all recruitment in the last 20 years and are now a third of all members. An exceptionally frank AFL-CIO report by a high-level and influential committee, *The Changing Situation of Workers and Their Unions,* concluded after 2½ years that major departures were needed.[4] Noting changes in the work force and in the economy, the report discusses "experimentation with new, non-adversarial forms of representation and with new categories of membership for workers not in an organized bargaining unit." Some workers may prefer a union "to negotiate minimum guarantees that will serve as a floor for individual bargaining." Unions might also offer employment-related services (such as job training) and fringe benefits (such as medical insurance) to workers who are not in a collective bargaining structure. There is emphasis, as well, on giving attention to "new issues of concern to workers," such as health and safety issues and pay equity for women workers. There is to be a new organizing attempt in smaller companies.

Although the fringe benefit topic is not treated in this report, the subject has had new attention. Early in 1986 the organization's Executive Council approved a "Work and Family Statement," based on a resolution at the 1985 convention. Affiliates are urged to pursue "family strengthening programs through the collective bargaining process." Special mention is made of day care, time off if a child or dependent is sick, and flexible working hours. A major part of the statement supports a range of federal social policies in employment, health, income maintenance, and other areas essential to a "decent family life." Here there is mention of a shorter work week and work year, legislation to support the funding of day care and parental leaves, and restored social service funding.

The initial benefits in the organization's "new image" program were announced in mid-1986: low-interest credit cards and discount legal services to be phased in until available to all members.

However, there also were other stirrings. The Steelworkers had written agreements into two major new contracts to explore child care options. The Mineworkers won a similar agreement to pilot a parental leave plan, a cause also adopted by the Newspaper Guild. Service employees, public workers, and others continued their union interest in such topics.[5] The sum total of all this remains modest, yet it may mean—as some union proponents argue—that the challenge of "family strengthening" benefits will

indeed be taken up in a major way in the future when unions once
again feel that they have leverage for action.

Public Policy

It is easy to forget that the benefit packages discussed are much
more than the products of management initiative or labor-
management bargaining. All of the plans and entitlements take
the legally mandated system as the point of departure. The chart
in chapter 2, which interrelates the statutory and the private
systems, reminds one of the significance of this point. What we
have been describing and discussing throughout this volume is
occupational welfare in the shadow of public policy.

Thus, pension plans are developed with social security in mind,
to ensure a target combined income replacement rate at the point
of retirement. Private disability insurance benefits are coordinated with social security disability insurance. Company supplementary unemployment coverage is written in the context of
the state's particular unemployment policy. The presence (in five
states) of temporary disability insurance (TDI) legislation in-
fluences how companies write their sickness and temporary
disability provisions and shape them so as to meet the need for income replacement coverage after childbirth. Medical coverage in
fringe benefit plans is written with full awareness of Medicare
eligibility at age 65. Nor are these the only illustrations.

Of particular importance has been the role of federal income
tax policies in creating and shaping this system (chapter 2).
Federal policy fostered the initial developments of the basic
fringe benefit system during World War II and the Korean War
by permitting growth in benefits while constraining wages.
Growth in the 1970s was fostered by expanding the tax-free status
of benefits at a time when inflation left wages subject to higher
taxes (e.g., ESOPs, legal services, van pooling, educational
assistance). Flexibility and family responsiveness were encouraged by developments in the 1980s: the regulations for establishing
cafeteria plans, approval of salary reduction plans, the establishment of Dependent Care Assistance Plans, and approval of child

care as a tax-free benefit. What the impact of the tax policy changes enacted for 1987 and beyond will be remains to be seen.

We are reminded, therefore, that the issue of the proper domains of government and the private sector are more than a matter of poor unions and low-paid workers, as contrasted with the circumstances of employees and powerful unions in the more prosperous sectors of the economy. Social security's old age, survivors', disability, health insurance (OASDHI); unemployment insurance; and Medicare are universal programs and have their own logic—they are not the residuals after private provision. Indeed they antedate and create the framework for private provision. The existence of TDI in five states offers an option to be considered by other state governments as well, quite apart from what individual employers may decide to do.

In short, the social insurance mandates of government affect what we now have. Other legislation shapes the policies that affect how private fringe benefit provisions may be interpreted. For example, we noted earlier how equal opportunity legislation and regulations affecting women's rights were the departure point for an elaborate program of fringe benefits and policies in a major manufacturing company. Also, as we have seen, any company with a fringe benefit covering temporary disability has had to interpret it since 1978 as including pregnancy and the period of disability following childbirth. Various Department of Labor rules and regulations and successive legislative amendments to the Employee Retirement Income Security Act of 1974 (ERISA) have reshaped much of the private pension system, spouse and former spouse and widow rights under private pensions, and employee access to information about their own fringe benefits —and this listing is only partial.

The private fringe benefit system continues to be shaped in the shadow of current law, potential changes in law, and new statutory initiatives. As one projects the future, the analysis must, therefore, go beyond private industry and unions. Government, too, will affect what happens in this field; government policies will have a considerable influence on the nature and size of the benefit systems and a variety of workplace policies.

Consultants and Active Organizations

Fringe benefits are complex. Health and hospital plans, pensions, disability insurance, various types of profit sharing, and life insurance involve huge sums of money in a large company. Actuarial talent, legal expertise, especially tax law expertise, and administrative experience, as well as knowledge of all specifics involved, are essential in designing and updating programs. A company may be large enough to employ its own staff specialists in these fields. Otherwise, it would be no more likely to make significant decisions without the help of expert consultants than a high-income taxpayer with many investments, multiple sources of income, and property in several states would be to prepare federal tax returns without the services of an accountant.

The major consultant firms, then, are extraordinarily influential in shaping the direction that the fringes take. These firms, whose core experts—in various proportions—are accountants, actuaries, and attorneys, may specialize with regard to types of benefits (life insurance, pensions, health) or approaches to benefit packages. Some cover everything of interest to an employer. Some specialize in particular types of employers (universities and hospitals, for example).

In the 1980s, a few identifiable companies have carried the cafeteria plan message and shaped the form that programs have taken. Until they became visible and used their newsletters and bulletins to educate client firms and potential clients, little occurred. Then, in a snowball effect, as they reported the adoptions, the process accelerated. This need not surprise. Federal tax legislation, we have noted, created possibilities; regulations were long delayed; the analytic work in a few companies and several consultant firms developed hypotheses and some sense of security. Most of the field awaited word of experience.

As the Johnny Appleseeds of flexible benefits, the consultant firms have performed a valuable service and shaped practice. In the interaction of pioneering companies with the Internal Revenue Service (IRS) and the Congress, as they have lobbied in the course of efforts underway in 1986 to rewrite the law and again cut flexibility and tax fringes, these firms have been able to shape agreements and compromises that now define acceptable plans.

Little of this has occurred with regard to work schedules and time off: flexitime, vacations, job sharing, part-time work, time for sick-child care, or the rest. There are no insurance policies to be sold here, no underwriting agreements. Here the messages are carried—sometimes even written—by public interest groups and professional or business associations. The most visible in this field have been the Conference Board (which created a special department to concentrate on "work and family"), Work in America (a research institute publicizing innovative practice), Catalyst (especially concerned with women in management), the Employee Benefit Research Institute (a private, nonprofit research organization concerned with new developments in employee benefits), the National Association of Junior Leagues, and the Bureau of National Affairs (whose publications disseminate information about practice, trends, and the law). All of these organizations have been active with regard to some of these issues by (variously) convening conferences and workshops, carrying out research, publishing task force reports and policy statements, and sometimes—as appropriate to their functions—advocating specific actions and legislation. Reported regularly in the media, their activities have challenged firms, suggested leads to employees and their unions, and kept the responsiveness issue on the agenda.

Adding It Up—with Uncertain Weights and a Future to be Shaped

The complex interactions, maneuvers, games, and individual initiatives that produce personal or family-responsive add-ons to employee benefit provisons and policies do not lend themselves to simple formula writing. We have decribed the field of forces, without pretending that it is possible even to capture fully the current action. It would be unrealistic to attempt to predict the specific pace of future change or the substance of innovations when many of the larger contextual variables, particularly the shape of the economy and the characteristics of emerging labor markets, remain unknown.

It is possible, nonetheless, to comment on the decision

dynamics to be considered by advocates of more adequate responses to the labor force and workplace developments we have highlighted.

First, however, we note the evidence from surveys and the testimony of interviewees about their needs and wants. Responsiveness to the daily problems and requirements of women who are shaping a new role for themselves in the labor force and of their families is a real issue, experienced as such, a source of much concern, stress, and pressure—and thus a potential subject for policy and provision. It is an important subject, with broad impact both on work and on family life. The affected are not only the two-earner or two-career families. There are also the single mothers, out working in the marketplace and rearing children, too. There are the members of one-earner families with at-home mothers daily facing the special medical needs of their handicapped children. There are the two-earner families with both working adults responsible for dependent parents whose adequate care is also a precondition to performing adequately at work by day.[6]

Management, unions, and government policymakers will need to have these circumstances as well as others in mind as they seek to allocate resources and energies in response to the new labor force diversity. Plans are not readily drawn or packages designed fairly without considerable sensitivity. A good data base is a minimum necessity; competent and concerned implementors are absolute prerequisites; a voice for those affected could be the critical safeguard.

It would no doubt be an error to place all of one's hopes in one pair of hands, although specific circumstances of company and time may at times dictate the obvious strategies. Clearly, with regard to large, important, visible companies with a reason or a desire to exemplify corporate responsibility, it is useful for government, civic groups, and professional associations, as well as employees, to appeal to corporate leadership as a collectivity and to individual leaders personally. The latter can often be determining.

At the same time organized employees need to find ways to express their own specific needs to union leadership, and leaders should be urged to move from the preoccupation only with traditional objectives toward these newer benefit possibilities. Obviously much in the larger environment, which shapes the power and role of unions, will determine how responsive they feel able to be. It would be in the spirit of the new AFL-CIO pronouncements for them to move further than they have in these new directions.

Corporate and union leaders, both, need information about what is possible, what works, what it costs; so the research centers, scholars, government data collectors, professional organizations, and interest groups in the field face a continuing challenge. As much may be said for consultant firms.

Very much needed as well are new ideas, new proposals, and successful demonstrations. The repertoire of innovative possibilities cited in chapters 2, 7, and 8 is not overwhelming. Is there not greater inventiveness possible in salary/wage policies, labor market practices generally, and in benefit plans? The flexibility theme is central to a responsive workplace, but its potential manifestations are many compared with what has as yet been begun.

Nor should the hard issues be avoided. Progress not only requires ideas, leaders, and exhortations; it also demands attention to central objectives, policy questions, objections, and obstacles. The following belong in the ongoing discussion:

- How can unions back flexible benefit schemes without undermining their relations with members? We see no intractable problem, but the issue needs discussion and exploration. The type of plan, a role in shaping options, and so forth could be part of bargaining.

- Do workers face hazards if flexible benefit schemes permit them to reject basic benefit protection? Yes, but not if the schemes ensure a minimal core of essential protections; most flexible benefit plans do. This is a concern of management generally, and unions could contribute to the solution.

- Is it discriminatory to expand benefits in which employees who are single are transferring (redistributing) resources to family members and those with dependents? Here, again, is the case for responsible, flexible plans. Nonetheless, we should note that much of our tax and social insurance system shares such characteristics with pension plans. Perhaps there are limits to the levels of solidarity to be expected, but should one not assume some foundations based on it? After all, although not discussed as such, most company fringe benefit health insurance, even if partially contributory, involves some pooling. Besides, if there were no families, no children, where would the future labor force come from to produce the payroll taxes to pay the social security benefits and pensions of the current unmarried workers?

- Isn't it possible for employers to respond to employees' family needs without being paternalistic and without fostering dependency on the firm? Earned and bargained benefits, personnel policies that respect the individuality and family responsibilities of employees, hardly need to be paternalism. The issue is what is offered and guaranteed, under what circumstances, and how it is administered. Benefits are a component of earned compensation. It is possible to have few benefits, yet much paternalism, and also to have a rich package that preserves autonomy and dignity. Many of the flexible schemes are in a libertarian mode and, as noted, may even be criticized as exposing employees to risk as the result of improper choices! It is because these are important concerns that benefit planning is serious business and must be shared by the several interests. If adequate pay is not paternalism, neither are responsive benefits. People should be recognized as earning them (and should be expectd to).

- But are there not some businesses so small, so unprofitable, so low paying that it is unrealistic to expect them to provide more than the minimum of benefit coverage? Does the encouragement for improved benefits not exaggerate the disparities between those in the privileged and those in the secondary sectors of the labor market? Yes, the problem could be very serious. The full agenda therefore must deal, as our final chapter does, with the role of statutory mandating of coverage by employers, as well as with public benefit systems.

10. Toward a Responsive Workplace

There are changes occurring at the workplace. Not only are more employees now provided with traditional benefits and in more generous measure (pensions, health insurance, life insurance, accident and disability insurance, sickness benefits), and not only do more employees enjoy leave policies (vacations, holidays, personal days), but there are also some employers now paying attention to such new types of benefits as parenting leaves, child care services, employee counseling services, preretirement counseling, flexible work schedules, and most especially, innovative approaches to structuring benefit plans either "cafeteria" style or in some other version of a flexible system.

Yet despite the growth in the range and scale of these benefits, generous benefits still characterize only the large, leading companies, and even among these, developments are modest for the new types of benefits. Employees in small or even medium-sized companies, where most women work, and employees in service sector jobs, overwhelmingly female too, are unlikely to have the advantage of good standard benefits and certainly not the newer, innovative ones. Indeed, the most creative benefit developments—the flexible benefit plans—are not even occurring at the firms employing the largest percentage of women. Since women continue to carry primary responsibility for most family tasks, especially child care and child rearing, if these benefits are not available to most working women, they are not reaching those most in need. Yet where the innovations occur, they can benefit male, as well as female employees, indeed all workers, regardless of family status.

We do not want to give the impression that all of the workplace departures discussed grow only out of conviction that the workplace must respond to the family needs of new types of employees. Although the family policy of the firm has been the focus of much of this book, and of much attention in the media, it is only one component of a complex phenomenon.

Another factor, much discussed in the European literature, is the need for workplace adaptation to occur if there is to be sufficient employment to go around. Thus, the argument goes, if high rates of unemployment are to be avoided, there needs to be a massive reorganization of work. Work—employment—must be distributed over a larger number of people.[1] One frequent recommendation is to shorten the workday and work week, a development that obviously could contribute to improving the family policy of the firm. A more modest suggestion with similarly modest results would involve extending workers' vacations and paid holidays. Encouraging earlier retirement, a policy that is growing in all the industrialized countries now, is another example of this approach to reducing work life and expanding the availability of work or sharing unemployment.

The proponents of workplace sensitivity to family needs of employees obviously welcome the flexibility made possible by potential workday and work week shortening, more vacation time, and phased retirement. None of this is a solution for most working families, however, if it is to be paid for by a concomitant decrease in take-home pay. Currently, only the more affluent can afford to trade off a bit of their living standard for flexibility. Most other workers will depend on productivity increases and economic prosperity (or some shifts in the sharing of that productivity among government, stockholders, managers, and employees) to pay for the greater responsiveness.

Still another factor influencing change at the workplace is the growing acknowledgment of the significance of the occupational/industrial/corporate welfare system, as a parallel to the social benefits provided directly by government, or funded by government and delivered by voluntary agencies. A leading political sociologist has suggested that the extent to which private welfare benefits may reduce the size and scope of public statutory benefits may reduce the size and scope of public benefits available. His hypothesis is that "In terms of public opinion, lush private benefits foster the cheerful illusion that stingy public programs are adequate. In terms of economics, the substitution effects between public and private health and welfare expenditures are very large."[2] There are others who now argue that one advantage of a mixed (public and private) social welfare system is that, in the U.S. at least, private delivery of publicly funded benefits is more acceptable and popular and therefore may lead to a more extensive overall system.[3] This implies that perhaps what is needed is to make more visible the public subsidy that supports fringe benefits.

Finally, there is the growing stress on private (occupational) welfare as a device for cost shifting from the public to the private sector. Tax expenditures do not show up on the federal budget. Here, the traditional view of the private sector as more efficient gets played out too. Providing benefits and services through employers may seem cheaper than providing them directly by government because the public cost is not very visible, and coverage is far more limited. That part of the cost not compensated through tax policy may be carried outside of government; usually, these costs are shifted either backward, in the form of lower cash wages for employees, or forward, in the form of higher prices to consumers.[4] To the extent that such cost shifting occurs, these private benefits in fact may not be provided any more economically than public provisions, although there may be some immediate shifting of part of the burden away from the public purse. Any significant financial savings that occur would do so because a large segment of the population that might be covered under statutory provision might not be under the private welfare system.

Regardless, the pressures from demography, the employment situation, and ideology have moved the focus of attention to the private sector and the workplace. The countervailing pressure is also, however, economic: the constraints on public expenditure and on the size of nonwage labor costs given the growing competitiveness of the world economy. Whether the issue is direct government expenditure or indirect, direct public provision or tax policies encouraging employer provision, the question of costs inevitably arises. Although at any one point in time there are limitations on what can be expended, over time the decision concerning how much to spend on social protection is at least as much political as economic. The U.S. is not among the high tax countries. Government spending is nowhere near as high a proportion of GNP as it is in many other countries, including some with rates of economic growth that are higher than those in the U.S. at present. Other countries have higher nonwage labor costs too, although some experts have argued that it is these costs that have precluded the European countries from increasing their supply of jobs.[5]

We see no convincing evidence from the data that nonwage labor costs are the critical variable in determining relative economic success of advanced industrial countries. As for economic competition among advanced industrial countries, the newly industrializing, and the developing world, overall salary levels are a more critical component of labor costs. The issues of world trade competition which have arisen will need to be solved in ways other than drastic lowering of living standards throughout the industrialized world!

The Changes at the Workplace

Changes that seem to be responding to the family needs of employees are occuring at the workplace; but they are modest changes, thus far. Moreover, systematic examination suggests that family responsiveness is at best only a serendipitous consequence.

At any given moment if there is an issue of recruitment or retention of scarce and attractive personnel, or of coping with a problem such as absenteeism or lateness, one or another topic may get attention and there may be a response. Sometimes these practices or benefits may become the subjects of collective bargaining or of company image making. Other times they may support a desire to shape a particular kind of company culture, believed to encourage creativity or good relationships with customers. Sometimes these policies are the subjects of paternalistic initiatives on the part of company owners or executives.

Family responsiveness is sometimes a rationale, often a by-product, occasionally a goal.

Certainly, issues of family responsiveness at the workplace have become part of the popular debate. Coverage of some issues is visible in all sorts of business publications, as well as in the popular media. Personnel and human resource managers are discussing such subjects as the pregnancy and maternity problems of working women and their child care needs. Executives in industry and labor-related organizations such as the Conference Board, the Work in America Institute, the Bureau of National Affairs, and the Chamber of Commerce are participating in exchanges on these issues, also. National women's organizations now routinely include these topics on their agenda, along with pay equity, occupational segregation, and job discrimination.

What has occurred?

Major companies are providing modest *paid disabili⁺y benefits at the time of pregnancy and maternity,* and some permit their female employees brief additional *unpaid but job-protected leaves.* Many are convinced that it is only a matter of time before large employers routinely provide a paid maternity disability leave and a supplementary unpaid but job-protected parenting leave for about three or four months all told. Unfortunately, small and meduim-sized firms rarely provide such benefits; and many employers say, only when it is a matter of law, when it is mandatory, will most employers provide them.

Good will and the best of intentions are not enough. Most employers cannot take on costs that their competitors avoid. Legislation has been proposed in Congress, and although it seems unlikely that it will be passed at the time we are writing, this is an issue that will not go away.

The 1970s saw a rapid expansion in the establishment of *flexitime* policies by many companies, but the trend has slowed down now. Yet there do not seem to be any good reasons why this policy shoud not continue to expand, and over time, we would expect to see this happen.

Part-time work, in contrast, is clearly growing, as is temporary work. Here the problem is to assure those who work part time of adequate benefits, at least prorating full-time benefits, and to assure those who prefer full-time work and/or permanent jobs that they can obtain them when they want them. Ultimately, it seems almost inevitable that the distinction between part-time and full-time work will disappear, in part because employers are now creating the distinction arbitrarily in order to pay lower wages or no or low benefits, and in part because the normal work week continues to become shorter over time, particularly in some manufacturing industries and services.

Counseling services have increased and seem likely to expand still more at the workplace. This growth is occurring largely because most of these services are short term and inexpensive and function more as a link with community resources than as a source of long-term help. In effect, the workplace provides an important access point to existing community resources, supplementing these resources in an emergency and assuring employees of necessary help. And from the employer's point of view, having these services available provides a way of dealing with employees with job-related, personal problems, even if most of the problems brought to these services are personal and not job related.

Child caring remains the family related service that is most discussed. The media are full of items on it—in TV programs, documentaries, newspaper articles, magazines. Every discussion of work and family life inevitably includes a discussion of child care. Employer-sponsored child care activities have grown substantially over the last five years, yet they remain very modest at best. Except for hospitals and military bases, few on-site child care services exist and few are planned. Employers have increased their support for child care information and referral services and for noontime seminars and lectures dealing with parenting and child-rearing issues. A few provide a modest subsidy—or negotiate a modest discount with providers—to help employees pay for child care, but this is not extensive, either. There does not seem to be any likelihood that employers will pay for a substantial part of this service or operate the service themselves. Most employees do not want worksite child care, in any case. Child care is an expensive service if it is done even reasonably well. Employers will not spend the amount of money that would be needed to make a significant difference so as to benefit what are likely to be a small group of employees who may not be very important to the company. Only the arrival of a tight labor market, or serious shortages in selective places, would be likely to change this.

What then does this add up to?

Employers still do not generally view work and family problems in a holistic sense. They tend to see only specific, discrete, categorical topics:

- Child care for working mothers with young children
- Relocation policies for two-earner professional or executive couples
- High turnover rates among female workers
- Recruiting and retaining able women in mid management positions.

Except for relocation, employers characterize these as "women's problems," not as problems experienced by all employees. And as the human resource vice president at Hi-tek told us, "women" is not a uniform category. Women are a heterogeneous group, especially in a large organization, with diverse needs and interests. Moreover, whether these problems are experienced by all women, or primarily by women in non-management jobs, makes a big difference, too. Management is concerned that if they establish a benefit that helps only a small group, it will be defined as "discriminatory." They might do something for their women managers, but thus far, although most non-aged women are in the labor force, very, very few are in management positions. Furthermore, those few who are in management still view their situation as very precarious. Most are convinced that they must project an image of "manager first, mother second" and therefore refrain from making visible the problems they experience in coping with job and family responsibilities.

The changes described—and which take place for all the reasons given—are not usually thought of as ways to respond to the *family* needs of workers. Employers would agree that the labor force has changed, and that it is important to respond to employees' needs, but they would argue that what has really happened to the labor force is that it has become far more diverse than ever before. It is not just that more women are working or that more employees have family responsibilities; it is that there are so many different types of employees with such a variety of personal needs that trying to develop a *uniform* benefit or personnel practice policy that will satisfy all of them is increasingly becoming impossible.

Once an employer could assume that most of his employees were men with wives and children at home. That is clearly no longer the situation. But neither are all workers members of two-earner couples. There are young single adults and childless couples, single women heading families, and single men in similar situations. There are two-paycheck families and traditional one-earner families. There are quasi-traditional couples in which the wife works part time while her husband makes the big investment in his career. And there are workers with babies and those with adolescent children, and increasingly, there are workers with responsibilities for aged parents. It is this extraordinary heterogeneity in the labor force that is driving some employers to become more innovative and more creative in their policies, and in so doing, to respond as well to those workers, in particular women, who have heavy family responsibilities. What these employers have recognized is that this great diversity of needs requires a new approach to designing benefit plans and employment policies generally—an approach that offers employees choice and autonomy in making those choices.

Flexible benefit plans are an obvious response. Designed to respond to a diversity of needs and to support choice, they offer a vehicle for maximizing responses to those employees who have demanding family responsibilities. Some of these plans even offer employees the right to "buy" more time off; some offer an opportunity to buy more or less generous insurance benefits. A package can be designed around special needs and preferences. Such a plan can offer advantages to dual-earner couples, for example, by facilitating complementary rather than duplicative benefit coverage, and to single parents by permitting the employee to select the most comprehensive coverage she/he can afford.

Flexible work schedules and flexible time-off schemes—all described in chapter 8—are similarly attractive, as are some experimental efforts at permitting a flexible worksite, including some opportunity to work at home, at least in transition periods.

Other aspects of work that impact on personal and family life are also beginning to be addressed. Job security, something that already exists to a far greater extent in Western Europe and Japan than in the United States, is at the top of the list. The trend in the United States seems clear,[6] even if developments are still modest.

If what is occurring is driven by an increased diversity in the work force, the question still remains, will this be sufficient to respond to the growing portion of the work force that has particularly extensive family responsibilities? Here our answer is that although flexibility is enormously important, it is a necessary but not sufficient response to the most important current family challenge—child rearing—and may not be sufficient to address what may be the next most urgent need, the care of aged parents. Furthermore, there are many in the work force who still do not have some of the most basic benefits, those taken for granted by employees in "good" jobs, with "good" employers. What can be done about them?

A Role for Government

We began by asking about employers but have found it necessary to ask: What, if anything, should be the role of government in all this?

We have described the important role government has in shaping and financing the corporate welfare system. Without supportive tax policies and subsidies, the system would collapse. Indeed, one point we have stressed is that this system is a "social welfare" system, paralleling the system of direct government financing and delivery of social benefits and services, but it addresses itself primarily to those with the best jobs.

Consequently, a strong argument could be made against the increasingly important occupational welfare system because of the inequities and unfairness of its distributional effect. Women, the unskilled, minorities, and young workers are especially likely to be closed out of the system or to derive the least benefit from it, because they work for small employers who provide no or few benefits, or they work in part-time jobs where benefits are usually not available, or they work in the service sector, where benefits if available are often poor.

From a social policy perspective, a rich package of employee benefits at a firm raises major equity issues for the vast majority of the work force. In effect, the best off become even better off as a consequence. Since many of the benefits are calculated as a percentage of wages, those with the highest salaries get far and away the most generous benefits. Strong unions that press for these benefits sometimes are aiding an elite group at the expense of the larger population.

Furthermore, there is concern that even greater stress on an enhanced fringe benefit package, before an adequate floor of statutory provision is in place, may undermine the public support for basic social protection. Those who "have" may feel they do not need the public system; the have-nots lack protected power. As a result, a significant portion of the society could be doubly deprived, first, because some are not in the labor force at all and thus do not have even the statutory coverage that is tied to work; second, some are in the labor force but in poor jobs. To tie social benefits to employment, and then only to good employment, is to create a two-tier society.

Since our society has not yet guaranteed employment to all, at least it must assure those who do work, and some who are in transitional situations (between jobs, temporarily unemployed), as well as those out of the labor force (children, the aged, perhaps the long-term unemployed), of certain basic benefits. Employers can, indeed should, supplement. This supplementation can be very important, but the workplace, which is primary in provision of money income, should not and cannot also be the primary source of social protection.

A mix of statutory and occupational welfare has yet another

basis for appeal. It can provide a social infrastructure that limits excessive dependency on either institution. Statutory provision, when universal, provides a kind of basic, at least minimal, social and economic protection, an essential foundation in industrialized countries. It may provide for those not yet in the labor force, already out of it, or not likely to be in it. It also covers interruptions and transitions. In effect, only when employees are assured of certain basic statutory rights can they be free to work for different employers; otherwise they are vulnerable to a new form of economic enslavement. Similarly, when some portion of benefits—whether public or private—becomes portable, the likelihood of excessive dependence on any one employer becomes lessened too. We will return to these issues subsequently.

What then is the basic social infrastructure we are suggesting? First, we look at the insurance benefits. Here we are talking about pensions, health insurance, short- and long-term disability insurance, and sickness benefits. These are the kinds of social benefits that everyone needs, regardless of family status or responsibilities. Almost all industrialized countries already provide these basic minima; the United States certainly could and should as well, where we are still lacking.

Whether the concern is with employees as individuals or as family members, some basic minimum health insurance is essential. When 15 percent of the population remains without the most rudimentary protection and still more have only the barest minimum, while some others have full and comprehensive coverage (often because of public tax policy or regulations), it seems reasonable to raise the question of fairness and of simple compassion. If we in the United States continue to depend only on employer-provided health insurance for the working population, clearly we are leaving a large group without any protection. At some point we must either require all employers to provide some basic minimum benefits to employees and their dependents, while government finds some way to cover the rest, or there must be a somewhat more nearly complete public plan that ensures coverage at least to those who are unemployed or underemployed or have no workplace health benefits. Several steps taken between 1984-1987 to expand Medicaid to all low-income children constitute an incremental step in the right direction. Mandating the availability of health insurance for the individual employee and his/her nonworking dependents, on a contributory basis, with an alternative plan available for very small employers, would be another. So would be the mandating of preventive health measures (well-baby care included) for children in all family health insurance.

For some years employees have listed health insurance as their most valued benefit. The country now needs to assure all workers of its availability, even while continuing the effort to control overall medical costs and expenditures. Recent (1986) legislation mandating continuation of health coverage after job termination and protecting benefits of separated spouses, dependents, and widows illustrates what present philosophies permit and their limitations. The new coverage protection requires that the potential beneficiary continue the premium. Those initially not covered are not helped.

Short-term disability or sickness insurance is a major form of social protection that is now missing at the workplace of most workers. As we have seen, not even all workers are now entitled to the very brief paid sick leaves of a few days or a week, let alone the more significant benefits needed in the case of something like a heart attack or a pregnancy. The kind of temporary disability insurance (TDI) plans that now exist in five states could make an enormous difference to many workers. These states require employers either to participate in a state insurance plan or to provide a plan of their own that is as good as or better than the state plan. Employees covered under these plans, who are not at work because of short-term disabilities (usually less than 26 weeks), get a portion of their wages replaced up to a specified maximum. As a social "security" or social insurance benefit, TDI is paid for by both employers and employees. The contributory tax is very modest, usually half of 1 percent of wages. Like unemployment insurance, the protection is most important for low and modest wage earners. In large firms, executives and professionals now usually have their full salary covered. TDI would, however, assure a floor of protection to all others. Given the work situations of most women who work, something like TDI is especially important as a device to assure income protection at the time of pregnancy and maternity, a protection sorely lacking now.

To recapitulate: If basic protection is to be assured, and if inequities are to be minimized, a core of benefits provided by government—or mandated by government—is essential. Most employers will not provide these as a matter of altruism, and the time will soon be past when the society can sit back and see a large group excluded from what is increasingly viewed as essential. We in the United States have basic statutory provision in some areas: pensions, life insurance, and long-term disability (OASDI); unemployment insurance; this is what our social security system is all about. Now, at the very least, we need to move toward basic health insurance and short-term disability insurance for everybody through some combination of statutory and workplace coverage, in one of several ways.

For the smallest employers, those who operate close to the margin, it may be that a bare bones plan with public backing would have to be developed or that some expansion of Medicaid could be made available to all low-income individuals even if not on AFDC. The same may be needed to cover the unemployed. Employers, too, could be innovative here. At FoodStores, health insurance is continued for one year when an employee/breadwinner dies, giving the family time to make alternative arrangements. Many large companies continue benefits for several months during layoffs or during transitions between jobs, whether as part of their policies or as specified in collective bargaining contracts. These are all interesting options, and perhaps there could be ways to require this of all employers.

The 1986 reforms protected coverage for some time for terminated workers and dependents, but permitted employers to require that premiums be paid by beneficiaries. This is a good start, but for some not practicable. Regardless, the fundamental objective should be to assure people of basic protection against excessive medical costs and against the loss of income when disabled. Supplementary coverage, richer coverage, more comprehensive coverage, and special coverage (dental or vision care) could still be provided by employers and enjoyed by those fortunate

enough to work for them. But at least the most grievous inequities would be reduced. And, even then, we in the United
States would still not be as generous as many other countries!

For many companies, there would be no additional direct costs
as a consequence of this recommendation; what we are suggesting as a government-mandated minimum is far less than most
medium-sized and large companies now provide. It could constitute more of a burden to small and some medium-sized
employers. Yet TDI already exists in some states, and those
employers have managed to adapt to this and to other laws also.
Many small employers say that if an inexpensive health insurance
plan were available they would participate; they cannot afford
their own group plan, and this would provide them the opportunity.

If the role of government in providing social benefits is to
assure a minimum—either directly or by mandating provision—what is the role of government with regard to service provision?

Here, as we have seen, employers have done very little thus far,
even if some services seem to be growing. Most of the counseling
services that are provided are delivered off the worksite, often
through contractual relationships with professional counselors
in the community. What is offered at the workplace is more likely
to be information, perhaps some advice and referrals to sources
of longer—term help. Similarly, with regard to child care services, there has been only modest increase in direct provision.
What has increased, albeit still only somewhat, is employer-paid
child care information and referral services, parenting seminars,
and some very modest financial aid, largely through flexible spending plans. There is no evidence that employers will provide
much more in direct service. Here, too, if what employers do is to
link employees with community services and support employees'
needs by advocating expanding community provision, they could
make a contribution to meeting their employees' needs.

Clearly, employers' efforts will yield very little without a strong
governmental role in financing and delivering child care services.
A variety of considerations, including attention to diverse parental
preferences and equitable distribution of costs among par-

ents, state-local government, and federal government, suggest the importance of: (a) immediate and considerable expansion of public preschools for 3 to 5 year olds, largely with state and local funding; and (b) expanded federal subsidies, both direct and indirect (through tax benefits), to help pay for the care of the younger children of working parents and for after-school programs.

Employers' support, in particular support by large employers of such improvements in the "social infrastructure" of the communities they are located in, is critical to resolving the work/family problem for many employees.

The Special Needs of Workers with Family Responsibilities

Our message in this book has been that to the extent that the workplace is changing it is due only in part to employers' deliberate decision to respond to the family needs of employees. Most of the changes that have occurred, even if modest, have been in response to the growing diversity of the labor force and to the variety of employees whose needs cannot be met through monolithic benefits and policies. We have demonstrated how inadequate and diverse these workplace responses are. Inevitably, in a market economy, the social policy of the firm, established as it is by individual employers or industries, is unbelievably fragmented. As a consequence, it is often unfair and inequitable in its impact on workers. Our response has been to highlight the need for a consistent social, public infrastructure to assure Americans of basic social protection. The minimum, whether delivered by government or only paid for through government, must be set by government. Employers may function as the delivery system, but the basic policy is one designed to respond to the public interest.

The social roles of employers remain significant nevertheless. These roles include "the public agent" and "supplementary" roles that have been assigned to the private sector for some time.[8] They also encompass the potential role of innovator.

Here we turn to the question: If government is the guarantor of the social minimum and employers are the instrument for delivering some social benefits and supplementing the minimum, how are the special needs of employees who have extensive, immediate family responsibilities attended to? What can/should be done for them?

In Japan, the firm copes with employees' families by coopting the family, along with the worker, into the culture of the firm.[9] The firm does not meet the family's needs so much as it creates an appreciation of the importance of the firm in the employee's life, and it also includes the family in various ways.

In the western industrialized world, there are those who are convinced that the workplace has become overwhelmingly important in people's lives, usurping the earlier central role of the family. One analyst worries about this trend because she is convinced that if it continues we will return to a system of feudalism, this time, however, tied by fealty to our employers instead of the lord of the manor.[10]

We would argue, in contrast, that the family can and will continue to be an important and autonomous institution and that the family and family members have already made extensive adaptations to the growing demands of work and home. Now it is the turn of workplace and communal institutions. The work force clearly is increasingly diverse, and the task for employers is to respond to this. Workers value autonomy, individual discretion, and flexibility. And workers have personal and familial needs, too. How can these be addressed?

We are convinced that for employees' autonomy to be protected at the same time as their personal and familial needs are being met requires a societal response that involves both employers and government contributing to a system of social protection—a public and private mix. It is as important to avoid excessive reliance on the firm as it is to avoid excessive dependency on the state.

Glendon and others like her are convinced that as larger employers provide more security, they also become more controlling. A political economist writes:

Increasingly, corporations serve as mini-welfare organizations, doing the things that individuals once expected to do for themselves: saving for retirement; paying health costs and in some cases, tending children in day care centers... As larger employers provide more security, they may become more enslaving. Accumulated fringe benefits make it more difficult to leave. As we assign more individual responsibilities to employers, we become more dependent. And dependence breeds not only loyalty but also resentment.[11]

He continues elsewhere:

A basic dilemma of our modern economic system is how to reconcile freedom with security... today's security-conscious world impedes change. The security lies less in public protection (unemployment insurance, various anti-discrimination laws) than in the private practices of employers. Big organizations require rules and create customs; the evolving rules and customs form a protective cocoon around many employees, especially those with long tenure.[12]

Essentially, Glendon, an expert in comparative family law, and Samuelson, a political economist-journalist, take the position that just as government welfare creates unhealthy dependencies, so does private, occupational welfare. The recipients may benefit, but over time they also come to lean more and more on the corporate social welfare system. Our argument is that if the social protection system includes both employer and government, and in somewhat varied patterns, since options could exist, the issue of dependency is deflected; at least it is shared. The foundation is government; the elaboration and enhancement are up to the employer.

An aside may not be completely out of order. Those who warn of the excessive dependence created by public programs tend to forget (chapter 9) that the employer's major motivation in offering benefits is to attract and retain personnel. He seeks quite deliberately to create dependencies through benefits as he does as well through generous compensation. Inevitably, the meeting of needs through any system, public or private, will create some reliance on that system. The real issues are whether the programs and benefits create undesirable motivations (with regard to work and family matters) or introduce rigidities into the system. Eligibility criteria, portability and vesting provisions, and administrative practices are the proper locus for protection both of people and programs in these regards.

The question remains: How can employers respond to the

special needs of those who have personal child care and parenting responsibilities that potentially conflict with work?

A Flexibile Workplace: Employers Adapt to Employees' Needs. Here the essential message is twofold. First we stress the goal of a flexible workplace. As mentioned earlier in chapter 8, the only way employers can respond to diversity is with flexible policies. And the only way employees who value autonomy and choice can be satisified, given their diverse characteristics, is with flexible policies. The flexible benefit plans that some large firms have developed are a splendid model of applying the flexibility principle to benefits. Flexible working schedules and flexible working hours are another. The option, where feasible, of working sometimes at home would add further to this concept of flexibility at the workplace.[13] The potential for reorganizing one's own work life more flexibly over time, to draw, for example, from one's retirement income in order to take time off from work, is still another.

There might even be the possibility of incorporating the principle of flexibility into statuatory social provision, permitting people in different circumstances to allocate some portion of their legally mandated benefits in different ways to meet special needs at particular stages of the life cycle.

Portability of employee benefits, especially private pensions, is another issue related to flexibility. Vesting has appropriately been speeded. Even with the new, 1986 restrictiohs, IRAs provide a device whereby some individuals can create private, personal pensions that remain with them wherever they work. Indeed, the portability of these pensions and their personalized nature could curtail the growth in employer-provided pensions. In any case, they offer another illustration of how important individualization and flexibility are; carrying one's pensions and health insurance with one when changing jobs could alleviate many problems at the time of job transitions.

Flexible career paths may be another approach. Women in management positions remain trapped by a linear career trajectory that may have worked for men—when they had wives at home—but will not work for many women and even some men today. A large national accounting firm finds itself with a top notch group of able women professionals. But after six years with the firm, just as the firm's investment in training is paying off, these women begin to leave in far higher numbers than their male colleagues. One hypothesis is that they now want to have children, and the job expectations and career paths they are expected to follow are too rigid to permit time for parenting. A more flexible approach might help to keep at least some of these women from leaving.

There is a groundswell of interest in flexibility throughout the western industrialized world now, generated in part by interest in that U.S. "job miracle," the creation of millions of new jobs. The Europeans believe that U.S. flexibility is the key. Some believe that European employee benefits are far more rigid than those in the U.S. The goal may be to increase flexibility even more than to reduce the cost of nonwage labor costs. Part of what some Europeans are looking at admiringly—while others look askance—suggests a move on their part to more part-time, peak-time, and temporary help and to less job security. In Europe, however, because of the more extensive floor of social protection, some of these short-time workers have better benefit protection than U.S. workers, and most have more job security. Some assurance of job and benefit protection for such workers becomes critical if the system is to remain fair. Here, we are addressing the need for *employers* to be flexible—not just to expect flexibility and adaptability on the part of their employees.

Other Europeans are examining the possibility of allowing people "flexible lifetime careers," with options for moving out of the labor force for brief periods of time and reallocating a portion of forgone retirement entitlements to provide current income.

Worker autonomy and greater worker discretion have been identified by several authorities as central to job satisfaction.[14] The workplace of the future may need to be more flexible if employers are to be able to recruit and retain employees and if employees are to be kept satisified.

Autonomy and individual discretion go hand in hand with being able to choose—at least within some parameters—one's working hours, worksite, and benefit options, and ultimately, with having some say in how one's job gets carried out. These measures may not guarantee increased productivity, but they definitely would assure an employer of a more satisfied work force and success in ongoing recruitment.

More Time Off. If one of our major themes is flexibility, the other is time. There is need to emphasize the growing importance of *time* — job-protected, additional time off as a workplace benefit.

When the prototypical worker was a man, usually a married man with a wife and several children at home, the primary concern was whether a job paid a "living wage." In many countries other than the United States, since wages are not related to family needs, family allowances and other income transfers were invented to provide wage supplements to compensate for the economic costs of child rearing. These child allowances were provided first at the workplace and paid for by employers. Only later were they provided by government. In-kind benefits of various sorts became increasingly important over the last two decades, provided by either employers or government: health insurance, housing allowances, counseling and other personal services, child care, and so forth. In some countries the primary responsibility was governmental, in others, the employer's.

From now on, we believe, a most important benefit area will involve providing workers with more nonwork time. For family income to be adequate, all adults — husbands and wives — must be in the work force. When this happens, the most important special benefit to employees will increasingly have to do with time: personal time, vacation time, leisure time, parenting time, time to care of a ill child, time to take care of a frail parent, time to take care of a personal emergency — paid and unpaid, but job-protected time off. For the increasingly large group of single parents in the society, this will be an even more important issue.

This growing pressure for more time off and more flexibility will come not just from women with young children but increasingly from older workers with elderly parents who need care and attention and from young single adults and childless couples who want to redress the balance between work life and personal lives. For years, one dramatic difference between many European countries and the United States has been the difference in paid vacation time. A few firms are now offering a kind of sabbatical. Elsewhere there are efforts going on to cost out policy options that would permit more flexible use of retirement benefits. We expect to see even more attention paid to all sorts of time-related benefits, including a move toward a shorter workday.[15]

For young worker-parents, the issue of time is often critical. Women, we have seen, now often take jobs for which they are overqualified, if the trade-off is greater flexibility of hours and greater willingness to allow time off. Many women accept part-time jobs with no fringe benefits, low pay, and no career potential because they cannot manage full-time work and childrearing/caring schedules, even when the loss of income constitutes a severe economic penalty. Many workers would be prepared to trade off some wages for more time, as long as all their benefits remain protected.

The Special Needs of Workers with Very Young Children

For employers to develop special policies for young parents is viewed by some observers as creating a potentially discriminatory policy—an inequity at the workplace. Where this issue of potential discrimination can be solved through flexible benefit plans, the equity issue may be dealt with at the level of the individual firms but not in the work force generally.

Parents of very young children are a growing minority in the work force. Fewer than 20 percent of all workers in the United States have children under age 6, the ages at which these problems are most acute. As more young women remain at work despite pregnancy, childbirth, and childrearing, this proportion may increase. Regardless, it will always be a small minority. Moreover, the life cycle stage devoted to intensive child care is very brief—a matter of a few years, especially with the one- and two-child families prevalent today. Workers in this situation are neither a large enough constituency nor powerful enough to shape policies at the workplace.

We would argue, however, that for this group with very young children, some protection of time must be mandated, in particular with regard to job-protected leaves after childbirth and for parenting purposes. It is hard to counter that such a policy would be costly or disruptive when it exists almost everywhere else.

The Workplace as Community

In many ways the workplace is becoming a substitute, if not for the family environment, then for parts of the local community environment. If people spend much of the day at the workplace, and if it is a workplace with many other people, it can and should help solve some of their family and personal needs and make life simpler. This is not a matter of large cost and can do much to create loyalty, stability of work force, and workers who are less harassed. Thus it is perfectly sound for a sizable company to provide information and referral services for child care and for long-term care in the community for the frail elderly or the handicapped; it is perfectly satisfactory to locate on company property amenities such as shops, as well as service offices that can take care of parking tickets and theater tickets. Why should there not be health clubs and recreation centers, too? One of the other things that companies can do in these contexts is to have services that answer people's questions about their benefits and entitlements. Employees need help about the way in which private pensions and public social security support levels come together; they need to know about how to coordinate their private health plan and Medicare if over 65 and still working; they may need help in knowing how to obtain state disability benefits or to package firm and state benefits.

There is yet another aspect to this. Even in large companies, there are many with quite small establishments, as we have seen represented by the supermarkets, coffee shops, auto repair centers, and banks that are part of national chains. We have also noted that in such places, often using part-time workers, decentralized administration brings local variations and employee-responsive adaptations in personnel practices. This is a sound kind of decentralization and might be enhanced and win further approval. In effect, the "street level administrator," part of a "community," is like the "street corner practitioner" needing to balance the pressure from a local work force that it now wants to hold loyal and the pressure from a central administration that tries to impose policies.[16]

Toward a New Rationale

In 1944, the United Auto Workers union (UAW) established a Women's Division and held a conference on issues confronting working women.

> Its 150 representatives passed resolutions asking for "in-plant" cafeterias to sell hot food and requesting counseling services that would include advice about family problems as well as work.... Members asked for maternity leaves without loss of seniority, insurance plans that included maternity benefits, improved child care facilities... a guaranteed annual wage, and unemployment benefit policies that did not discriminate against women.[17]

The agenda does not seem dated. More than 40 years later we have still not achieved these goals.

The plea of the 1980 White House Conference on Families, for employers to become more responsive to the family needs of employees, is far more recent. The agenda, which included flexitime schedules, part-time jobs with full benefits, maternity and parenting leaves, and child care services, is only slightly more elaborate. The likelihood of achieving these goals in the short term seems only slightly greater.

Some employers will argue that the policies here recommended are expensive to employers and to the society and may be disruptive to the workplace, too. Some insist that more extensive benefits have created an obstacle to greater economic growth in several European countries. Generous public benefits and high nonwage labor costs are said to create a noncompetitive situation.

Many employers insist that these policies can be introduced only if and when productivity increases can be demonstrated. As we noted at the beginning of this book, in the long term there may yet be produced rigorous, well-documented evidence of significantly increased productivity resulting from the introduction of such policies. To the present, however, no definitive evidence of such quality can be marshaled. We would argue that this is the wrong issue. We have now learned that corporations do not use productivity as the measure of many other policies they introduce. For example, they do not use productivity as the measure of whether or not they support executive training; they simply do it. Productivity is not used to justify an attractive headquarters building. Although alleged, it cannot scientifically be the basis for some levels of executive compensation. Increased productivity was not the reason for establishing health insurance and private pensions in the 1940s, nor for the subsequent growth of these benefits; tax policies and pressure from organized labor were the major factors.

There is need for a new perspective—a new rationale for supporting a changed culture and a more responsive employee benefit and service system—other than scientifically proven improved productivity.

Recruitment and retention of personnel is a key factor in all companies that voluntarily establish responsive workplace policies. Women are expected to constitute close to 70 percent of new entrants into the work force for the rest of this decade and for some time into the 1990s. The cohort of young people entering the labor force is declining in size, now that the baby boom cohort has already completed its transition into the labor force and the baby bust generation is entering adulthood. The competition for new labor entrants is increasing. If employers do not want to be closed out of obtaining the best among the new entrants, for all levels of jobs and types of responsibility, they are going to have to do something about recruiting women.

With regard to one high level of qualification, women MBAs and lawyers are graduating in almost equal numbers with men. When professional firms are hiring almost as many women as men, and investing heavily in their training, they want and need to be able to retain these young female professionals, not lose them in their 30s when they want children and find that the job expectations in some of these firms preclude any possible personal or family life.

The issue of family responsiveness at the workplace remains

largely a euphemism for the problems of women. If women continue to be more actively concerned about their children than men are, and continue to bear more responsibility for their care and upbringing, the work/family tension will remain far more of a woman's problem than a working parent, work and family, or employee responsiveness problem. If this continues, far less will occur at the workplace until women move up the management ladder—until women have more power and feel more secure about acknowledging the inequities in their lives.

Ultimately, for the conflicts between work and family life to be resolved, the issue must be transformed from a woman's problem to a societal problem. We have begun this process by labeling it an employment problem, but that is only part of the task. Resolving the conflicts between work and family life cannot be the responsibility of employers alone any more than it can be the responsibility of individual parents/employees—as it has been until now. Whether adults have children, how they rear the children they do have, as well as the kinds of workers they are, will be determined in large part by how difficult it is to manage work and family roles simultaneously. Society has an investment in the outcome; protecting it requires government action and initiatives as well.

Our society has changed, the work force has changed, and clearly the workplace has changed; but there is far more that needs to be done, if the goal is a more responsive workplace.

There is a role for all the major institutions in our society: the family, the community, the workplace, and government. In this book, we have focused largely on the role of employers. The process of adapting to major social change is not easy and takes time. But surely the time to move ahead is now.

Notes

1. Why Employers Should Care

1. See, for example, Helen Axel, *Corporations and Families: Changing Practices and Perspectives* (New York: The Conference Board, 1985); Sheila B. Kamerman, *Meeting Family Needs: The Corporate Response* (White Plains, N.Y.: Pergamon Press, 1984); Children's Defense Fund, *A Corporate Reader* (Washington, D.C.: Children's Defense Fund, 1983). See also two leading national women's magazines: *Working Women* and *Working Mother*, which regularly publish articles on this subject.

2. For a discussion of the new BLS measures of productivity and the factors influencing long-term trends, see Jerome A. Marks and William H. Waldorf, "Multifactor Productivity: A New BLS Measure," *Monthly Labor Review* (Dec., 1983), 106(12): 3-15. See also Irving H. Siegel, *Productivity Measurement in Organizations: Private Firms and Public Agencies* (New York: Pergamon Press, 1986).

3. See Ira C. Magaziner and Robert B. Reich, *Minding America's Business: The Decline and Rise of the American Economy* (New York: Vintage Books, 1982); Economic Policy Council, United Nations Association (UNA) of the United States, *The Productivity Problem: U.S. Labor-Management Relations* (New York: UNA, 1983); also Siegel, *Productivity Measurement in Organizations.*

4. Thomas G. Peters and Robert H. Waterman, Jr., *In Search of Excellence* (New York: Harper and Row, 1982), ch. 1.

5. Ibid., see ch. 8. The other seven attributes cited are "a bias for action"; remaining "close to the customer"; facilitating "autonomy and entrepreneurship"; adherence to basic values; concentrating on what is known best; maintaining a simple organizational structure; and maintaining a flexible balance between centralization and decentralization.

6. Ibid., p. 14.

7. Rosabeth Moss Kanter, *The Change Masters* (New York: Simon and Schuster, 1983).

8. William G. Ouchi, *Theory Z: How American Business Can Meet the Japanese Challenge* (New York: Avon Books, 1982), p. 165. See also Magaziner and Reich, *Minding America's Business;* Robert Reich, *The Next American Frontier* (New York: Times Books, 1983); and James O'Toole, *Making America Work* (New York: Continuum, 1981).

9. See, for example, International Labour Office, *Workers' Participation*

Within Undertakings (Geneva, Switzerland: International Labour Office, 1981). For a different approach from the perspective of management and a discussion of "participatory management," see Robert Townsend, *Further Up the Organization* (New York: Alfred Knopf, 1984).

10. Martin L. Weizman, *The Share Economy* (Cambridge, Mass.: Harvard University Press, 1984).

11. O'Toole, *Making America Work;* Daniel Yankelovich, "New Rules in American Life: Searching For Self-Fulfillment In A World Turned Upside Down," *Psychology Today* (April, 1981), 15(4): 35-91. See also Florence Skelly, "Changing Values and Their Effect on Employee Attitudes, Expectations and Requirements," in Dallas L. Salisbury, ed., *America in Transition: Implications for Employee Benefits* (Washington, D.C.: Employee Benefit Research Institute, 1982), p. 1.

12. O'Toole, *Making America Work.*

13. Ibid., pp. 57-58, 184.

14. State of the Union speech, January 26, 1982.

15. American Association of Fund-Raising Counsel, Inc., *Giving U.S.A.* (1954), pp. 31-39, 42. See also Doug Bandow, "Misdirecting Corporate Philanthropy," *Journal of the Institute For Socioeconomic Studies* (Spring, 1983), 8(1): 57-66.

16. Archie B. Carroll, Professor of Management, University of Georgia, "Corporate Social Responsibility: Will Industry Respond to Cutbacks in Social Program Funding?" *Vital Speeches of the Day*, 49(19): 604-608.

17. Milton Friedman, *Capitalism and Freedom* (Chicago: The University of Chicago Press, 1962), pp. 133-136.

18. Sandra Burud, Raymond Collins, and Patricia Divine-Hawkins, "Employer-Supported Child Care: Everybody Benefits," *Children Today* (May-June, 1983), p. 429.

19. John P. Fernandez, in his book, *Child Care and Corporate Responsibility* (Lexington, Mass.: Lexington Books, 1986), is a strong advocate for corporate action in the child care field. Although he insists that this call is based on evidence of increased productivity, the data he presents are largely employee beliefs or fragmentary studies that do not prove the case. For a more rigorous analysis of the productivity issue, see Thomas I. Miller, "The Effects of Employer-Sponsored Child Care on Employee Absenteeism, Turnover, Productivity, Recruitment or Job Satisfaction: What Is Claimed and What Is Known," *Personnel Psychology* (1984), 37: 277-289. Forthcoming work by Arthur Emlen and others is said to document such undesirable consequences of lack of supportive provision as personal stress on the job and problems in attendance.

20. Katheryn Troy, *Meeting Human Needs: Corporate Programs and Partnerships* (New York: The Conference Board, 1986). Also, U.S. House of Representatives, Select Committee on Children and Families, *Child Care: Beginning a National Initiative; Child Care: Exploring Private and Public Sector Approaches; Working Families: Issues for the 1980s*

(Washington, D.C.: U.S. Government Printing Office (GPO), 1984).

21. We draw here on published and unpublished data from the U.S. Department of Labor, Bureau of Labor Statistics.

22. U.S. Bureau of the Census, Current Population Reports, Series P-20, No. 395 *Fertility of American Women: June 1983* (Washington, D.C.: GPO, 1984). Updated. See also Howard Hayghe, "Rise in Mothers' Labor Force Activity Includes Those With Infants," *Monthly Labor Review* (February, 1986), 109(2): 43-46; Hayghe, "Working Mothers Reach Record Number in 1984," *Monthly Labor Review* (December, 1984), 107(12): 31-34. See also S. B. Kamerman, A. J. Kahn, and P. W. Kingston, *Maternity Policies and Working Women* (New York: Columbia University Press, 1983).

23. Janet Norwood, Commissioner of Labor Statistics, Testimony, U.S. House of Representatives, Select Committee on Children, Youth and Families, Hearing, *Work in America: Implications for Families*, April 17, 1986.

24. Yankelovich, "New Rules in American Life"; Skelly, "Changing Values and Their Effect."

25. O'Toole, *Making America Work*, p. 5. Emphasis in original.

26. Richard Kinney, "The White House Conference on Families: Implications for Management," in Clifford Baden and Dana E. Friedman, eds., *New Management Initiative for Working Parents* (Boston, Mass.: Wheelock College, 1981), p. 11.

27. General Mills, The American Family Report, *Families at Work: Strengths and Strains*, (Minneapolis: General Mills, 1981), p. 12.

28. Peters and Waterman, *In Search of Excellence*, p. 26; see also, "Who's Excellent Now?" *Business Week*, November 5, 1984.

29. Public Agenda Foundation, *Putting The Work Ethic To Work* (New York: Public Agenda Foundation, 1983).

30. Of some interest are the differences between men and women in their assessment of what makes for a good job and what will motivate them to do more work.

31. Charles Reich, "The New Property," *Yale Law Journal* (April, 1964), 73(5).

32. Peter Drucker, *The Unseen Revolution: How Pension Fund Socialism Came to America* (New York: Harper & Row, 1976).

33. Mary Ann Glendon, *The New Family and the New Property* (Seattle, Wash.: Butterworths, 1981).

34. Ibid., p. 96.

35. Glendon, *The New Family*. Her thesis is that changes in family structure and family composition, coupled with changes in family law, have left familial relationships more fragile a source of economic support than either employment or government.

36. William Serrin, "Companies Widen Worker Role in Decisions: Management Turns to Sharing Decisions With Workers for Benefit of Both," *New York Times*, January 15, 1984.

2. Employers' Responses

1. Howard Hayghe, "Working Mothers Reach Record Number in 1984," *Monthly Labor Review* (December, 1984), 107(12), table 3. See also U.S. Bureau of the Census, Current Population Report, Series P-20, No. 398, *Household and Family Characteristics, March, 1984* (Washington, D.C., Government Printing Office, 1985), table 18.

2. From a different perspective, wage policy in Australia and the initial establishment of a minimum wage in 1907 were predicated on the assumption that (1) wages were the primary means of assuring minimally adequate family income and (2) an adequate minimum wage should cover a male worker, his nonworking spouse, and two dependent children. See also Meir Avizohar, "The Family Wage," *Journal of Social Policy* (1977), 6(1): 47-54.

3. Family or child allowances, provided by the government as an income supplement to offset some of the economic costs of rearing children and delivered through the income transfer or tax system, exist in 67 countries today. For some discussion of the French benefit and its history, see Nicole Questiaux and Jacques Fournier, "Family Policy in France," in Sheila B. Kamerman and Alfred J. Kahn, eds., *Family Policy: Government and Families in Fourteen Countries* (New York: Columbia University Press, 1978). Also, Alfred J. Kahn and Sheila B. Kamerman, *Income Transfers for Families with Children* (Philadelphia, Pa.: Temple University Press, 1983).

4. That labor market policies focused specifically on achieving full employment exist already in other western countries, such as Sweden and to a lesser extent West Germany, suggests that such a goal is possible. Job security, too, is receiving growing attention here, but not nearly to the extent that it has in Europe. See also Mary Ann Glendon, *The New Family and the New Property* (Seattle, Wash.: Butterworths, 1981); Work in America Institute, *Employment Security in a Free Economy* (New York: Pergamon Press, 1984).

5. Stuart D. Brandes, *American Welfare Capitalism, 1880-1940* (Chicago: University of Chicago Press, 1976). See also Tamara K. Hareven and Randolph Langebach, *Amoskeag: Life and Work in an American City* (New York: Pantheon Books, 1978); Tamara K. Hareven, *Family Time and Industrial Time* (Cambridge, Mass.: Cambridge University Press, 1982); Anthony Wallace, *Rockdale* (New York: Alfred Knopf, 1978); Sheila B. Kamerman and Paul W. Kingston, "Employers' Responses to the Family Responsibilities of Employees," in Sheila B. Kamerman and Cheryl D. Hayes, eds., *Families That Work* (Washington, D.C.: National Academy Press, 1982), pp. 144-208.

6. Walter Trattner, *From Poor Law to Welfare State* (New York: The Free Press, 1984).

7. See Morris Heald, *The Social Responsibilities of Business: Company*

and Community, 1890-1960 (Cleveland, Ohio: Case Western Reserve Press, 1970); and Daniel Nelson, *Managers and Workers: Origins of the New Factory System in the United States 1880-1920* (Madison, Wisc.: University of Wisconsin Press, 1975).

8. See, for example, Jane Addams, *Twenty Years at Hull House* (New York: New American Library, Signet Classics, 1961).

9. Richard Ely, in Heald, *Social Responsibilities of Business,* p. 6.

10. Brandes, *American Welfare Capitalism.*

11. Hareven, *Family Time and Industrial Time,* pp. 38-39, 40.

12. The first personnel department was introduced in the National Cash Register Company after its 1901 strike. Although many companies introduced welfare and efficiency plans between 1911 and 1915, systematic personnel offices did not emerge until after 1915.

13. Hareven, *Family Time and Industrial Time,* p. 40.

14. Brandes, *American Welfare Capitalism,* pp. 143-144.

15. Walter W. Kolodrubetz, "Two Decades of Employee Benefit Plans, 1950-1970: A Review," *Social Security Bulletin,* 35(4): 11-22.

16. Richard Titmuss, "The Social Division of Welfare," in Richard Titmuss, *Essays on 'The Welfare State'* (Boston, Mass.: Beacon Press, 1969) pp. 34-55.

17. Timothy Smeeding, "The Size Distribution of Wages and Nonwage Compensation: Employer Cost Versus Employee Volume," in J. Triplet, ed., *The Measurement of Labor Cost* (Chicago: University of Chicago Press, 1984) pp. 237-277.

18. U.S. Department of Labor, Bureau of Labor Statistics, *News* (Washington, D.C.: August 9, 1983).

19. Greg J. Duncan, *Years of Poverty, Years of Plenty* (Ann Arbor, Mich.: Institute for Social Research, 1984), pp. 103-105. The deprivation is serious even if employment of other family members eases the deprivation. For estimates, see Deborah P. Klein, "Trends in Employment and Unemployment in Families," *Monthly Labor Review* (December, 1983), 106(12): 21-25. There was other income in 66—70 percent of families with unemployment.

20. U.S. Chamber of Commerce, *Employee Benefits 1982* and *Employee Benefits 1985* (Washington, D.C.: 1983, 1986); Bureau of Labor Statistics, *Employee Benefits in Medium and Large Firms, 1983; Employee Benefits in Medium and Large Firms, 1984; Employee Benefits in Medium and Large Firms, 1985* (Washington, D.C.: Government Printing Office, 1984, 85, 86); Mitchell Meyer, *Profile of Employee Benefits: 1981* (New York: The Conference Board, 1981). Robert Frumkin and William Wiatrowski, "Bureau of Labor Statistics Takes a New Look at Employee Benefits," *Monthly Labor Review* (August, 1982), 105: 41-45. Robert P. Quinn and Graham L. Staines, *The 1977 Quality of Employment Survey* (Ann Arbor, Mich.: Institute for Social Research, 1979). Emily S. Andrews, *The Changing Profile of Pensions in America* (Washington, D.C.: Employee Benefit

Research Institute, 1985).

21. Lucia F. Dunn, "The Effects of Firm Size on Wages, Fringe Benefits, and Work Disability," in Betty Brock, et al, eds., *The Impact of the Modern Corporation* (New York: Columbia University Press, 1984), pp. 5-58.

22. Timothy M. Smeeding, "The Role of Employment-Related Benefits in the Social Safety Net," November, 1985, publication pending. Summarizing a U.S. Chamber of Commerce analysis for 1983, the *National Journal* reported (February 2, 1985, p. 286) that for the firms studied, benefits cost $3.69 per payroll hour on average. Fringes were computed as 36.6 percent of payroll, down from 37.3 percent in 1981. In 1983, the cost of employer-paid benefits for all private and public employees, covering both salaried and hourly workers, reached $550 billion.

23. Major sources are U.S. Bureau of the Census, *Current Population Reports*, Series P-60, No. 150, *Characteristics of of Households and Persons Receiving Selected Noncash Benefits: 1984* (Washington, D.C.: Government Printing Office, 1985). Also: Wesley S. Mellow, "Determinants of Health Insurance and Pension Coverage," *Monthly Labor Review* (May, 1982), 105: 31; Robert J. Blendon, Drew E. Altman, and Saul M. Kilstein, "Health Insurance for the Unemployed and Uninsured," *National Journal* (May 28, 1983), pp. 1146-49, quotation p. 1147; Wesley S. Mellow, "Determinants of Health Insurance and Pension Coverage," *Monthly Labor Review* (May, 1982), pp. 30-32; Ann K. Taylor and W. R. Lawson, "Employer and Employee Expenditures for Private Health Insurance," *Data Preview 7, National Health Care Expenditure Study (NHCES)*, National Center for Health Services Research, DHHS Publication no. (PHS) 81-3297. Also Gail Lee Cafferata, "Private Health Insurance: Premium Expenditures and Sources of Payment," *Data Preview 17 (NHCES)*, DHHS Publication no. (PHS) 84-3364; Ann K. Taylor, "Inpatient Hospital Services: Use, Expenditures, and Sources of Payment," *Data Preview 15 (NHCES)*, DHHS Publication no. (PHS) 83-3360. Also, Pamela J. Farley, "Private Health Insurance in the United States," *Data Preview 23 (NHCES)*, DHHS Publication no. (PHS) 86-3406.

24. Melvin A. Glasser, Psychiatry, Industry and Labor-Retrospect and Prospect," *The Psychiatric Hospital* (August, 1982), p. 88.

25. U.S. Senate, Committee on Finance, staff report, *Health Benefits: Loss Due to Unemployment* (1983), p. 2. Also, *Characteristics of Households and Persons Receiving Selected Noncash Benefits, 1984*, p. 4 and tables 15-20.

26. Ibid. For documentation, see table 20 of *Characteristics of Households and Persons Receiving Noncash Benefits*.

27. See tables 2.7 and 2.8 of *Health Benefits: Loss Due to Unemployment*.

28. The Urban Institute, "Who Has Been Without Health Insurance," a

summary of two studies, *Policy and Research Report* (Washington, D.C., October, 1984), 24(2): 5-6. The 1984 update is from an unpublished Urban Institute report by Katherine Schwartz.

29. Taylor and Lawson, "Employer and Employee Expenditures."

30. R. J. Blendon et al, "Health Insurance," p. 1148.

31. *INC.* (August, 1982), p. 106.

32. Blendon et al, "Health Insurance."

33. Ibid. The 1986 legislation also protects benefits for divorced or separated spouses, dependents of workers, and widows for 36 months, but they may be required to pay premiums plus a 2 percent administrative charge.

34. Gail Lee Cafferata, *Private Health Insurance: Premium Expenditures and Sources of Payment. Data Preview* 17 *(NHCES)*, DHHS, 1984.

35. Bureau of Labor Statistics, *Employee Benefits* (1982, 1983, 1984, 1985 reports).

36. The Conference Board, 1981. The sample is mostly very large firms with 1,000 or more employees (71 percent), and 96 percent are firms with more than 250 employees.

37. "Updated Report on Access to Health Care for the American People," *Special Report* (Princeton, N.J.: Robert Wood Johnson Foundation, 1983).

38. Quinn and Staines, *The 1977 Quality of Employment Survey.*

39. BLS, *Employee Benefits: 1985.* See also *National Journal* (June 9, 1984), p. 1158; and Daniel Beller, "Patterns of Worker Coverage by Private Pension Plans" (Washington, D.C.: U.S. Department of Labor, 1983).

40. *Characteristics of Households and Persons Receiving Selected Noncash Benefits: 1984,* p. 4.

41. The major recent source is Andrews, *The Changing Profile of Pensions in America.* Also see: Dallas L. Salisbury, "Will You Ever Collect a Pension—Yes," *Across the Board* (September, 1982), 19(8): 50-53. Employee Benefit Research Institute, *Women, Families and Pensions* (Washington, D.C., December, 1985). Also, John Woods, "Working Women and Pensions," *Social Security Bulletin* (May, 1986), 49(5): 33-34. Haveman and Lasker, using two computer simulations, project that by the year 2000, only between 48.5 and 54.1 percent of male workers and between 24.3 and 30.2 percent of female workers will receive private pensions. Fifteen years later the male coverage will be 50-60.5 percent and the female, 40.5-46.5. See Robert Haveman and Jeffrey Lasker, "Discrepancies in Projecting Future Public and Private Pension Benefits," *Special Reports Series,* 31(Madison, Wisc.: Institute for Research on Poverty, University of Wisconsin, 1984). This analysis of course does not consider the vesting reforms enacted in 1986.

42. Employee Benefits, 1983, 1984, 1985

43. Dallas L. Salisbury, "Tax Expenditures for Pensions—Questions of Equity and Efficiency," *National Journal* (April 7, 1984), p. 694. A similar

projection is offered by Sanford Ross in "Private Sector Retirement Security," *National Journal* (March 31, 1984), p. 642.

44. Employee Benefit Research Institute, *Fundamentals of Employee Benefit Programs* (Washington, D.C., 1985).

45. Daniel B. Price, "Cash Benefits for Short-term Sickness, 1979," *Social Security Bulletin* (September, 1982), 45(9): 15-19. Also, "Cash Benefits for Short-term Sickness: Thirty-five Years of Data, 1948-83," *Social Security Bulletin* (May, 1986), 49(5): 5-19.

46. Price, "Cash Benefits for Short-term Sickness... 1948-83."

47. Sheila B. Kamerman, Alfred J. Kahn, and Paul W. Kingston, *Maternity Policies and Working Women* (New York: Columbia University Press, 1983).

48. For a summary of international developments, see Sheila B. Kamerman, "Maternity, Paternity, and Parenting Policies: How Does the United States Compare?" in Sylvia Ann Hewlett, Alice S. Ilchman, and John J. Sweeney, eds., *Family and Work: Bridging the Gap* (Cambridge, Mass.: Ballinger Publishing Co., 1986) and "Maternity and Parenting Benefits: An International Overview," in Edward Zigler and Meryl Frank, eds., *Infant Care Leaves* (New Haven, Conn.: Yale University Press, forthcoming). For a worldwide overview, see *Woman at Work*, no. 2,(Geneva, Switzerland: International Labour Office, 1984).

49. Gerald G. Gold and Ivan Charner, "Another Piece of the Financial Aid Puzzle: Tuition Aid Offered by Companies and Unions," *The Chronicle of Higher Education* (September 29, 1982), vol. 20; and Beverly T. Watkins, "Post-Compulsory Education by U.S. Companies May Be a $10 Billion Business," *The Chronicle of Higher Education* (September 22, 1980), vol. 18. The 1986 tax law eliminates the privileged tax status of these benefits.

50. Meyer, *Profile of Employee Benefits: 1981.*

51. Bureau of Labor Statistics, *Employee Benefits: (1982, 1983, 1984, 1985 reports).*

52. Meyer, *Profile of Employee Benefits: 1981.*

53. Janice H. Hedges, "The Workweek in 1979: Fewer But Larger Workdays," *Monthly Labor Review* (August, 1980), 103(8): 31-33.

54. General Mills, *The General Mills American Family Report 1980-81, Families: Strengths and Strains at Work* (Minneapolis, Minn.: General Mills, 1981).

55. Fred Best, *Flexible Life Scheduling* (New York: Praeger, 1980).

56. Stanley D. Nollen, *New Work Schedules in Practice* (New York: Van Nostrand Reinhold, 1982).

57. Stanford G. Ross, 'Public and Private Aspects of Social Policy: What Are the Appropriate Roles for Public and Private Sector Programs?" *The National Social Conscience,* Conference Proceedings (Waltham, Mass.: Florence Heller Graduate School for Advanced Studies in Social Welfare, Brandeis University, 1986), pp. 31-62.

4. Big Companies Can Be Flexible

1. The relevant federal legislation is the 1978 Pregnancy Disability or Pregnancy Discrimination Act. TDI offers, of course, protection for all short-term, non-job-related disabilities, for both men and women, not just for pregnancy and maternity.

2. For some discussion of the use of TDI for pregnancy and maternity and maternity policies in private industry, generally, see Sheila B. Kamerman, Alfred J. Kahn, and Paul W. Kingston, *Maternity Policies and Working Women* (New York: Columbia University Press, 1983).

5. Trading on Tradeoffs

1. "Waterside," our New York community, is largely residential, on the periphery of New York City. It is rich in educational, religious, and medical resources and has several landmark buildings. The stable population is 100,000, more than 30 percent minority. One third of the labor force is in the retail trades, one third in the service industry. Most local businesses are retail. Interviews were carried out in the community's central commercial area.

"Milltown," in Massachusetts, is an old community in Boston's orbit and has a population of 58,000. Almost 300 industries are within city limits, as well as two major universities, numerous churches, and medical facilities. There are few citizens of minority background. Unlike Waterside, Milltown has 42 percent of its labor force in manufacturing, much of it in high technology, the remainder in retail trades and services. The interviews took place in the substantial downtown business district.

Both communities are above the median national income.

The New York interviewer was a community resident. The Massachusetts interviews were carried out by an outside team. The former had 10 refusals, the latter, 64.

6. Smaller Is Not Always More Beautiful

1. Janet L. Norwood, *The Female-Male Earnings Gap: A Review of Employment and Earnings Issues* (Washington, D.C.: U.S. Department of Labor, Bureau of Labor Statistics, Report 673, September, 1983).

2. Ibid., table 4, p. 7.

7. New Needs, New Responses: Child Care and Employee Counseling

1. "Work and Families: A Report to Corporate Leaders on the White House Conference on Families, October 22, 1980" (Washington, D.C.: Department of Health and Human Services, 1980).

2. In our own writing and lecturing we had developed the agenda earlier. See, for example, Sheila B. Kamerman, *Parenting in an Unrespon-*

sive Society: Managing Work and Family Life (New York: Free Press, 1980). The White House Conference was the first major public statement of the issue, and the media picked up the theme immediately.

3. Alfred J. Kahn and Sheila B. Kamerman, *Helping America's Families* (Philadelphia: Temple University Press, 1982); Martha Ozawa, "Development of Social Services in Industry: Why and How?" *Social Work* (June, 1980), 25: 464-470.

4. Clifford Baden and Dana Friedman, *New Management Initiatives for Working Parents* (Boston, Mass.: Wheelock College, 1981).

5. Sheila B. Kamerman, *Meeting Family Needs: The Corporate Response* (Elmsford, N.Y.: Pergamon Press, 1984).

6. Rosalie Babalinsky, "People vs. Profits: Social Work in Industry," *Social Work* (June, 1980), 25: 471-475; James O'Toole, *Making America Work: Productivity and Responsibility* (New York: Continuum, 1980); Norman Wyers and Malina Kaulukukui, "Social Services in the Workplace: Rhetoric vs. Reality," *Social Work* (March-April, 1984), 29(2): 167-172.

7. Robert Samuelson, "A Rebel with Cause," *National Journal* (April 28, 1980), 12: 690.

8. Kathryn Senn Perry, "Child Care Centers Sponsored by Employers and Labor Unions in the United States" (Washington D.C.: Women's Bureau, Department of Labor, 1980).

9. *Personnel* (November-December, 1980), p. 45; see also, *Community Focus,* the United Way magazine (February, 1981), p. 3.

10. Perry, "Child Care Centers."

11. Sandra L. Burud, Raymond C. Collins, and Patricia Divine-Hawkins, "Employer-Supported Child Care: Everybody Benefits," *Children Today* (May-June 1983), vol.12; *Child Care Programs in the U.S. 1981-1982* (Pasadena, Calif.: National Employer-Supported Child Care Project, 1982). A 1983 survey of a selected group of 80 major employers in New York City found that 3 hospitals had on-site or nearby child care centers, 5 employers had some form of flexible spending or benefit plans that included child care, 5 provided information and referral services, and 6 had offered some kind of parent education seminar. This is not a discrete count of employers; in some cases the same employer provided a child care benefit, information and referral service, and parenting seminars. See Kristin Anderson, *Corporate Initiatives for Working Parents in New York City: A 10 Industry Review* (New York: Center for Public Advocacy Research, 1983).

12. Dr. Dana Friedman, personal communication, 1986; also see Bureau of National Affairs, *Employers and Child Care: Development of a New National Benefit,* A BNA Special Report (Washington, D.C.: Bureau of National Affairs, 1984). Dr. Friedman notes that the 1982 number was 600. Early in 1984 the estimated total was 1,500. She notes that there are 44,000 U.S. employers with more than 100 employees.

13. For some descriptions of these, see Baden and Friedman, *New Management Initiatives;* Dana E. Friedman, *Encouraging Employer Supports to Working Parents: Community Strategies for Change* (New York: Center for Public Advocacy Research, 1983); "Employers May Find It Easier To Help Working Parents With Child Care," *World of Work Report* (September, 1983), 7(9); and Sheila B. Kamerman, "Employers Sponsor Child Care Services," ibid. (November, 1983), 8(11); Bureau of National Affairs, *Employers and Child Care.*

14. Dana E. Friedman, "Is Business Good for Child Care? The Implications of Employee Support," *Child Care Information Exchange* (January, 1986), no. 47, pp. 9-13 (table, p. 11). To underscore the softness of current data on these employer-supported/sponsored child care services, we note that nowhere is there a list of the employers referred to. Furthermore, there is a significant amount of overlap across categories, since some employers are counted as having a near-site program, as well as having a contract with an independent provider; most who provide information and referral services also have held parenting seminars. See also Friedman, "Child Care for Employees' Kids," *Harvard Business Review* (March-April, 1986), 86(2): 28-34.

15. "AT&T: Two Experimental Day Care Centers That Closed," *World of Work Report* (February, 1977), 2(2): 16.

16. Burud et al, "Employer-Sponsored Child Care: Everybody Benefits."

17. Friedman, *Encouraging Employer Support to Working Parents.*

18. Friedman, "Child Care for Employees' Kids."

19. The Taft-Hartley law was amended in 1969 to permit unions to include child care as a bargainable item when negotiating contracts.

20. Sheila B. Kamerman and Alfred J. Kahn, *Child Care, Family Benefits and Working Parents* (New York: Columbia University Press, 1981).

21. Baden and Friedman, *New Management Initiatives.*

22. "TV Stations Join Forces To Provide Day Care," *New York Times,* January 12, 1980.

23. BNA, *Employers and Child Care.*

24. Ibid., p. 28.

25. The Ford Foundation has a special brochure describing the company's plan; the Polaroid plan is described in Baden and Friedman, *New Management Initiatives;* and by Joann S. Lublin, "The New Interest in Corporate Day-Care," *The Wall Street Journal,* April 20, 1981.

26. Catalyst, *Child Care Information Service: An Option for Employer Support of Child Care* (New York: Catalyst, 1983); Baden and Friedman, *New Management Initiatives;* Friedman, *Encouraging Employer Supports to Working Parents;* Press release Work/Family Direction, Boston, Mass, 1984. Also see Alfred J. Kahn and Sheila B. Kamerman, *Child Care: Facing the Hard Choices* (Dover, Mass.: Auburn House, 1987), chapter 2.

27. See Baden and Friedman, *New Management Initiatives;* see also

Lublin, "The New Interest in Corporate Day Care."

28. Jacqueline S. Anderson, "Who's Minding the Sick children?" *Children Today* (January, February, 1984), 13(1): 2-5.

29. Commerce Clearing House, *Tax Incentives for Employer-Sponsored Day Care Programs, 1982;* Leonard Sloane, "Cutting Cost of Child Care," *The New York Times,* June 11, 1983.

30. Roy Leavitt, *Employee Assistance and Counseling Programs: Findings from Recent Research on Employer-Sponsored Human Services* (New York: Community Council of Greater New York, 1983).

31. James T. Wrich, *The Employee Assistance Program: Updated for the 1980s* (Center City, Miss.: Hazelden, 1980).

32. Paul M. Roman, "Pitfalls of 'Programs' Concepts in the Development and Maintenance of Employee Assistance Programs, " *The Urban and Social Change Review* (Summer, 1983), 16: 9-12.

33. Robert C. Ford and Frank S. McLaughlin, "Employee Assistance Programs: A Descriptive survey of ASPA Members," *Personnel Administrator* (September, 1981), 26: 29-35.

34. Robert T. Hellan and William J. Campbell, "Contracting for EAP Services," *Personnel Administrator* (September, 1981), 26: 49-51.

35. "Xerox Renews FSAA Contract," *Highlights,* FSAA (January-February, 1981), vol. 7, no.1.

36. Not real name.

37. Personal communication.

38. Leavitt and MacDonald, 1983, as cited by Brenda G. McGowan, *Employee Counseling Services,* Work in America Institute, Studies in Productivity (Elmsford, N.Y.: Pergamon Press, 1984).

39. Ibid.

40. Ibid.

41. Ibid.

42. Louis Harris, *General Mills American Family Report 1980-81, Families At Work: Strengths and Strains at Work* (Minneapolis, Minn.: General Mills, 1981).

43. For a useful overview, see McGowan, *Employee Counseling Services,* and "Employee Assistance," a series of three articles in the *New England Journal of Human Services* (Fall, 1984), 4(4): 20-31; Cathy J. Brown, "Building an In-House Service"; Karen S. Haynes, "From Workplace to Outside Agencies"; Mignon Sauber and Roy Leavitt, "Some Research Findings."

8. New Needs, New Responses: Time Off and Flexibility

1. Robert D. Cooper, Research Director of the International Foundation of Employee Benefit Plans, *Benefit News Spotlight,* vol.2., no.1. For a recent collection of case studies of corporate initiative in the areas covered

in this chapter and in child care, see *Work and Family: A Changing Dynamic*, A BNA Special Report (Washington, D.C.: The Bureau of National Affairs, 1986).

2. Bureau of Labor Statistics, *Employee Benefits in Medium and Large Firms, 1985* (Washington, D.C.: Government Printing Office, 1986).

3. Sheila B. Kamerman, Alfred J. Kahn, and Paul W. Kingston, *Maternity Policies and Working Women* (New York: Columbia University Press, 1983).

4. Sheila B. Kamerman, "Time Out for Babies," *Working Mother*, September, 1985; and "Maternity, Paternity and Parenting Policies: How Does the U.S. Compare?" in Sylvia Ann Hewlett, Allice Illichman, and John J. Sweeney, eds., *Family and Work: Bridging the Gap* (Cambridge, Mass.: Ballinger Publishing Co., 1986), pp. 53-65.

5. Stanley Nollen, "What is Happening to Flexitime, Flexitour, Gliding Time, the Variable Day? and Permanent Part-time Employment? and the Four Day Week?" *Across the Board* (April, 1980), 17:6.

6. R. T. Golembiewski and C. W. Proehl, Jr., "A Survey of the Empirical Literature on Flexible Workhours: Character and Consequences of a Major Innovation," *Management Review* (October, 1978); vol.3.

7. This introductory material is from Sheila B. Kamerman and Paul W. Kingston, "Employer Responses to the Family Responsibilities of Employees," in Sheila B. Kamerman and Cheryl D. Hayes, eds. *Families That Work: Children in a Changing World* (Washington, D.C.: National Academy Press, 1982).

8. See Earl F. Mellor, "Shift Work and Flexitime: How Prevalent Are They?", *Monthly Labor Review* (November 1986), 109(11); Jerome M. Rosow and Robert Zager "Punch Out the Time Clocks," *Harvard Business Review* (March-April 1983), pp. 12-30. See also Rosow and Zager, *New Work Schedules for a Changing Society* (Scarsdale, N.Y.: Work in America Institute, 1981).

9. U.S. Department of Labor, "10 Million Americans Work Flexible Schedules, 2 Million Work Full-Time in 3 to 4-½ Days," *Office of Information News Release* (February 24, 1981).

10. Stanley Nollen, *New Patterns of Work* (Scarsdale, N.Y.: Work in America Institute, 1979).

11. Nollen, *New Patterns of Work*.

12. Stanley Nollen and V. C. Martin *Alternative Work Schedules Part 1: Flexitime* (New York: AMACOM, 1978).

13. Golembiewski and Proehl, "Survey of Empirical Literature"; Stanley Nollen, "Does Flexitime Improve Productivity," *Harvard Business Review* (September-October 1979).

14. Richard Winett and M. S. Neale, "Results in Experimental Study of Flexitime and Family Life, " *Monthly Labor Review* (1980), 103(11): 29-32.

15. Halcey Bohen and Anamaria Viveros-Long, *Balancing Jobs and*

Family Life: Do Flexible Work Schedules Help? (Philadelphia: Temple University Press, 1981).

16. Nollen, "What is Happening to Flexitime, Flexitour...," p. 11.

17. For a description of the different types of part-time work and the relevant research, see Stanley D. Nollen, *New Work Schedules in Practice* (New York: Van Nostrand Reinhold, 1982).

18. Thomas Plewes, "Profile of the Part-Time Worker," *Part-Time Employment in America* (McLean, Va.: Association of Part-Time Professionals, 1983). Data for 1985 were provided by the Bureau of Labor Statistics. See also Deborah C. Wise and Aaron Bernstein, "Part-Time Workers: Rising Numbers, Rising Discord," *Business Week* (April 1, 1985). Also, "Part-Time Work, New Labor Trend," *New York Times,* July 9, 1986. Also, Thomas J. Nardone, "Part-Time Workers: Who Are They?" *Monthly*

19. Plewes, "Profile of the Part-Time Worker."

20. Louis Harris, *The General Mills American Family Report 1980-81, Families: Strengths and Strains at Work* (Minneapolis, Minn.: General Mills, 1981).

21. A. Cohen and H. Gadon, *Alternative Work Schedules: Integrating Individual and Organizational Needs* (Reading, Mass,: Addison-Wesley, 1978); Diane S. Rothberg, "Part-Time Professionals: The Flexible Workplace," *Personnel Administrator* (August 1986), 28-39, 104-6.

22. W. Deuterman and S. Brown, "Voluntary Part-Time Workers: A Growing Part of the Labor Force," *Monthly Labor Review* (1978), 101(6): 3-10.

23. M. Meyer, *Women and Employee Benefits* (New York: The Conference Board, 1978); M. Meyer, *Profile Of Employee Benefits 1981* (New York: The Conference Board, 1981); Stanley Nollen and V. C. Martin, *Alternative Work Schedules Part 2: Permanent Part-time Work* (New York: AMACOM, 1978).

24. The federal government offers one model for its part-time employees. Annual and sick leaves are prorated by both hours and years worked; retirement and life insurance are based on earnings. For health insurance the government pays 60 percent for both full-time and part-time workers. Part-time workers who are covered through a spouse (or otherwise) do not have any incentive to participate; thus, the government saves the entire cost of health insurance for these workers. Companies could also turn to the cafeteria system of providing employee benefits. The total value of employee benefits could be prorated for part-time employees, who could then make choices to fit their personal and family needs. Before cafeteria plans can be generally offered to part-time employees, though, life and health insurance companies must overcome their reluctance to include part-time workers in group plans. See E. Lazar, *Constructing an Employee Benefit Package for Part-time Workers* (New York: Catalyst Career and Family Center, 1975), for a detailed

description of a benefits package designed to be equitable for part-time workers. See also chapter 6, FoodStores and NortheastBanks.

25. Nancy Barrett, "Part-Time Workers Among the Adult, Non-Aged," in *Part-time Employment in America*, Highlights of the First National Conference on Part-time Employment (McLean, Va.: Association of Part-time Professionals, 1984).

26. Gretl Meier, *Job Sharing: A New Pattern for Quality of Work Life* (Kalamazoo, Mich.: Upton Institute, 1978).

27. Ibid. Also, Nollen, *New Work Schedules*, including Meier, "Professionals and Supervisors as Part-timers and Job Sharers."

28. Sheila B. Kamerman, *Meeting Family Needs: The Corporate Response* (New York: Pergamon Press, 1983), pp. 13-14.

29. Catalyst, *Human Factors in Relocation: Practices and Attitudes from the Corporate and Employee Points of View* (New York: Catalyst, 1983); Carl H. Driessnach, "Spouse Relocation: A Creative Approach to Recruitment and Employee Transfer," *Personnel Administrator* (December 1982), 27: 59-65.

30. See, for example, H. C. Collie and P. DiDomenico, "Relocation Trends—Moving into the 80s," *Personnel Administrator* (September, 1980), 25: 19; Runzheimer and Company, *A Study of Employer Relocation Policies Among Major U.S. Corporations—1979* (White Plains, N.Y.: Merrill Lynch Relocation Management, 1979).

31. Dreissnach "Spouse Relocation,"p. 59.

32. Catalyst, *Human Factors in Relocation.*

33. Ibid.

34. Thomas P. Gullotta and Kevin C. Donohue, "Preventing Family Distress During Relocation: Initiatives for Human Resource Managers," *Personnel Administrator* (December, 1982), 27:37-43.

35. An outstanding source is David Bloom and Jane T. Trahan, *Flexible Benefits and Employee Choices* (White Plains, N.Y.: Pergamon Press, 1986). Also, Carson E. Beadle, "Cafeteria Benefits: A Commentary on Process," *Employee Benefits Journal* (September, 1981); Robert B. Cockrum, "Has the Time Come for Employee Cafeteria Plans?" *Personnel Administrator* (July, 1982), 27:66-72; Albert Cole, Jr., "Flexible Benefits Are a Key to Better Employee Relations," *Personnel Journal* (January, 1983), 26:49-53; Mitchell Meyer, *Flexible Employee Benefit Plans: Companies' Experience* (New York: The Conference Board, 1983).

36. American Can Company, *The American Can Company Flexible Benefits Program* (Greenwich, Conn.: American Can Company, 1980).

37. National Women's Law Center, "Comments and Testimony on Employer Cafeteria Plans" (Washington, D.C.: July 13, 1984).

38. "Chemical Bank's Flexible Benefits Work for Working Parents," *BusinessLink: The Report on Management Initiatives for Working Parents* (Spring, 1984), 1(1). See also *Benefits News Analysis*, 5(2).

39. John A. Haslinger, "Why Employers Choose Flexible Compensation," *World of Work Report* (November, 1984), 9(11):6-7.

40. Pat Choate and J. K. Linger, *The High-Flex Society* (New York: Alfred Knopf, 1986).

41. "Of Men and Machines: The Outlook For Jobs," *The OECD Observer*, (September, 1986), p. 10.

9. What Shapes Developments?

1. Richard B. Freeman and James L. Medoff, *What Do Unions Do?* (New York: Basic Books, 1984), ch. 4.

2. Ibid, pp. 65-67.

3. *The New York Times*, February 10, 1985.

4. *The Changing Situation of Workers and Their Unions* (Washington, D.C.: AFL-CIO, 1985).

5. *The Wall Street Journal*, December 2, 1986.

6. We note here the emerging interest in employers' roles in sponsoring care of elderly family members, now termed "elder care," as a parallel to employer-sponsored child care. See for example, Dana Friedman, "Eldercare: The Employee Benefit of the 1990s?", *Across the Board* (June, 1986), 23(6):44-51, and Glenn Collins, "Many in Work Force Care for Elderly Kin," *The New York Times*, January 6, 1986.

10. Toward a Responsive Workplace

1. Wassily W. Leontief, "The Distribution of Work and Income," *Scientific American* (September 1982), 247(3):188-204; Jonathan Gershuny, *Social Innovation and the Division of Labor* (London: Oxford University Press, 1981); Robert Hart, "Meeting of Management Experts on Adjustment of Working Time: Economic and Employment Implications," Discussion Paper (Paris, France: OECD, 1981).

2. Harold L. Wilensky, *The Welfare State and Equality* (Berkeley, Calif.: University of California Press, 1975), pp. 63-64.

3. Marc Bendick, Jr., "Privatizing the Delivery of Social Welfare Services," in Sheila B. Kamerman and Alfred J. Kahn, eds., *Privatization and the Welfare State*. Forthcoming.

4. OECD Working Party No. 1 of the Economic Policy Committee, "Nonwage Labour Costs," Paris, France: OECD, Draft Paper, (September 30, 1981). See also Robert A. Hart, *The Economics of Non Wage Labour Costs* (London: George Allen & Unwin, 1984).

5. Leslie Wayne, "U.S. Job Surge: Envy of Europeans," *International Herald Tribune* (June 27, 1984).

6. See, for example, Jerome M. Rosow and Robert Zager, eds., *Employment Security in a Free Economy* (Elmsford, N.Y.: Pergamon Press, 1984)

and the companion casebook, Jocelyn F. Gutchess, *Employment Security in Action: Strategies That Work* (Elmsford, N.Y.: Pergamon Press, 1985). For a more "radical" proposal, see Martin Weitzman, *The Share Economy* (Cambridge, Mass.: Harvard University Press, 1984).

7. Alfred J. Kahn and Sheila B. Kamerman, *Child Care: Facing the Hard Choices* (Dover, Mass.: Auburn House, 1987).

8. Sheila B. Kamerman, "The New Mixed Economy of Welfare," *Social Work* (January-February, 1983), vol. 28, no. 1.

9. Ronald Dore, *British Factory—Japanese Factory* (London: George Allen and Unwin, 1973).

10. Mary Ann Glendon, *The New Family and the New Property* (Seattle: Butterworths, 1981).

11. Robert J. Samuelson, "A Rebel With a Cause," *National Journal* (April 26, 1980), p. 690.

12. Robert J. Samuelson, "Make Room For The Individual," *National Journal* (July 18, 1981), p. 1300; see also Samuelson, "Private Welfare," *National Journal* (July 12, 1982), p. 1062.

13. About 9 million persons were reported as working at home in 1985 for 8 or more hours a week as part of their sole or principal job. These are mostly full-time workers who do a small part of their work at home, and men are more likely to follow this pattern than women. See "BLS Survey Reports on Work Patterns and Preferences of American Workers," Advance Report (August 7, 1986).

14. Jeylan Mortimer, University of Minnesota, as quoted in Phillip M. Boffey, "Satisfaction on the Job: Autonomy Ranks First," *New York Times* (May 28, 1985); see also William Mares and John Simon, *Working Together* (New York: Alfred Knopf, 1983).

15. See, for example, Margarethe Landenberger, "Flexible Work Forms and Social Security," (Berlin, F.R. Germany: Wissenschaftzentrum, 1984). John Logue points out that a reduction of working hours of about two hours a week per decade (or adding two weeks vacation per decade) would be sufficient, also, to bring labor force and employment opportunities back into balance, provided that overtime were restricted in the United States. "Love that Robot? American and Swedish Attitudes Toward New Technology on the Job," *Working Life in Sweden* (May, 1986), no. 31.

16. Michael Lipsky, *(Street Level Bureaucracy* (New York: Russell Sage Foundation, 1981).

17. Alice Kessler-Harris, *Out To Work* (New York: Oxford University Press, 1982), pp. 291.

Index

ACE 2215   BuS

HF5549
K253
1987